ZIONISM

To Randy

Comrades in struggle now and in the future. With appreciation

11/9/94

ZIONISM

The Limits of Moral Discourse in Israeli Hebrew Fiction

Yerach Gover

University of Minnesota Press
Minneapolis
London

Passages from *Akud*, by Albert Swissa (Tel Aviv: Hakibbutz Hameuchad Publishing House, 1991; published in English as *The Bound*) reprinted with permission from the publisher; passages from *Aravi Tov*, by Yoram Kaniuk (Tel Aviv: Kineret Publishing House, 1984; published in English as *Confessions of a Good Arab*) reprinted with permission from the author; the quotation from "The First Million," by Nathan Alterman reprinted with permission from Acum Ltd.

Published by the University of Minnesota Press
2037 University Avenue Southeast, Minneapolis, MN 55455–3092
Printed in the United States of America on acid-free paper

Library of Congress Cataloging-in-Publication Data

Gover, Yerach, 1931–
    Zionism: the limits of moral discourse in Israeli Hebrew fiction / Yerach Gover.
        p.   cm.
    Includes bibliographical references and index.
    ISBN 0-8166-2412-7. — ISBN 0-8166-2413-5 (pbk.)
    1. Zionism in literature.   2. Jewish-Arab relations in literature.   3. Israeli fiction—History and criticism.   4. National characteristics, Israeli.   5. Israel—Civilization.   6. Jews—Israel—Identity.   I. Title.
PJ5030.Z55G68   1994
809'.93358—dc20   94-2527

para Raquel

Contents

Acknowledgments

I am deeply grateful to my colleagues and friends. I would like to thank Michael Brown for his unfailing support and sincere enthusiasm for this project, which has benefited immensely from his careful and provocative reading, his methodological suggestions, and his superb sense of style as well as from his interdisciplinary and cross-cultural awareness; and Stanley Aronowitz for his encouragement and care in reading and commenting on the chapters. My thanks also to William Kornblum for his dedicated teaching, generosity, and concern for his students who may do work in unconventional fields of research. I am also grateful to Edward Said, who early on found interest in my work, followed its progress, and initiated academic discussions with Israeli and Palestinian intellectuals and writers in international forums; to Tuvia Shlonski of the Hebrew University of Jerusalem; to Lena Jayyusi, whose acute awareness opened for me new international professional vistas; to Ella Shohat and Ammiel Alcalay for their solidarity and scholarly suggestions from within similar academic and philosophical perspectives; to Benjamin Beit-Hallahmi of the Haifa University; and to the Palestinian-Israeli writer Anton Shammas.

I would like to express my deep appreciation to the *Social Text* editorial collective, as well as to Bruce Robbins, Andrew Ross, and Randy Martin, for their encouragement along the road. I owe special gratitude to the entire team of librarians and staff of the Jewish Theological Seminary of America Library, in New York. Also, my thanks to members of the staff at the University of Minnesota Press: Biodun Iginla, my editor; Elizabeth Stomberg; Laura Westlund; and Judy Selhorst, my copy editor.

The publishers of two of the books I discuss extensively in this volume kindly gave me permission to quote generously from those novels. My thanks to Hakibbutz Hameuchad for permission to quote from *Aqud*, by Albert Swissa; and to Kineret Publishers for permission to quote from *A Good Arab*, by Yoram Kaniuk.

Finally, I extend my utmost gratitude to my wife, Raquel, who stood at my side with unlimited generosity of heart, intellect, and practical matters during this endeavor.

Introduction

The Relationship of Israeli Hebrew Literature to Israeli Culture

Today, Israel's cultural elite is still relatively broadly based. Much of its political vision is still articulated, or rather, represented literarily—in prose, poetry, or drama. Israeli writers are still deeply involved in current political events, and their books are evaluated in terms of politically charged standards. Politicians seek the approval of literary figures, and publics are swayed by their statements. Hebrew literature in Israel is still read as an authoritative interpretation of real life, still with the expectation that it remain loyal to the Zionist vision.

The study of Israeli Hebrew literature provides the quintessential object for a critique of Israeli political discourse precisely because of its highly spiritualized yet embodied referents, a historical people and a living utopia beyond which lies an unanalyzable but concrete, hence dangerous, otherness of being. Through the literary heightening of the symbolic and allegorical aspects of this myth, Israeli hegemonic culture presents itself as a historical force that can be taken as an object of critique, therefore as an object of an altogether different subjectivity.[1]

However, the relationship of Israeli Hebrew literature to Israeli culture provides sociology with a strong variant in its general theory of culture. On the one hand, it is not compatible with the traditional distinction between high

1

and popular cultures. The circulation of literary texts in Israel is so widespread, and the texts and their authors so much a part of public life, that what in another society would be "high" and elite is in Israel popular and public. On the other hand, it seems to challenge two largely unexamined assumptions in the sociology of culture: (1) that what *appear* as cultural forms constitute in fact the key elements of culture, and (2) that culture operates in society as a "latency."[2]

In regard to the first, what makes Israeli Hebrew literature cultural is not simply that it is literary, but that the instances of it are features of a greater public discourse. This is true, however, only in regard to a particular sense of "features," namely, that literary texts are, as Clifford Geertz might say, "thickly" implicated in that discourse and cannot be extricated from it, even for the most elementary understanding of their form and content. Indeed, Israeli literature lacks the degree of autonomy—of text, genre, significance, and position—that is attributed to what is usually called "literature." One of the most important consequences of this for my investigation is that a "close" critical reading of Israeli texts is essentially intertextual and interdiscursive, and only secondarily textual.

In regard to the second point, Israeli Jewish culture manifests an assertiveness, an unwillingness to take for granted anything that has to do with the relationships between the individual and society and between society and history. This deprives it of the capacity to provide a basis for consensual spontaneity, and leaves the categories of familiarity and plausibility, normally so important to what Riffaterre calls "fictional truth," relatively open and indefinite.[3] This aggressive tendency to become explicit in all respects gives Israeli culture something of the force of a threatened return of the repressed: more—ambivalence, anxiety, desire—edges onto and disturbs the surface than in most other cultures. One important consequence is that it should be possible to find a singular moral tension present in all Israeli cultural forms, particularly in the most widely read novels. In what follows, I will illustrate the pervasiveness of this tension and the ways in which it gives shape to moral and political reflection in contemporary Israeli literary Hebrew fiction.

My investigation suggests that this tension has to do with what might be called the politicoethnological history of the Jews, and with the incessant need to make manifest for each individual, in each voice, in regard to every assertion, an identification with a certain version of a very different kind of Jewish history. It expresses itself, as one might expect, through representations and through the discursive operations of their signs, and, for reasons I hope to make clear, it allows for no positive point of rest. This accounts, in part, for why Israeli culture has always been so distinctively ideological. This must be understood, again in part, to be motivated by a need to reduce the tension intrinsic to identification on so expansive a scale. Such a reduction involves the management of representations in detail. As a result, the normal operation of Israeli culture can be seen to be aimed at reducing the relatively uncontrollable latency typical of culture in other societies and at other times. That is, its normal operation entails a positioning of culture against itself.

There are certainly historical causes of this regression of the latent in the service of the manifest, but it needs to be noted and investigated as such if one is to understand contemporary Israeli culture. Given this hypothesis, I expected to find in the texts that I chose for analysis an irreducible unease or ambivalence about any representation having to do with Jewish history and identity and all that is currently associated with them. Further, I expected to find in each text compromises testifying to this unease insofar as it aims to revitalize criticism within the body politic that is in Israel also a body cultural. The key elements in this postmodern cultural formation—culture against itself—are Zionism and representations of otherness.

Zionism, the significance of the Holocaust, and the poetics of Arab-Jewish relations are important elements indicating a way of thinking—but they only indicate it. The ways in which these elements make themselves textually known imply deeper, more general, cultural operations having to do with the relation of self to other, the relation of state to society, and the relation of subjectivity (including society) to history. In what follows, I will attempt to explicate these operations against the background of contemporary Israeli history and the geopolitics of Arab-Jewish relations, as well as inter-Jewish ethnic relations. I will focus especially on the ways in which dissident literary fiction in Israel both challenges Zionist moral and political themes and, despite itself, ends by reiterating the episteme upon which those themes are based. This inevitably raises the issue of ideology.

Ideology, Culture, and Material Life

It is difficult to define ideology satisfactorily for all purposes, but for my project, ideology refers to a repetitive discourse that, unself-critically, expresses a particular interest in such a way that it mediates other discourses, particularly those whose concerns are primarily moral or political. As a practical matter, such a discourse aims to refamiliarize its audiences with what they have already received as incorrigible knowledge, and to do so monologically, in a way that places it beyond the challenges of different points of view and different, dialogical, means of knowing and claims to know. The most obvious examples are class-based ideologies in which a particular interest is expressed as a structure or inclusive narrative—as if no further work needs to be done in order to establish and clarify the latter.

The success of any ideology, the extent to which it colonizes other discourses, depends in large part on its capacity to constitute and synthesize formations of meaning and feeling, integrated elements of legitimation and motivation.[4] Because of the role played by Zionism in contemporary Israeli culture, it is necessary to consider the ideological aspect of Zionism. In this regard, I intend to show how Zionism constitutes just such a synthesis; how it conforms to the model of ideology as a countergenerative, repetitive, thematically discursive unit; how it serves as a basis for predication within the discourses that it informs; and in what way it can be seen as pervasive to or unavoidable within Israeli culture. My method will involve analyzing literary fictional texts in such a way that these features of Zionism are pronounced. In this way, it will be possible to highlight the interactions of these features with other epistemic elements present within each text.

If a *prima facie* case can be made for the ideological and cultural force of Zionism, it is reasonable to assume that the study of Zionism is crucial to the study of contemporary Israeli political and moral discourse. However, the relations among ideology, culture, and sociality are different in Israel than in other national societies. If, as I argue, Jewish Israeli society is grounded in its culture, and if that culture is mediated by Zionist ideology, then political decisions, attitudes toward other groups, patterns of authority and obligation, and the limits of political and moral dialogue must be examined as they take form relatively independently of the rational instrumental base of the Israeli national political economy.[5]

The hypothesis that culture in Israel has an explanatory weight not derived from or reducible to material factors is not inconsistent with a more comprehensive theory that sees material base as the most general condition of culture, sociality, and consciousness. Nor does it imply that Israeli society cannot be studied profitably from the perspective of its political economy. Rather, the analysis of Israeli politics must examine certain attributes of political and moral discourse implicit in all Israeli institutions. Among the most important of these are the figurative categories by which populations are defined and then seen as essentially in opposition; that opposition, taken as part of a universal historical drama; the moralization of politics according to this drama; and the totalization of conscience in all political and moral discourse according to this moralization.

Politics and Morality

We usually think of political discourse as distinct from moral discourse and only loosely related to it. Typically, political discourse is said to have little to do with the more general morality children are taught in school. In Israel, on the other hand, political and moral discourse are never distinct. People learn to think politically and morally simultaneously, in regard to referents, images, and conceptions that are deeply and persistently moralized. This is illustrated in a study of the pedagogy of prejudice by an Israeli social psychologist.

In 1963, Dr. George R. Tamarin, then professor of social psychology at Tel Aviv University, studied "the influence of ethnic and religious prejudice on moral judgment" in Israel. Tamarin investigated the effects of chauvinism on moral judgment in regard to the presence of prejudices in the ideology of youth and the effect of uncritical teaching of the Bible on the tendency to form prejudices particularly associated with the notion of the "chosen people," the superiority of monotheistic religion, and the study of acts of genocide by biblical heroes. The questions were as follows:

1. Do you think Joshua and the Israelites acted rightly or not? Explain why you think as you do.

2. Suppose that the Israeli army conquers an Arab village in battle. Do you think it would be good or bad to act toward the inhabitants as Joshua did toward the people of Jericho and Makkedah? Explain why.

Tamarin selected, as he says, "the most extreme forms of prejudice: extermination of the out-group." Pupils were "asked in direct confrontation" to comment on a text taken from the Book of Joshua (6:20–21; 10:28–32) that described Joshua's genocide of the people of Jericho and Makkedah.

As an additional exploration of the influence of ethnocentricism on moral judgment, Tamarin presented another (control) group with a different text. This group consisted of two subgroups, parallel classes of the seventh and eighth grades of another school in the same city. The first subgroup was presented with the above-mentioned biblical text (and asked only the first question); the second group read a text analogous to Joshua, but presented in a "Chinese version" featuring General Lin. The question for this group was: Do you think that General Lin and his soldiers acted rightly or not? Explain why.

Joshua's genocide is not the only instance of genocide recounted in the Bible, but Tamarin selected this particular example "because of the position the Book of Joshua has in the educational system, both as national history and as one of the cornerstones of a modern national mythology that includes such concepts as 'the generation of the desert', etc." Tamarin concluded that the approval of Joshua's genocide and the relative disapproval of General Lin's shown by his study indicates

> the influence of chauvinism and nationalist-religious prejudices on moral judgment. The answers indicate the existence of a highly prejudicial attitude among a considerable number of the respondents. . . . The uncritical teaching of the Bible—to students too young—even if not taught explicitly as a sacred text, but as national history or in a quasi-neutral atmosphere concerning the real or mythological character of its content, no doubt profoundly affects the genesis of prejudices . . . , even among non-religious students, in accentuating the negative-hostile characters of strangers. . . . The overestimation of statehood as a supreme value and the idea that assimilation is the greatest evil, and the influences of militaristic values in ideological education, are further sources of discriminatory tendencies.[6]

As ideology, Zionism is singularly self-conscious and therefore more dependent than other ideologies on what we might call literary values. There is a curiously intellectual quality to Zionism, and a tendency to emphasize the mode of expression as much as what is expressed. These qualities make Zionism more complex and theoretical than is normally the case with ideologies. Israeli culture reinforces that complexity by its own tendency to leave nothing inexplicit and unspoken. Thus, if the defining characteristic of culture in regard to other institutions is said to be its "latency," Israeli Jewish culture tends always to *manifest itself* as the consciousness of its people. Because a culture of reflexively manifest values requires that all institutional action be morally accountable, Israeli culture lacks what Talcott Parsons believed was the inherently conservative disposition of culture. Instead, it shows a degree of volatility and tendencies toward ambivalence that lead less to the comforts of consensus than to a self-conscious and only superficially satisfying utopianism.

Zionist discourse is riven with a distinctive figurative language, particularly evident in literary texts, that corresponds to the need to represent contemporary Israel as a totality and as a living utopia—"actually existing Zion." The demand for so abstract and constant a referent creates an extraordinarily complex ideological formation, one that supports the exclusivist attitudes of which Tamarin wrote, in particular attitudes that preempt recognizing what is at any moment defined as Other and, therefore, that can only leave the issue of self-identity itself morally unsettled. This lack of settled identity is what makes Israeli politics incorrigibly a politics of identity.

Political discourse taken by itself looks outward. It does not produce ambivalence or self-doubt in the self-consciousness of its subjects so much as a sense of uncertainty and doubt about the world. This mix of confident subjectivity and a sense of the world as unreliable and problematic promotes an instrumentalist rather than a self-reflective and dialogical outlook.

Similarly, moral discourse taken alone is self-reflective, but only in the abstract: the reduced self of isolated moralism is impractical, unable to learn or to teach. Therefore, its mode of self-reflection cannot be critically reflexive in the sense of being impelled by the desire to make its own terms immediately problematic in their use. If it were to be self-critical in this sense, moral discourse would have already implicated politics, and the two hypothetically distinct discourses would be, in effect, one. In that case, ambiguity and ambivalence would be part of politics, motivating political discourse toward questions pertaining to identity and significance at least as much as efficiency and instrumental effectiveness.

This unavoidable synthesis of morality and politics provides, therefore, a heightened awareness of the productive aspects of discourse and a totalizing attitude toward the society to which this refers. This is progressive only if the inclusive referent is a universal humanity rather than a segment of a population. It is regressive and reactionary if the posit of a living utopia is particularized and sectarian. The language of Israeli Hebrew literature has to do work of a higher order than is normally required of other linguistic cultures where literature appears distinct from the subjective conditions of writing, reading, and discoursing—that is, from society. Israeli Hebrew writing can never be seen simply as a matter of technique, distorted as it then would be by the distance thereby established between itself and its community. Nor can it be seen simply as expressive and artifactual, as a symptom that successfully conceals its conditions.

However, it does not follow that Israeli literature is somehow more honest to itself. It is only that it cannot avoid its own dishonesty, which derives from its elision of the sociology, the civil society, of the living utopia to which Israeli writing constantly refers. Nor should the inability to avoid this pathos of the self be thought of as an "Eastern" trait. It may well be specific to any historically mechanical unification of people in which the collective forms of subjectivity and the socially practical orders of moral obligation derive their validity from the same source, an identity asserted beyond space, time, and experience, as in the Zionist episteme. The study of Israeli Hebrew literature provides the quintessential object for the critique of Israeli political discourse precisely because of these highly spiritualized yet embodied referents, a historical people and a living utopia beyond which is an unanalyzable otherness of being. It is through the literary heightening of the symbolic and allegorical aspects of this myth that Israeli Jewish culture presents itself as a historical force and can be presented as object for the critique of ideology.

The Selection of Texts

One may still ask whether or not literature, in the form of published books, written by authors who are said to be more or less canonical, is too narrow an empirical domain for an analysis that aims to connect ideology to culture and the latter to politics. And, of course, even if the argument were granted, how would it be possible to sample this literature or to read it in general through the analysis of a few works? And if this is possible, how can an analysis of selected texts demonstrate, without simply being tendentious, the specific overlay of morality and politics, the limitations of criticism, and the pervasiveness of Zionist ideology that my argument and working hypothesis had led me to expect? I attempt to show in the chapters that follow that the perspective in which Israeli Hebrew literature and culture are taken together, in the context of what is deceptively called "Arab-Jewish relations," provides plausible accounts of certain key limitations of Israeli moral and political discourse, specifically those having to do with the irreducible themes of inclusion and exclusion so far as they bear on self-criticism.

Part I (chapters 1 through 6) concentrates on one literary text, *A Good Arab*, by Yoram Kaniuk. Through this text I explore the construct of the Arab as "moral subject" in Israeli Hebrew literature. In Part II, my analysis broadens to include the depiction of Arabs by three Arab-Jewish writers, Shimon Ballas, Sammy Mikhael, and Albert Swissa, and, in parallel, their positions vis-à-vis the Israeli Hebrew literary "canon."

Briefly, my method involves what might be called close reading, and it identifies points at which extratextual materials are unavoidable if the material of the text is to be understood. By *close reading*, I mean reading in detail, for the internal relationship between the rhetorical and the substantive, and for the ways in which narrative elements achieve what Hayden White might call an affect of plausibility.[7] Interpretive inferences are subject to the tests of consistency and coherence, by which I mean that they are initially posed as hypotheses and tested against the narrative in all other respects. By *the identification of points of intertextuality*, I mean the identification of specifically symbolic and allegorical moments that are essential for the plausibility of the presumptions, intimations, and analogies that appear at the surface of the text. To a large extent, this involves paying close attention to juxtapositions of figures of abstraction and concreteness, lapses in the temporal sequencing of events or in the intentionality with which events appear to be grasped, and the ways in which a given text challenges its own boundaries (e.g., by problematic titling, by ambiguities in designation of authorship, by the method[s] used to refer to extranarrative historical or sociological contexts, or in the means by which a text carries its reader from passage to passage). It also involves addressing the critical context itself from the perspective of its being read, as no novel can be said to speak with a single voice.

Israeli Hebrew literature, ostensibly Israel's "high culture," presents its representations and narratives in such a way that the morality of writing itself is always on the surface—in the poetics of representation and in the constant absorption and reabsorption of narratives by metanarratives. The "subtexts" of Israeli Hebrew fiction—of the return of those who are lost, of the mediation of history by memory and of memory by the conflict of questions, of the cultivation of the land by a chosen people, and so on—are "sub" in name only. In fact, they operate as supertexts, metatexts, there before what is read and not merely brought surreptitiously into the text as something extra.

In this sense, one must acknowledge that the "meaning" of any Israeli novel, if "meaning" is the issue, is always outside of itself, the novel being a vehicle for that "meaning" rather than a distinct and permanent presence geared to defending itself against all extratextual ascriptions. Although this dependency might be attributed to any novel, the characteristics of Israeli culture described above imply that the way in which "meaning" lies outside of the Israeli Hebrew text is different from what could be said about the instances of other national literatures. It is "outside" in the sense of being a feature or moment of a greater manifest center of meaning, not merely in the sense of reflecting an unstated idea. The heaviness of the symbolic in Israeli fictional writing testifies to this, as does the constant return to allegory as part of the way in which its narratives achieve their plausibility and therefore a sense of community among readers.

Hegemonic and Counterhegemonic Formations

In order to understand better the relationship between Israeli society and Zionist ideology, it is necessary to show how the literary textualization of Zionism glosses over polarities of hegemonic and counterhegemonic formations in Israel. One question I will address in this regard is how texts can both refer to something significant and exclude it at the same time. In other words, in what way does the reference to Israeli Jewish identity exclude the Other on which that very identity is predicated? I will also consider ways in which certain dilemmas peculiar to the exclusionist consciousness appear in literary fiction as limitations of moral self-reflection.

An example of the latter may be seen in the potentially subversive interactive themes of virtue and strength. David Ben Gurion expresses them with a certain forcefulness: "Reliance on ourselves means two things: on our strength and on our being in the right. Just one of these two will not sustain us."[8] Yet, it seems clear that the need to exercise strength and its actual exercise are not the same thing. Whereas the former may be consistent with virtue, the latter can be only if it is possible to justify the surplus of destruction and the elision of the difference between the innocent and the involved that are unavoidable whenever force is used to protect virtue. Even in the case of self-defense, force may be understandable, but it is not and could not be virtuous. For that, one would have to appeal to the aristocratic principle of "honor," and that can only replace virtue, not include it.

In the context of an exclusionist ideology, the need to be strong and the need to be right are already contaminated because there is no definite point at which one needs to deliberate about whether or not and when force is necessary. They are contradictory because the use of force to implement a categorical exclusion is inconsistent with its regulation by the universalistic requirements of virtue. How is this dilemma reflected in Israeli literature?

> Of course, how could it be otherwise? On the contrary! Why didn't I think of it right from the beginning? Our Hirbet Hizah. Questions of housing and problems of absorption! And hurrah! We'll house and absorb, and how: we'll open a co-op store, we'll build a school, maybe a synagogue too. There'll be political parties here. They'll debate plenty of issues. They'll plough fields and sow and harvest and do great things. Long live Hebrew Hizah! Who would guess there ever was a Hirbet Hizah before, that we have evicted and thus inherited. We came, we shot, we burnt, we bombed, we pushed and shoved and expelled.[9]

"Hirbet Hizah," the name of a fictional Palestinian village as well as the title of Yizhar's short story, tells about a detachment of Israeli soldiers sent to evacuate the Palestinian inhabitants. Yizhar is protesting not only the brutal use of force, but its use to evacuate the Palestinians from their homes, their communities, and their land. It is an atypically intense critical text. However, the protagonist's reflections are not subject to any play of voices, to a dialogical process in which criticism can discover its own history and obligations. The story is told as an inner monologue of a soldier who participates in the evacuation despite his reservations, who in effect "follows orders." This separation of theory and practice, considerations of virtue and considerations of strength, deprives the monologue of what it needs if it is to represent a self-critical, and therefore virtuous, recognition of the humanity of the "other."

If the narrator were to be provided that recognition, if he were to have recognized not only the violation of the principle in the exercise of force but the significance of that violation for his own sense of self as well as for the victims, he would have been unable to continue inflicting pain and unable to sustain the sense of self that had permitted complicity in it in the first place. That is, if the monologue were to be the reflection of a subject, one whose recognition of the other permitted a recognition of the self, too, as other, it could not have remained an interior meditation. By remaining so, the monologue speaks only of the particular others beyond the morally constitutive interpretation of selfhood and otherness.

In this way Yizhar's story illustrates the sentimentality and hollowness of hermetic reflection, of exaggerated and one-sided self-consciousness, once force and virtue are associated and given glib articulation as such. Once they are, subjectivity can only become utopian, apart from practice and indifferent to the history of practice. Yizhar's protagonist thinks, finally, only for those who do not dare speak, which is to say, for those who cannot speak and therefore cannot constitute themselves dialogically.

Similarly, consider the related themes of unity and creativity—community and fecundity or generativity. Through the "ingathering and assembling of exiles," diversity, through which a people discovers its own need to progress and discovers the dependency of progress on the inclusion of yet greater diversity, is qualified by the putative national unity that gives them the abstract and impractical identity *exiles* need to enjoy, to exult in, the "ingathering and assembling." This abstractive joy of community cannot sustain generativity; but generativity, diversity, can guarantee neither joy nor community, both of which *exiles* might desire more than anything else. The two can be sustained as absolutes only without the burdens of self-reflection. Above all, they can be sustained as such only at the cost of historical memory.

Jacob Kellner, of the Hebrew University of Jerusalem, has published an enlightening study of this cost of imposing the contradictory ethos of "the Exile" onto the nation of what must, despite itself, aspire to be a diversely composed people. Kellner analyzes two attitudes toward the administration of the Jewish refugees entering Palestine in the late nineteenth and early twentieth centuries. The first considers the physical and social "redemption" of the land as the fundamental point of reference, with the individual as a means of achieving that goal. The second considers the "rescue" of the individual as pri-

mary and the "redemption" of the land as a means of accomplishing that rescue on a societal scale.

According to Kellner, the first attitude has prevailed from the beginning
(the 1880s) to the present. As a practical matter, it entails systematic surveillance and control, an orientation of education to increasing productivity, and
the allotment of resources primarily to those who can sustain themselves. This
choice, according to Kellner, led to the development of "an ideology which
turns the collective into a sacred ideal and allows conscious indifference
toward the individual person," and an ominous tendency on the part of settlers
to "obey their leaders without question."[10] Emblematic of this ideology is the
ancient injunction, "Any man who is afraid and has lost heart shall return
home, or his comrades will be as discouraged as he is" (Deuteronomy 2:8).
Kellner writes that this slogan was used at the time of the Second Aliyah by
Yosef Witkin and A. D. Gordon, two early Labor Zionist leaders, to promote
halutzim (pioneers), and that Martin Buber had, in 1916, also agreed with it.[11]
But it is clear that the demand for unity can only support at best a demand for
the expenditure of energy, the concrete labor appropriate to extreme scarcity
and subsistence rather than to a mode of productivity consistent with the
creative and socially progressive use of resources. Although conditions may
control the degree to which the demand for unity outweighs the need for generativity and progress, Kellner argues that the ideological realization of conditions went far beyond these principles.

Thus, Kellner cites M. Usishkin, an early Russian Zionist leader, who proposed, in 1905,

> to establish all-Jewish workers associations of young single men, healthy and
> strong in body and spirit. Each member of the association has to immigrate to
> Palestine for three years and to fulfill his army duty for the People of Israel, not
> by the sword or by the gun, but by the spade and the plough. These thousands
> of young men will have to come to the Hebrew colonies and to offer their ser-
> vices—as if they were laborers—for the exact same salary as the Arab laborer,
> to live in the most arduous conditions, as those provided to the army in its bar-
> racks. (p. 32)

Kellner concludes that "the daring attempt to organize the transfer of the
Yemenite Jews to Palestine at the time of the "Second Aliyah" is a perfect
example of the tendency to use the forced dependency of individuals on their
absorbing institutions, and to make of them tools" (p. 28). He points out that
this plan was conceived when the mass Jewish emigration from Palestine
would have jeopardized the survival of the Zionist community there (p. 39).

This dichotomy has been captured by Joseph Hayyim Brenner.[12] In his novella *Mikan u-Mikan*, Brenner's main protagonist, Oved Etsot, says:

> A ridiculous marvel hung above their heads. Here, they came not very long ago, to an eastern and alien distant land, people of low stature and pale face, and they say they want to be peasants, laborers, and most of them call themselves "pioneers," "idealists"—on the face of it, this is very nice of them; on the face of it, it seems to be heroic and to show determination; on the face of it, it has the glory of *Yesod*, but within? Does it have a foundation?[13]

Brenner was extremely skeptical of the future prospects of Jewish cultural generativity. He was the first Zionist iconoclast writer, and a cynic. The literary critic Baruch Kurzweil has argued that, in his philosophical disposition, Brenner resembled those European Jewish thinkers and writers who "had lost their faith in Judaism and in its power to provide the spring for healthy and moral life." For them, Kurzweil says, "Judaism appears as disastrous, defective, and as the source of evil."[14]

In the novella, Oved Etsot says, "I do not retract my main object: my negative perception of an essentialist history of ours, [or] my heresy regarding the greatness of our heritage" (p. 1:338). And, in a letter to his friend Diasporin,[15] who lives in the United States, Oved Etsot writes:

> This is an old reckoning. I always had an utmost hatred for renaissance preachers who, instead of theology, instead of faith in God, which we have all lost forever, invented some sort of a new faith, blind, a faith in our great, hidden, nationalist powers, that they, as it were, do not fear the Diaspora, that they have shown, and that they are still about to show their wonders. (p. 1:338)

Oved Etsot is telling his friend about the Zionist community in Palestine:

> There is a congregation here of a few thousand Jews, dispersed and divided, which should not be granted preference over any similar Jewish congregation anywhere else. The same ghetto with all its attributes: idleness, a mixture of languages, Jewish occupations, foreign workers, dependence on Gentiles' discretion, a minority among a majority, fear of neighbors, emigration, strangeness, strangeness. (p. 1:338)

Then he deplores Diasporin:

> But if there were Jews in the world, if it were worthy speaking and if my voice could be heard, I would have shouted at them: they should not cast their fate on this dream. It is a horror dream. A false dream anyway. If any remnants of the people still exist and if they can establish a land for themselves wherever they are—let them have the strength and establish their revival anywhere. (p. 1:338)

There was very little tolerance for such ideological heresy. The Zionist Hebrew literary establishment in Europe was not only reserved, but even sneering. Brenner's critics argued that he was "more of a publicist than an artist."[16] They resented his dark, ascetic spirit: "Literature, and specifically young literature, should emphasize the joy of life," they argued (p. 16).

"If the tone of Brenner's criticism prior to 1907–1908 was foul," says Yitshak Bakon, "it became rather thick after his immigration to Palestine in 1909" (p. 18). The reaction to Brenner's new novel, *Between Water and Water* (1910), was negative and even wrathful." In a letter to Brenner, the poet H. N. Bialik, who was already probably the most prominent figure in the Hebrew cultural center of Odessa,[17] "categorically condemned" his novel, saying, "and your 'Between Water and Water' is water in water." Bakon says that "if the same artistic defects criticized in this novel were found in a story about the Jewish ghetto of London, for example, the vociferous rage would be of much lower volume" (p. 18). For those critics, says Bakon, "a story that takes place in the Holy City of Jerusalem," that reflects the "life [of the Zionist community] in Palestine, demands majestic respect and sacred praise" (p. 18). Another critic, Y. L. Baruch, demanded that Brenner should "leave the country and go and trade his rotten literary merchandise in the ghettos of London and Levov" (cited by Bakon, p. 19).[18]

Brenner's death, however, made of him a Zionist martyr. Writing about him became ceremonial, biographical, and ideological. Distinctions between Brenner, the person, and his literary protagonists were blurred. "Some began to apply his literary anti-Zionist pathos to support their own Zionist pathos, especially socialist-Zionism and the kibbutz movement" (Bakon, p. 25).

In his work as a publicist, Brenner did not fare any better.[19] On 24 November 1910 he published a critical article in his column in *Hapoel Hatzair* (The young worker) magazine regarding the current phenomenon of Jews converting to Christianity. Brenner expressed the opinion that religious conversion does not present a danger to the survival of the Jewish people, and added:

> As far as I am concerned the Old Testament too, does not carry such great value as everyone shouts, being the "Book of Books" the "Eternal Book," etc., etc. For a long time already I had liberated myself of the *hypnosis* of the twenty-four books of the *Biblia*. . . . By now . . . the New Testament—is our book as well, a bone of our bones, and a flesh of our flesh. And I do not consider the fact that I include . . . the "New Testament" in our spiritual heritage as a revolutionary act.[20]

This article caused a major storm among the the Hebrew literati, and was called the "Brenner Affair," or the "Apostasy Disputation."[21] Brenner was accused of "instigating an apostasy," and of being paid by Christian missionaries. Ahad Haam initiated a decision by the Hovevi Zion Committee in Odessa, headed by Menachem Usishkin, to discontinue its financial support for *Hapoel Hatzair*.[22]

A Brenner renaissance began in the 1950s and 1960s, when a younger generation of Israeli literary critics no longer considered the historical and political context of Brenner's work relevant to evaluating him as a writer. "After a long eclipse of Brenner's sun," wrote Dan Miron, "literary critics are required to emphasize the artistic-aesthetic meanings by which he inculcated his sense of the world with a distinctive artistic reality, but seemed to be regarded as a publicist" in the past.[23]

Statist Idealism and the Plight of Refugees

In 1984, the Israeli historian and journalist Tom Segev published a book titled *1949: The First Israelis*.[24] About one-fourth of it deals directly with the issue of the Jews' immigration and their absorption in Israel during its first three years as a state. Segev is regarded by some as one of Israel's "revisionist" historians. In fact, with the opening of some of Israel's historical archives to the public, documents not available before were examined, providing in some instances a different perspective on Israeli history.

Segev argues, for example, that in promoting mass immigration to Israel, Zionist leaders, many of whom also served in the government, were motivated by their statist idealism as much as by the plight of the refugees. This is indicated by the ways in which they provided for the refugees' needs. Segev provides ample evidence of the harsh and critically dangerous conditions of transportation suffered by the refugees from Europe. For them, and for those coming from Arab countries in the Middle East and North Africa, their new life resembled life in a concentration camp. Segev quotes an Absorption Department official telling the Zionist Executive Board that "it is no exaggeration to say that conditions were better in the refugee camps in Germany, after the war" (p. 124). Segev argues that although there were undeniable difficulties in administering the influx, the methods used to control the immigrants did not derive from conditions of general scarcity or a lack of financial resources. Rather, they reflected a design justified ideologically and guided by the purposes of the state. Thus, Ben Gurion argued that the main thing is the absorption of immigrants. . . . This embodies all the historical needs of the state. . . . We might have captured the West Bank, the Golan, the entire Galilee, but those conquests would not have reinforced our security as much as immigration. Doubling and tripling the number of immigrants gives us more and more strength. . . . That is the most important thing above all else. (quoted by Segev, p. 97)

The attitude of the "first Israelis" toward the newcomers was complex and self-contradictory, charged with emotion and infused with prejudice, reflecting their self-images as Jews and Israelis. The key lay in their evaluation of the Diaspora. Segev writes that "most tended to regard themselves as Israelis first and Jews second. Israel was above all." They often talked of the "elimination of the Jews," or "being eager to finish off the Diaspora" (p. 104). In this, Segev notes, "they discarded ancient Jewish cultures," and did so "without compunction, for they believed that they were making the only relevant history; the state of Israel meant more to them than the preservation of Jewish culture abroad" (pp. 117–18).

The number of Jewish refugees who went immediately from Europe to Israel after World War II was relatively small. Thus, it became urgent for Israel and the World Zionist Organization to encourage Jews to emigrate from their home countries, sometimes creating panic and at times near catastrophe. In the early 1950s and 1960s, Eastern Europe, North Africa, and the Middle East were the most likely places of origin for immigrants. The "emptying" of Jews from Arab countries was considered by the Israeli government to be an exchange of populations for the Palestinians expelled or otherwise displaced during the 1948–49 war.[25] This also justified expanding the war against the Palestinians into neighboring countries, a policy that eventually dragged all other Arab nations into the conflict. In many instances, emissaries of the Zionist Organization and Mossad functionaries operated illegally in those countries, often intimidating Jews in the effort to get them to emigrate.

Before the establishment of the Israeli state, the World Zionist Organization had no specific interest in Jewish life in the Middle East and North Africa. Once the country was established, however, there was no limit to that interest. Segev claims that, through bribery and other covert arrangements with governments of those countries, the actions of Zionist and Mossad agents contributed to increased hostility toward Jews, creating in some cases situations in which Jews had to flee in haste, only to arrive in Israel bewildered and impoverished. The explanation Segev offers for these policies are, first, the belief of the Zionists that the only legitimate place for Jews was Israel, and second, the belief that there would be no opportunity later to emigrate. The fact that the more affluent Jews chose to migrate not to Israel, but to France and other countries in Europe and to the United States (Segev, pp. 117–18),[26] gave the immigration a class as well as an ethnic character, which no doubt contributed to the direction taken by its administration. The mass of immigrants therefore arrived in Israel perplexed and immediately dependent upon the bureaucracies of the political parties. They often became clients of and constituencies for these parties, in the hope of at least solace for the abuse they regularly experienced as they searched for jobs, housing, health insurance, education, and other social services.

In contrast to this harsh reality, the poet Nathan Alterman wrote sentimentally about the immigrants whose arrival raised the Jewish population of Israel to about one million:

> It's good to be a million
> You look at them and your eyes grow moist
> Tears twinkle. And why?
> For we've said it, brother—Statistics
> Is not always something dry.[27]

Analogous to biblical prophecy in ancient times, Zionism reinforced itself with dire predictions in the form of what Neil Smelser has called "generalized beliefs"[28] about the future of world Jewry and the prospect of yet another Holocaust. "New catastrophes, no less dreadful, may yet happen," said Ben Gurion. And the writer S. Shalom warned: "This is an age of annihilation, of utter peril. We are facing the question whether or not we will exist as a people" (quoted by Segev, p. 115).

Dan Laor, an Israeli literary critic writing in 1988, saw a trend in the fact that "not only 'veteran' writers such as Nathan Alterman and Haiim Hazaz responded to the historical challenge of immigration and the ingathering of the exiles . . . but this matter was legitimized by the younger 'native' group of Israeli writers of the 1950s as well." Moshe Shamir, in 1946, demanded of those younger writers that they "go down to the people" and help "shape the real life of the country, express the values of Zionism, and build the Land."[29]

In 1954, Hanoch Bartov published a critically acclaimed novel focusing on immigration titled *Each Had Six Wings*. In 1958 it was adapted for the stage by the Habima, Israel's National Theater, and in 1987 it appeared in a new edition. The story takes place in an abandoned Palestinian neighborhood at the southern outskirts of Jerusalem, immediately after the 1948–49 war, an area that was in the process of being resettled by Jewish newcomers. For Bartov, it provided a paradigm for presenting the total life of the "new immigration."

The protagonists were represented as instances of complete social entities—the "Seventy Jewish Diaspora": social classes, fathers against sons, newcomers against veterans. Bartov attempted to create situations that could illustrate and provide an image of the new immigration in all its complexity. These included daily life, linguistic diversity, social differentiation, the experience of strangeness, the experience of alienation between veterans and newcomers, and confrontations with Israeli authorities.

The biographies of the various characters that appear in the course of the narrative were intended to represent the broad diversity of Jewish "destinies." But

> the representational spread of the mass immigration with all its aspects and components was guided in this work—as in those of Alterman, Hazaz, and other writers—by ideology. Although Hanoch Bartov is well aware of the reality of the 1950's, with all its problematic angles, he attempts to interpret it as a constructive social process, leading in an almost linear progression toward the assimilation of the newcomers into the "melting pot" of Israeli society, and to an almost instant achievement of the "Ingathering of Exiles."[30]

In contrast to the nationalist and Zionist pathos that characterized the approach to the "new immigration" by Alterman, Hazaz, Bartov, and M. Shamir, and in contrast to more recent writers, such as A. B. Yehoshua, Amos Oz, and David Grossman, who similarly present in their writing a hegemonic voice, one must mention a different tendency, represented by, among others, writers such as Yitzhaq Shami, Yehuda Burla, Shimon Ballas, Sammy Mikhael, Anton Shammas, Yitshaq Gormezano Goren, and Albert Swissa. They represent an alternative vision of the issue of immigration and, as Ammiel Alcalay has pointed out in a slightly different context, such "conceptions as a new national entity, the formation of a new state, the collective adoption of a new tongue, and the actual formation of a new culture."

> The construct, in this case, is that of Labor Zionism, with its particular version of a "master narrative." Here even the diversity and range of *mainstream* contemporary Israeli writing—and thus what is available to Jewish culture as a whole—has been greatly "abbreviated."[31]

Part I

1

Israeli Hebrew Literature
and Zionist Historiography

Sacred Texts as Material Force

Following the European "Jewish Enlightenment" (mid-eighteenth century), modern Hebrew literature positioned itself as a vehicle of cultural, social, and political criticism. Simon Halkin summarizes this trend in terms of its aim:

> Convinced that it preached the salvation of the group, it lashed out against what it considered social ills of the Jew's own making—against the obscurantism of Jewish orthodoxy, against the supineness of the Jewish masses under the "oppressions" to which they were subjected by the ghetto oligarchy, against the inertness of the community in the face of constant economic insecurity and cultural stagnation.[1]

But this aim was, according to Halkin, predicated on yet a greater project. He argues that, based on the prevailing bourgeois ideologies and literary genres of the epoch, and following the granting of political emancipation to Jews in major Central and Western European countries, the writers of the Enlightenment assigned themselves the task of revising Jewish history to establish an immediate link between their image of a humanist-rational "Renaissance" Jew, which they thought was demanded by their epoch, and the Israelite pastoral shepherd-king of the biblical narrative specifically depicted in the books of Judges and Kings. This provided the framework within which the millenarial aspect of Zionism took root.

Following the fall of the "Israel Northern Kingdom" in the late eighth century B.C., and the destruction of the "First Temple" in Jerusalem early in the sixth century B.C., the Jewish diaspora that already existed in ancient Mesopotamia and Egypt, as well as other countries in the region, was greatly enlarged. At the same time, other peoples were settled in the country by the kings of Assyria. In 538 B.C., a charter granted by Cyrus, king of Persia, permitted the restoration of Judea as a relatively autonomous protectorate. Consequently, Judea, like a few other small states, was able to remain relatively autonomous, first under Hellenist and then under Roman rule, until about the middle of the second century A.D.[2]

During this time, the diaspora grew much larger than the Jewish population of Judea itself, and developed networks of social and cultural institutions with internal legislative and representative bodies in the various countries of its sojourn. However, as for most of this epoch neither Judea nor its Diaspora developed an independent base for the exercise of political power, the learned word of the "sacred texts" served as the only authority in the conduct of life, and in community affairs. If any historic connection at all may be assumed between these ancient communities and Jewish communities living today, it can be attributed only to the material force of what otherwise seems merely idea or notion, namely, the sacred texts themselves.[3]

For such traditions to develop, a broad and widespread system of popular education must have been in place since very early times, and education, from the elementary to the extremely esoteric, had to have been institutionally secure beyond even the question of content. One should not underestimate, however, the mediating force of non-Jewish thought in the development of Jewish culture. Initially, Aristotelian, Hellenist, and neo-Platonist thought were important, replaced later by the early Greek-Christian schools. Following the emergence of Islam and the rise of Muslim-Arab culture in the mid-seventh century, thinkers such as Rabbi Sa'adia Gaon, Isaac ha'Israeli, Solomon Ibn Gabirol, Ba'Hayaii Ibn Pekuda, Yehuda Ha'Levi, Abraham Ibn Daud, Musa Ibn Mimon (Maimonides), Levi ben Gershon, and Hasdai Karshkash, all of whom lived in Muslim countries, brought to bear on Jewish thought the works of the great medieval Muslim philosophers, including Ibn-Sina, Al-Kindi, Al-Farabi, Al-Khawarizmi, and Ibn Rushd.[4]

Until the middle of the eighteenth century, all Jewish texts founded their legitimacy in the religious codex. At that point, a process of secularization began within the European Jewish community, evidence of which is manifest in the departure of younger scholars from tradition in favor of "external" studies. Because the political and material conditions for such a change had been emerging in Europe for at least a century under the auspices of the newly assertive bourgeois class, these revisionists were able to achieve high intellectual stature in various countries, even outside of Jewish settings (for example, in Germany, Moses Mendelssohn).[5]

The emergence of a secular bourgeois nation-state following the Napoleonic Wars, and the ensuing popular struggles for national liberation in Europe, led many "reformed" modern Jewish intellectuals to endorse the prevailing nationalistic sentiments of their time. Rabbis, the first to articulate such aspirations, used the lexical and metaphorical field of theology to give "providential" legitimacy to worldly, political, human action. A millenarian, messianic movement emerged as the herald of this new liberatory spirit.[6]

Those who succeeded the revisionist rabbis were, in most instances, their sons, but they included others as well who were willing and able to leave their traditional homes and orthodox schooling at a relatively young age. Most attended secular institutions of higher education as unaccredited students, and their scholarship was, to some extent at least, amateurish and intuitive relative to that which they criticized. They were more versed in the writings of Goethe, Schiller, Heine, Dostoyevsky, and Tolstoy than in those of Kant, Hegel, Marx, and Nietzche. They became "modernists," "rationalists," "liberals," and "socialists" as a reflection of their existential position in a new global social constellation, and they did so by means of belles lettres, rather than through systematic and scientific study.[7]

This was not in itself a disadvantage. Close to the surface lay the Bible; the messianic idea, the "millenarian promise" embodied in the Hasidic temperament, provided tremendous spiritual as well as emotional energy. Not having access to mainstream institutions for maintaining an immanently Jewish social order, Jews of the time spilled great quantities of ink, rather than blood, in fighting their internal wars. This may help to explain why modern Hebrew literature assumed so prominent a role in Jewish life at the expense of theology, thereby appropriating for itself an almost unchallenged authority over secular discourse for the past one hundred years. Many of the earliest of these literary works can be seen as pre-Zionist texts, articulating specific Zionist-like themes that easily translated into the Zionist "master narrative." The specific modalities of this articulation are evident in novels and constitute in the novel form itself the ideologically representational constitutive divisions that developed within and in relation to Israeli national society.[8]

When the Zionist movement came into being, the corpus of modern Hebrew literature was well established as a center of cultural authority for a relatively coherent frame of reference that provided Zionism with the means to disseminate its message and a context in which the legitimacy and the motivational force of that message were already prepared. The notion of a return to the "promised land" merely made explicit what was already a "structure of feeling," and its transformation from a historical promise to a moral obligation, from a matter of sensibility to a matter of republican virtue, gave it a distinctly modernist politicality. This is indicated by the participation of eminent writers in the Zionist Executive, in prominent Zionist social and cultural institutions, and as delegates to Zionist world congresses following the early lead of such figures as Herzl, Ahad Haam, N. Sokolov, E. Ben Yehuda and H. N. Bialik. The overlap of literature and politics, and the special cultural significance of the former, led in many instances to writers' playing a more important role than politicians in the formation of constituencies and policy.[9]

In late medieval times, and in the culture of the shtetl, however, secular Hebrew books were forbidden.[10] Even the study of the Prophets was restricted and permitted only for the more mature, as one was not supposed to read the Bible for pleasure or for its literary content. Jewish culture in Central Europe had for centuries been anti-intellectual, under the control of harsh rabbis who scorned any modern knowledge. Yet, the Hebrew word for *writer* derives from the act of copying the Bible (counting the letters of the text). Hebrew publishing was not seen as ordinary commercial activity, but was looked upon almost as a calling, especially during earlier times, when the only purpose for writing books was to interpret and be instructed by the Scriptures. Thus, modern Hebrew literature found itself operating institutionally at the most generalizing level of the superstructure. This is why Gershon Shaked concludes that this history of textual presence is most eloquently represented by Zionist "renaissance literature."[11]

Hebrew Literature in Palestine and Israel

When we turn to Hebrew literature in Palestine, and later in Israel, it is necessary to distinguish between two separate periods, first from the early 1900s to the late 1950s, and since then to the present. The event that marks the division is the mass immigration of the late 1940s and 1950s, which in ten years tripled Israel's Jewish population. The sudden numerical swell dramatically changed Israel's social fabric. Before the establishment of the state, the Zionist community in Palestine was, in many respects, more or less homogeneous. The majority of its members came from Europe, primarily from Eastern Europe. Many had experienced some education and training in Zionist camps and communes, and though most lacked formal higher education, they were avid readers of European classic literature and, secondarily, Jewish and non-Jewish history. Some became versed in philosophy and social science and, probably most important for the quality of their participation in Zionist active life, modern Hebrew literature. Many of the German Jews who migrated to Palestine in the early 1930s and during the years immediately preceding World War II were professionals and academicians. These constituted the first Zionist intellectual elite in Palestine.[12]

By then, Hebrew literature in Palestine had positioned itself at the apex of cultural life (classical music and art were just emerging as national cultural media). However, the legacy of such writers as A. Mapu, M. J. Berdichevsky, J. H. Brenner, and A. N. Gnesin, and later H. N. Bialik, S. Tchernichovsky, S. Y. Agnon, and H. Hazaz, in the final analysis, limited the boundaries of Hebrew literature to a distinct national setting, linking politics and literature in ways supported by the Zionist leadership itself.[13]

Aside from the few modest private publishers, institutions such as the Zionist Organization, the Federation of Trade Unions, and most political parties had their own publishing houses. Almost every party had its daily newspaper and weekly literary supplements featuring original prose, poetry, and literary criticism oriented toward Zionist life in Palestine. From this point of view the times were revolutionary, and literature was held to that standard.[14] The eventual structure of this deeply literary political culture provided no clear distinction between the "high" and the "popular," and, increasingly, left little room for the implicit or the latent.

The migrations of the 1950s initially represented a break in the continuity of this structure. The majority of the newcomers could not speak, read, or write Hebrew, and for many years literature, Hebrew or non-Hebrew, was the least of their existential priorities. But this was momentary. Although so decisive a demography was bound to threaten the hegemony of the established literary culture, it may, paradoxically, have given it a yet more definite institutional position in Israeli society than before.

The Imaginaire of the Living Utopia

I am interested in studying how literary texts pose the less obvious moral dilemmas of Israel's culture, in particular those that have to do with relations of self to society, and of society to history. Thus, I am especially concerned with dilemmas arising from how subjects are thought to be related to the Law, those that bear on the subjective aspect of Israeli civil society. Whereas interpersonal relations ignore their own moral problems for individual actors, I am interested in that level of moral thought that constitutes rather than merely manifests the normative order, such as it may be. Thus, the civil subject precedes the interpersonally responsive subject, in Israeli culture as in many others, though in Israeli culture the division between civil and juridical subjects is particularly fraught with alterity, and hence laden with opportunities for a deeply guarded bad faith.[15] Thus, the issue of historical "value," difference, is immediately presented within Israeli moral/political discourse and unavoidable from the standpoint of all parties to that discourse. Relations of civil subject to civil subject are relations that individuals manifest in general, as representatives. Therefore, they carry the weight of an exclusion as well as inclusion. The other is, in a sense, the object of the civil subject, and the latter expresses the subjectivity beyond what an individual can claim on her or his own. It follows that the overriding relation that presents itself as one of *Subject* to *Subject* changes when one term refers to an *other* beyond moral society. When this other is nevertheless acknowledged as a subject, the relation is that of the moral citizen of the living utopia to the merely juridical citizen of the state. The former appears as an authentic subject, whereas the latter is, as it were, a merely practical subject who is always an instance of a category, never an authentic representative. The authentic moral citizen's relation to the living utopia is not available to the juridical subject as such, for whom society is a practical but never a moral community.

These relations, and the dilemmas they constitute, appear in virtually every canonical literary work as the textualized presence of a greater cultural reality and as features of a greater discourse on the universal significance of the Israeli and Jewish experience. A preliminary test of this hypothesis lies in the comprehensiveness with which these relational presences operate within specific texts. My analysis focuses on the morally deceptive key relations of the Jewish person as moral citizen to the non-Jewish person as juridical citizen. This requires accounting specifically for ways in which "the Arab" is represented in Israeli Hebrew literature. It requires, as well, exploring the field in which these representations constitute the quintessential non-Jewish person of Israeli Hebrew literature, and how these two ostensibly equal subjectivities are stratified from the point of view of the Jewish civil subject. The latter is the major finding of my investigation.

At the same time, I argue that through the *imaginaire* of the living utopia, which for historical reasons has become a dominant and substantive field of reference throughout Israeli Hebrew literature, the texts dramatize and re-create the relationship of Israeli society to itself, to "its" history. They thereby encompass the less-than-utopian obligations of people as citizens to the living society of which they are part—that is, they inscribe a practicable "general will" on an embodied lesser world of counterwills, ostensibly affirming a community of Law and a unity of theory and practice. This argument draws upon historical research suggesting that Israeli society presents itself, by virtue of its elevation of Law to the status of a moral and practical imperative, as a virtuous "republic."

But, for one reason if for no other, Israeli republicanism fails to guarantee itself. It spatializes and temporalizes its posit of a general will by the qualification of lineage and therefore, in the modern reference of lineage to a type of person, hence a population, "race." Thus, it is difficult for an Israeli Jew to understand other Jews who are not Zionists, and the difference can be represented only negatively, as one of identity versus a lack of identity.[16] In this sense, the non-Zionist is, for Zionism, neither lapsed, nor absent, nor missing. He or she is not to be mourned, but is erased from memory, and, in the moment of that erasure, is reconstituted as a moral Other, therefore an enemy of morality itself. That is, the rejection of the non-Zionist by the Zionist, in the name of both the republican form and the living utopia that is its Israeli content, is conceived fundamentally as a matter of moral revelation, a charismatic moment rather than a result of a deliberated resolution of a difference of opinion or principle.[17] This antidialogism, this monologue that challenges the possibility of sociality in its very assertiveness, establishes an ethical foundation for what otherwise would appear to be merely intolerance or absolutism. It is the point at which Israeli Jewish culture draws a boundary aimed at delineating and protecting the possibility of a *Jewish* discourse, a Jewish moral universe, and an ethos of conviviality necessary for the experience of equilibrium and a balance of expectation and obligation.

As with all such boundaries, this one measures its own futility. The cost of those ethnic virtues and resources is ultimately the possibility of boundedness, hence, the interiorizing vitality and centering associated with the boundary-dependent notion of a living utopia. Its very secularity, as a device aimed at security, betrays that visionary notion by making of membership itself an obligation and the object of *a test*, something that cannot be lived with the pleasure of practical day-to-day sociality. This self-alienation that is built into the effort to cure alienation provides a core problematic for the liberal branch of Zionist morality, which wishes to escape the exclusivist strictures of Zionism and to recover the universalism by which alone the living utopia can find its moral justification. But the best it can do, as I will try to show, is to defer the crisis of identity in which the Other by which the community defines itself is revealed as community itself. Thus, the utopian community must ulti-

mately sacrifice itself as a practical reality, or form of life, to its own dreams
and fantasies. Tragically, it can hardly avoid first sacrificing those "external"
others against which it had hoped to define itself as an ethically complete
totality.[18]

It would be relevant to mention here the Israeli High Court's 1989 decision
on the challenge to the right of the Progressive List for Peace to run in the
elections. The challenge was rejected, three to two, on narrow grounds, based
on the claim that it had not been definitively proven that the PLP was calling
for equal rights for Arab citizens of Israel. But the position of Justice Menahem
Elon, that "it is necessary to prevent a Jew or Arab who calls for equality of
rights for Arabs from sitting in the Knesset [Parliament] or being elected to it,"
appears to have been upheld by a four-to-one majority. The charge that the
PLP program calls for full equality between Jewish and Arab citizens, and, fur-
thermore, that the party intends "to act to realize equality in all aspects of
life," was not considered to have been proven. But the majority appears to
have agreed with Justice Dov Levin that such commitments (which he
thought *had* been proven) would suffice to bar the party from the political system. As Justice Dov Levin put it, the PLP members "completely deny that the
State of Israel is the State of the Jewish people," so, although they have the
right to express their opinions, if these opinions "conflict with the Basic Law
of the Knesset" by calling for equal rights, the party is barred from participation in the political system—or would be barred according to the Court majority, if those transgressions had been fully proven.[19]

The utopian aspect of Israeli Jewish culture, in regard to which Zionism
asserts a power—to define, to know, to declare—that ultimately depends on
the unattainable pleasures of exclusivist community, provides a special ideological articulation of history. Class (internal) and race (external) are finally
constituted as a synthetic abstraction that operates to delineate, as fundamentally distinct, the relations of juridical citizenship and moral being. Zionism
was, at the outset, in certain respects a class ideology as well as one imbued
with a moralism of race.[20] The synthesis of the political and the moral incorporates class and race in an essentialist configuration of otherwise ambiguous
terms of exclusion. This configuration relies on the attribution of traitlike dispositions and assures the validity of trait signs and identity names. When it is
taken in its orientation to the non-Jew, it bears the aspect of "racialism," an
intellectual propensity to see others in terms of rigidly stratified principles of
difference and disposition. It rationalizes social divisions in a way that dis-
qualifies, as a moral imperative, the mixing of groups.

For example, the difficulty of acknowledging "the" Arab as a possible partner in a "general will" may be understood as an expression of the absolute distinction between moral citizenship (a matter of identification) and juridical citizenship (a matter of enforced obligation) in the context of the historical conflict on which the validity of the absoluteness of the distinction depends. This complex formation frames moral decision in such a way that it is possible spontaneously to think ethically only if the thought is supported by a self-reflection that is also a moment of the utopian reflection of society on itself. It effectively transforms every moral decision from an instance of a specialized rationality to a total reflection on self and society, to a contentless rationality as such. The three "tropes," identity, utopia, and boundary, make it difficult if not impossible to avoid a hypermoralization of politics in which what is *of* politics but external to morality—that is, the Arab—is subject in principle to exclusion on the basis of race.

Israel is not unique in this structure of rationalization for policies of exclusion. South Africa can be described in somewhat similar terms, as generating a white racialist culture inconsistent with expansion—for example, by negotiation—of the body politic in the direction of a greater moral inclusion of its putative "other."[21] I want to show how the critical intention of certain Israeli Hebrew novels is similarly undermined by the imperatives of its informing ideology, in specific regard to depictions of "the Arab" and, through those, of the Jewish self.

Briefly, the Arab cannot be conceived of as an authentic moral being (unless, as A. B. Yehoshua argues against Shammas, he or she "moves to a Palestinian state").[22] He or she exists only in the formlessness of a nonsubject assimilated to the generally negative category of the *other than us* and its concomitant moralistic evaluation—*unable to be us*. This has its abstract political aspect in the attempt to assert a moral universe as a condition of claiming a territorial realization of Jewish history. In this way, the questions surrounding conquest are resolved by asserting a polity that can stand for the moral universe itself, therefore one based on the identification of exclusion with moral rectitude.

The exclusionary attitude of Zionism toward "the Arab" is understandable in these terms, and it may be that one can extend this understanding to account for yet different but equally morally charged exclusions—Christian, Moslem, non-European ethnic Jews (Sephardim and Arab Jews)—and the tendency to place at least in the margin the "Diaspora" Jew and the Israeli Jewish emigrant. In all of this, exclusion and marginalization are accompanied by an extraordinarily self-conscious but unself-critically idealist historiography in which the living utopia of Zionism's Israel is at the center of an epic and epochal narrative, the course of which is strictly allegorical, and whose persuasive force lies in its accumulation of a seemingly endless stream of confirming anecdotes and cases.

The national history that appears in Israeli Hebrew literature and the historiography of the Holocaust are both relevant to an understanding of the significance of Israeli Hebrew literature to and within its cultural context. Yet neither defines that context to the extent to which it is understood in terms of its informing ideology. The Holocaust and national histories are, in the discourses that now prevail, products of, rather than sources of evidence for, Zionism.

The Israeli Hebrew novel walks a very different line between fiction and reality from that drawn in most American literature. Its audience requires something more than narrative plausibility, the subjective possibility that events within the narrative *could* have happened as represented whether they did or not, what Riffaterre calls "fictional truth."[23] What it requires above all is *historically* objective plausibility, namely, that such events *probably* happened and that events of the given type certainly *must* have happened.[24]

In the canonical Israeli literary text, the use of historical materials is intended to be informative as well as moralizing, *and* to inform about history as a whole, as is appropriate for a people that claims to make its own history and therefore "history" as such. This use of history has properties in common with the traditional epic, but the attempt to define a universal praxis, to display an obligation to history, defines it as a distinct genre. One can see this clearly by comparing the Israeli novel to familiar and ahistorical genre traditions of popular American literature. Unlike the North American writer, the Israeli Jewish writer cannot plausibly construct a plot around isolated ironist heroes who move, barely noticed, within settings of unlimited extent—such as, "the Far West" or "bourgeois society." He or she cannot simply dwell on a character's predicament without a historical account of it as a general condition, or on such conspicuous challenges as those that lead protagonists to utterly individualistic modes of action, or on those journeys that pit the subjectivity of the hero against the limits of place and time in the sort of universally indifferent allegory of personal growth and development typical of modern romance novels in the West. The Israeli writer must always position the present *as a whole* in the consuming context of a *total* history, and reconstitute the individuals of the present as agents but never as principals or sources of principle.

This allegorical mode of constituting a semblance of praxis, with its sense of movement from the past toward just this very moment of ethnic society, this living utopia, provides the foundation for the historically "explanatory affect" that invariably accompanies every other pleasure in Israeli Hebrew literary fiction.[25] The Israeli Hebrew author resolves the putative historical order to a narrative order in which moral priorities are stated in reference to a cumulative series of oppressions and resistances superintended by the telos of the living utopia, the Zionist's Israel. This integration of telos and experience has the look of a dialectic, but it operates only as an incomplete version, producing what Hegel called mystical enthusiasm rather than enlightenment. Thus, it has the effect of making present experience both tolerable in its pain and exhilarating in its prospect. The most recent Jewish oppression becomes yet another demonstration of that telos of total history that transcends the suffering of mere others and any history that such others might, on their own behalf, create.[26]

Today, the Holocaust has become the Israeli Jewish writer's standard of suffering. Therefore, it is also the legitimate standard moment in which resistance makes itself visibly heroic and heroism appears as visibly historic. By definition, no other people can justify resistance and struggle because no other can claim an equal grievance, an authentic beginning that makes this struggle necessary and universally significant. Thus, the writer is free to explore the terms under which Arabs and Jews actually communicate in Israel, but never terms of a possible negotiation based on mutual recognition. The latter presupposes rights, a sense of violation, and justifications external to the Jewish experience as defined, precisely what Zionism cannot admit for any other people.

It is, in that light, possible to understand why the Zionist conception of Jewish history is systematically lacking in the compassion evident at least in some other Jewish traditions of self-knowledge. Thus, we have the paradox of the narrative of the Holocaust erasing all other instances of modern genocide—of Palestinian Arabs, Africans, Latin Americans, American Indians—as in the long narrative of Jewish history, with its endless and ungenerous sectarian sadness. This is why no amount of suffering can be permitted a definition that would expand the "genocidal universe" of which only the Holocaust is permitted to be the definitive instance. This is why no struggle can be justified as part of a universal struggle but that of the Jews for Israel. To be sure, this is a narrative that, in other contexts, would preserve the universal idea of the voice of humanity, a morality virtually infinite in compassion. But the possibility of articulating this theme is altogether subverted in the context of Zionism.

To see this, one needs to look at the history presented in Israeli Hebrew literature in terms of how it contributes to and substantiates the project of

Zionism. What does this history present such that the Israeli Jewish Hebrew reader must choose between recognizing "the Arab" as absolutely nonidentical to the Jew and finding a Jewish aspect only in those Arabs who are not culturally or politically endowed? Either "the Arab" is morally empty or he or she is like "the Jew." In either case, "the Arab" can only be good or bad, never a morally practical being. In the first case, the good Arab is totally predictable, or dead; the bad Arab is arrogant, intrusive, ungrateful, insistent, alive. In the second case, the good Arab is tormented, guilt-ridden, self-doubting, eager for Jewish recognition, or self-destructive. The bad Arab either betrays his or her people (e.g., by becoming a Jew) or lives ambiguously but without guilt or self-reflection.[27]

What cannot occur is the recognition of a moral other in whose gaze the Jew would find him- or herself suddenly objectified as a Jew, made an essence, in the face of the then existentially vital, subjective, and self-reflective Arab. In such a turning of tables, "the Arab" would not be merely *deserving* of respect, but would suddenly be the *measure* of respect. Instead of a Jewish morality to which the Arab must but can never conform, there would be an Arab morality or moralities in the light of which it would be the Jew who would lack the right to claim, without question, moral substance and the corresponding capacity to sustain a morally significant identity. Suddenly the Jewish reader would feel, apodictically, that only the Arab can judge, can grant recognition to that reader as a moral subject.[28] Such a "dizzying" reversal of fortune is nowhere found in the canonical Hebrew literature of Israel. Its lack constitutes the most important critical limitation of that literature and stands as a fundamental paradox of Israeli Jewish culture. It defines the inability of that culture simultaneously to assimilate the principle of universalism on which its claim of the moral priority of the Jewish experience rests with the exceptionalist theme by which that priority is and can only be experienced.

2

The Problematic of a "Good Arab"

The Inability to Turn the Tables

The moral limitations of Zionist ideology are poignantly displayed in Yoram Kaniuk's novel, *Confessions of a Good Arab*. Kaniuk's protagonist is "part" Arab and "part" Jew. In this ontological ambiguity, he encapsulates the moral and political chaos of a geopolitical reality and lives the contradiction of that fact as a course of self-loss and self-discovery. The novel presents a political fact—the confrontation of Jew and Arab—as an allegory of authenticity. In this regard it is a meditation upon and engagement with the moral dimension of politics aimed at instituting a disposition toward universal compassion within the putatively authentic self of "post-Diasporic" Israeli Jewish society. However, the ambiguity of self that afflicts the novel's protagonist ultimately substantiates an image of a utopia that can be enjoyed in a morally gratifying way only by the unambiguously Jewish Israeli reader. The ambiguity that initiates an essentially moral quest is denied by the very success of the quest, leaving the good conscience produced in the text unable to remember how it came to know itself as good. In *Confessions of a Good Arab*, only the Israeli Jewish reader can experience the coming to fruition of a moral self compatible with the view of history. But, as will become clear, even that remains in doubt. Its systematic conflation of morality and politics reveals in the development of Kaniuk's narrative the most radical limitations of his project.

One attribute that gives *Confessions of a Good Arab* its place at or near the center of Israeli culture is the size and visibility of its audience. Its author is a canonical writer, which means that his work informs the work of other writers; it participates as object and as point of view in significant literary, political, and social discourses; and it has become part of critical reflection on Israeli national literary traditions. *Confessions of a Good Arab* presents the actual polity of the opposition of Arab and Jew in an idealized relation between moral and juridical selves that can only favor the former over the latter.

The story traces an allegory in which the protagonist's failure of identity is overcome through his exploration of a division—of Arab and Jew—within his experience of himself, by his acknowledgment of an absolute otherness in regard to which the self must measure its authenticity. This absolute is then distinguished from the merely relative otherness with which one ("we") must and can live in a condition of mutual understanding against the absolute other. But this resolution begs two questions: (1) On whose terms, and with whose sense of problem is the problematic self authorized to discover *and* convey the truth of its history? (2) How can it know that history as its own and as true?

The tendency to resolve the ambiguity of the self is mediated within and enforced by a political reality that defies compassion and a social reality that defies mutual recognition, and by a societal unity that appears as virtually neutral, universal, and prior to politics. Kaniuk narrates a dilemma of self-recognition that virtually exhausts the spirit. His novel, like its protagonist, ultimately falls victim to its own circumstances. It memorializes valor—"honesty"—at the cost of the memory of the dilemma in the light of which valor was possible in the first place. Whatever success the protagonist has in confronting what, in his dual identity, he represents to Jewish Israelis is betrayed by his failure to recognize what compels someone like him to confront identity as a problem in the first place.

Thus, a self divided against itself becomes allegorically complete, as if returning to an original wholeness the initial departure from which is then only an error or accidental. This is in one respect analogous to the Zionist illusion of a final and complete Israel. But, perhaps more important, this recovery of origins at the expense of history is the only way in which selfhood can be achieved within the Jewish culture of contemporary Israel. This is why the allegory is poignant and not merely a sham.

How then does it operate? The allegory is the undertext, or the telos, of a series of narratives. The relationship between this undertext and the narratives is revealed in many ways throughout the book, but it is presented imme-

diately as a problem by two otherwise curious devices: its title, which combines the pathos of confusion with the savage irony of racial slur, and the
adoption of an Arab-like pseudonym, Yosef Sherara, by the Jewish author.

The book is, then, even before it is read as a novel, allegorical. It manifests
in its two most objectlike traits, title and authorship, an underlying contradiction between the culturally idealist conditions of recognizing the other and
the relatively practical conditions of self-recognition. In this way, the object-
book sets the stage for the novel-text to address a key issue for the Israeli liberal conscience in regard to the "Arab-Jewish question": How can one be both
Zionist and moral in the existential, self-reflective sense of the term?

Despite the author's desire to confront and overcome the essentialisms of
self and other in the midst of their deployment within the essentialist politics
of contemporary Israel, the novel fails internally to fulfill its project. It lacks
what it most requires, namely, an acknowledgment of this particular constitution of self and other. Yet it is clear that Kaniuk has made a serious attempt to
explicate a point of view that, at least arguably, can be recognized, not merely
acknowledged, as the other's. To the extent to which the other of the novel
resembles the other that is "the Arab," the self-sufficient Arab, Kaniuk might
be said to have succeeded. However, it is not possible to demonstrate such a
resemblance; nor could such a demonstration guarantee that the "real" Arab
could be described beyond the semblance, therefore neutrally, and then be
held up as a whole, without the limitations of perspective, as a test of the
fictional image of the "recognizable" other. Therefore, one must still ask how
the Arab is constructed by the novel as one that a Jew can claim to recognize
as a subject, and what is involved even in so limited a recognition.

Clearly, the recognition of another as subject requires, at least momentarily, experiencing the self as object. But the problem of recognition itself
emerges in a context that precludes tolerance for such a turning of the tables:
self, other, and mutuality appear in the way they do only for a subjectivity that
can know no alternative to itself. This, at least, is what I hope to show—that
the possibility of a subjectively valid recognition is caught in the same
predicament as the failure or inability to recognize, and, therefore, that this
novel could have succeeded only by turning against the Zionist subjectivity it
had hoped to reform and, by reforming, conserve.

For the tables to have been turned, the Jew in Kaniuk's self-divided protagonist would have to constitute an experience of self as an instance of its own
originally posited otherness. It would have to have found, at least momentarily, the terror of lapsed subjectivity, a helplessness of the self in the face of total
definition from without. Only then, in the midst of its own hostile objec-

tification, could this self find the possibility of self-criticism. In that case, it would reemerge as a full subjectivity on the side of its former other, the Arab, and therefore against the Zionist ideological emphasis on difference and exclusion. What Kaniuk intended as a reform of the self could have succeeded in a reform greater than mere self-affirmation only if it could have become radical vis-à-vis its own presuppositions. It would then have come to know as itself what it had once taken for its enemy. That is, it would have *recognized* the other in regard to a history of its own denial of that other's subjectivity. This would also be a history of a defense of the self against self-recognition, therefore of the reasons for and contradictions of such a defense. Thus, as a matter of principle, defense against a possible reversal of fortune reveals the inherent instability of a self made definite as an identity only by its rejection of an other.

As I hope to show, *Confessions of a Good Arab* nevertheless challenges Zionism from within by insisting on questioning the principle by which only Jewish Israeli subjectivity is included in the moral universe claimed for Israeli society. It suggests that exclusionism is inconsistent with the universalism claimed by Zionism in the light of the Holocaust as justification for the inherently primary morality of the Jewish experience, and requires an untoward suppression of any attempt to expand the moral universe to include those defined as other. This suggestion, implicit in the novel, that Zionism has not lived up to its own metaethics allows us to read *Confessions of a Good Arab* as posing as poignantly as possible the question of whether or not Judaism can survive Zionism. The problem is that the poignancy of this implicit critique is only an instant in a system of thought determined to protect itself from any and all moral challenges. Thus, the novel's critique is only momentarily unsettling; in the aftermath of reading it, the reader finds him- or herself in the same position he or she was in before the dilemma was posed. The novel's bad faith lies in its cancellation of the very self-critique that it introduces as the object of its project. But it is a bad faith within the project itself, not that of the author alone. Reform within any exclusionist formation can only end by setting conditions of inclusion that reaffirm exclusion.

Title, Pseudonym, and Criticism

The Hebrew edition of Yoram Kaniuk's novel *Confessions of a Good Arab* was published in 1984, under the pseudonym Yosef Sherara. This curious *nom de plume* is composed of Hebrew and Arabic elements in an altogether awkward amalgam. It is a pseudonym, but, because of its elements and their combination, it is also an impossible name. The novel's Hebrew title is *Aravi Tov*, meaning "a good Arab." The Hebrew title of the book ends with a comma, the full phrase suggestively incomplete: *A Good Arab,*.[1] The comma provocatively signifies the Hebrew colloquialism, "A good Arab is a dead Arab."

According to the narrator, *A Good Arab,* is a confessional narrative in the first person: "The words I am sending to the reader are supposed to be a confession, probably a partial autobiography" (Heb. 5; Eng. 2).[2] Its principle, what motivates the *book* (text plus title, plus "author"), is the desire to create suspicion on the part of the reader—suspicion about identity in general. This is done first by coupling the uncertainty of authorship (of the book) with the ambiguity of the narrator's identity (in the text). Suspicion is also created through a constant ironic subversion of action. For example:

> If they finally catch up with me and somebody decides, in spite of everything, to settle accounts with me, I'll laugh. I've come to the end of my tears, and of my fears too. If I weren't the victim of the executioner who was my own self, I would have written an amusing farce. (Heb. 6; Eng. 2)

The accumulation of such instances of ironic alienation reverses the usual moral order of agenda and content. The imagination of the act is more important than the act and, as a result, what might have been a morality or a politics is finally established as an untrustworthy consciousness, but one that is threatening. Our capacity to identify with so picaresque a character lies in the fact that his critique of "us" is one in which he does not believe. It is one that can be entertained without having to be thought through or lived. We will see, finally, that the truly, recognizably, "good Arab" is the Arab as such, and no one in particular. Therefore the "good Arab" is only a possibility never materialized. The Arab is good only when he or she is no one in particular, is beyond situation, lacks politics, is without vitality or life. With neither agenda nor the capacity to respond to situations, with neither memory (connected speech, discourse) nor practice (connected activities), the essential Arab becomes the truly dead, objectified Arab of the occupation. As a practical matter, the good Arab can be only *for another;* therefore he or she can exist only institutionally, as an abstraction of law and its sanctions. In this case, the reform offered by Kaniuk can be only something between pity and compassion, an abstract acceptance and a momentary indulgence in sentiment for a victim of an unacknowledgeable perpetrator.

The novel recounts the life of an Arab Jew, Yosef, who was born in Paris in 1950.[3] His father was a Palestinian Arab born in 1904, in the town of Acre. His Jewish mother was born in Berlin, in 1930. The plot opens in the Cafe

Kassit in Tel Aviv, apparently in late autumn of 1971, and moves back to World War I, when Franz Rosenzweig (born in 1895) met Azouri Sherara on the Haifa seashore at the foot of Mt. Carmel. Sherara, a Christian Palestinian Arab, was then thirteen years old. An immediate bond of love is established, which they would not admit to each other and which would eventually come to muddle their lives. Azouri marries Franz's daughter, Hava, and they have a son, Yosef, who is the novel's protagonist.

Yosef graduated from art school in 1971. He had just ended an intimate relationship with Dina that had continued from their early adolescence. Dina, a young and renowned Jewish poet living in Tel Aviv, is the daughter of Holocaust survivors. Yosef occasionally sleeps with Laila, an Arab woman who lives in Haifa. His friends are for the most part derelicts, or "bums," who hang out in the disreputable Cafe Kassit. Frustrated by his rejection for military service, because his father was an Arab, Yosef goes to work for the Mossad. His rejection by the army confronts him with a problem he never knew he had, the lack of a clear identity. Instead of being an Israeli of mixed parentage, he is suddenly and dizzyingly reconstituted as an *Arab claiming to be a Jew*. For a Jew there can be no separation of self from citizenship. From the standpoint of the Jew, the Israeli Arab self is by definition separate from Israeli society; though subject to the law, he cannot be moral, only obedient. He thus owns none of the moral entitlements of society's history.

Yosef is a Jewish Arab who becomes—through the micropolitics of identity—both Jew and Arab and therefore cannot be a Jew. Indeed, Yosef discovers himself as a purely negative identity, the non-Jew. This is his problem: an ambiguity of essence comes to infect his subjective life, determine the prospects of his freedom, and define him for the Israeli Jewish reader not so much as a character but as an impractical *field* of moral dialogue. The novel's ethical project is to create the opportunity for Jews to be compassionate toward Arabs by guiding the Jewish reader toward an identification with the duality of Yosef's self, in itself a simulacrum of the historical dualism, so much discussed, of Jewish identity as such. In *this* identification, the Israeli Jewish reader can ostensibly experience an "Arab" anxiety as if it were his or her own, and "Arab" needs, desires, and even suffering.

Yosef still loves Dina, but he persuades her to marry Rammy, who, in his symmetrical identity scheme, Yosef considers his Jewish "double."[4] After that, Yosef resigns from the Mossad and leaves Israel to work for the Palestinian "Organizations" in civil-war-torn Beirut, though we are never told what, if anything, he does. He had no physical contact with "enemy agents," nor apparently any direct access to "secrets." His work for the Mossad involved "forecasting" and recording his "forecasts" on tape.

He does some translation for the Palestinian "Organizations." He is as uncomfortable working for the "Organizations" as he had been working for the Mossad. For whatever reason, he comes to believe that he has been "burnt," first by the Mossad and later by the Palestinians, and that he must flee from both the Israelis and the Palestinians. The true reason for so impossible a flight is never altogether clear to the reader. It is one of many unsolved mysteries in A Good Arab,.

Yosef finally arrives at the city of his birth, Paris, where he finds a safe place to hide. From there, in autumn 1982, he sends his manuscript, presumably written while he was on the move, to a publisher in Tel Aviv. This manuscript is titled A Good Arab,.

Yosef's name, lineage, liaisons, and adventures, and his manuscript, are filled with mystery and laden with a sense of failure. Falling between categories, without clear location, Yosef is a slippery character, a special kind of monster—demographically one of "us," yet not of any community. He is inside and outside at the same time. His always modest ironic critique of the relationship between Arab and Jew is unthreatening, but the definiteness of his marginality makes him, as a fictional character, a dangerous concept.[5] The reader can identify with him only in the abstract; all that is concrete in this unavoidable intimacy of Arab and Jew is, as we shall see, suppressed.

Yosef embodies a self-alienation with which the reader is encouraged concretely to identify and to reflect upon, as at a distance. In this way, the reader can experience a fall and then salvation through a final ironically claimed resolution of difference. However, as we will see, this salvation is, under the circumstances, an event external to the novel: only the reader can live it and, therefore, it can be lived only after reading. Yosef himself is fallen, condemned at the moment of his conception—by his parents, by the author, and at the moment of the first knowledge the reader has of him. We will discover also that he provides an opportunity for redemption, therefore grace, for the Israeli Jewish reader that is not available to the Arab. The novel inserts "the Arab" into Yosef's subjectivity only to deny "Arabness" as a form of life beyond its category.

Knowledge of the date of the novel's publication is crucial to an understanding of the uproar it caused in Israeli literary circles, in the media, and among the public at large. During the spring of 1984, Israel was still in control of the greater part of Southern Lebanon, including the cities of Tyre and Sidon. Its invasion of Lebanon, in June 1982, had led to a momentary collapse of consensus about the "Palestinian problem." The invasion was termed Israel's first "war of choice," a characterization in sharp contrast with previous wars, which were regarded as "wars of no alternative."[6]

It should be noted that the Peace Now movement was established soon after the right-wing Likud coalition took office in 1977, displacing, for the first time, Labor and the other left-of-center partners. But it was also an opportunity for those on the left to argue that the stagnation of the "peace process" could no longer be thought of as solely caused by "Palestinian intransigence," but as the work of the "extremists" of "right-wing Zionism," including some of the same religious parties that had once been Labor's own partners.[7]

From the pace of Kaniuk's literary production, one must assume that he wrote A Good Arab, during 1983. By then, there was considerable opposition in Israel to the invasion of Lebanon, and many Zionist ideological tenets had, as a result, lost some degree of legitimacy among Jewish Israelis. Nevertheless, the fundamental principles of Zionism still held sway across the political spectrum, or what is otherwise termed "the Zionist consensus" from which only the Communists and the Israeli Arabs were and remain excluded.

It is in this context that Yoram Kaniuk disguises himself, presenting his novel as if its author were Arab.[8] Given the circumstances, the decision to use a pseudonym might have been reasonable for at least two reasons: the desire of the author to protect himself in anticipation of controversy, and/or his desire to protect the novel from the possibility that readers would doubt that a Jew could write from an Arab's point of view. On the other hand, Kaniuk might have intended the pseudonym as a qualification of the text, as part of its project. In this regard, I will try and show that the use of "Yosef Sherara" as the author's name is a vital aspect of the text itself, mediating the process of reading and qualifying all the content that could be said to compromise the text.

Even before its author's actual name was revealed, A Good Arab, had become a media event. It was not, however, universally acclaimed. For example, Heda Boshes, a Haaretz cultural affairs commentator, stated: "The great curiosity regarding the true identity of the mysterious author cannot yet turn this novel into a meaningful document, nor assign it literary value. The current comparisons with Emile Az'ar and B. Traven belong, at best, in the gossip columns." She added: "Literary criticism welcomed the novel with one of its most enthusiastic outbursts, and considered it an original 'discovery.' Perhaps it is the law of 'guilt' that operates here: it is much more comfortable to challenge literature than reality."[9]

Whatever the agenda of its critics, the novel was often taken to task for what appeared to some to be its peculiar and overwhelming display of "style."

But the exaggeration of the distinction between "style" and "content" implicit in this criticism may have been itself a way to neutralize the danger the book posed for Zionism's attempt to manage Israeli Jewish culture in the interest of its interpretation of Jewish history. This danger was recognized by some critics. For example, after condemning what she saw as mere tricks and idiosyncrasies, Michal Sela attributed the initial reception of A Good Arab, to the fact that

> it brings up again a problem that is at the center of the political and social debate here, in the country—although at times only implicitly. It is the story of an Israeli of "mixed marriage" (what an irony. A people of Holocaust survivors is pondering all sorts of mixed marriages!). . . . This novel has, however, an additional aspect: an ironic criticism of Israeli society's ways of thinking, pardon—Jewish society—in Israel, regarding the entire set of relationships with Arabs.[10]

Yet this account separates the "problem" from the experience of which it is part. Perhaps this tendency of so many critics to neutralize the novel's moral significance led Amnon Navot to claim that A Good Arab, conveys meanings not easily reduced to propositions and argument:

> from any point of view A Good Arab, is an exceptional work: not only in various poetic aspects, but also, and mainly, in terms of its materia [content]: meaningful engagement with "border line" materia which are outside of the routine and customary consensus of contemporary Hebrew fiction, and outside of the real and imaginary area of the familiar "topical canon." The degree of success and failure, though, in this case is secondary when compared with the breakthrough of an Israeli canonical writer into textures and materials that were never in the consciousness and conceptual vocabulary of contemporary Hebrew fiction. We have here a singular and impressive challenge with the problematic of a threshold sensitivity issue.[11]

Navot concludes that A Good Arab, is notable for its "excellent artistic and literary quality," and its exposure of "an existential friction in Israeli society felt in the dimmest layers of reality involving two peoples" in a single nation. At the same time, he criticizes the author for not having controlled the ambivalent and sensationalist aspects of his novel, for making "a priori automatic assumptions" in what Navot calls "the external layer" of the novel, and for failing finally to shed light on "the consciousness of the Other."[12] This lies, in Navot's view, in Kaniuk's failure to have provided alternative consciousnesses or perspectives. But this view of the novel as monologue is at the expense of seeing it as a radically ironic, self-critical text. For Navot, Kaniuk's choice of point of view, that of a "first-person confession," provided "a great deal of credibility." But the "attachment to a single consciousness narrowed down its perspective and reduced the scope of its prism."

Thus, Navot concludes that, though the novel touches on "controversial and traumatic aspects of our existence," it ultimately fails to make "us" sufficiently self-conscious. But this is a failure of Israeli literature itself, not merely of Kaniuk. Admitting this, Navot ends with a question: "What is the element that is lacking in Hebrew literature in order for it to make a conscious and wide breakthrough toward new and all inclusive textures?"

Although it may seem that Navot leaves the question unresolved, in fact, his analysis suggests that he has an answer. Apparently drawing on Bakhtin's distinction between monologic and dialogic discourse, a single voice and the intrinsically self-critical mixture of voices that constitutes a moral/political subjectivity, Navot compares A Good Arab, to Faulkner's Light in August:

> When Faulkner was seeking to make a general statement regarding the tragic dilemma of "black" and "white" by means of "black on white" (Joe Christmas is a hybrid), he did not cling to one consciousness, nor even to one dominant consciousness but as the case might be, to many consciousnesses which in their accumulation formed the internal tragedy that evolves out of negro and white existence in a violent and shattering milieu.

On the other hand, he argues that

> the private tragedy in A Good Arab, is not illustrated by, and not connected to other consciousnesses. Those could have provided a broad and many-faceted framework in which the private predicament of the novel's protagonist could have acquired a proper frame.

But a multiplicity of consciousnesses can as easily merely add perspectives or force them into convenient synthesis as lead to a discovery of their internal connections. The appearance of objectivity in Faulkner lies, for Navot, in a kind of journalistic summing of differences—one voice, then another. Such a process could leave the reader, the final agent of such a summation, untouched by any particular voice, or touched in a way that creates an impersonal distance from all experience. What gives Kaniuk's novel its force is its irony, not its "objectivity" or inclusiveness as such. If it fails, A Good Arab, will have had a higher aim than objectivity, namely, to negate distance so that the reader him- or herself may hear and speak with a different voice. In this, Kaniuk succeeds. His failure lies in the way in which the novel enforces a prior hierarchy of voices, which I want to show is a failure of the national literature and its culture that the novelist could hardly avoid.

Author, Form, and Content versus Text, Context, and Reading

All literature operates in contexts. This is certainly the case with literature in Israel. What in my view is powerful if not unique in Israel is the way in which its literature manifests an interpenetration of the extraliterary discourse of morality, politics, identity, and history. This provides an unusual connection of what otherwise would be seen merely as a minority phenomenon, "high culture," to the interest of the community in its own solidarity. This is why debate within and about Israeli literature so easily revolves around the question of policing boundaries.

I wish to show how this policing becomes part of the literature itself. Kaniuk's novel is a case, and my investigation is an exploratory one. Despite the profound unease caused by A Good Arab, among its Jewish Israeli readers, its images, representations, and narratives display the constraints of an unusually dominant ideology, Zionism, that defeat the novel's moral purpose. It is these interior constraints that I believe lie behind the general inability of Israeli Jewish culture to acknowledge the Arab in authentic self-critical acts of recognition and self-recognition.

The inability to escape so exclusionist an ideology as Zionism resembles the predicament of writers in all of what are called "colonial-settlers' states," for example, in Algeria before its independence.[13] I will examine Zionism as an instance of this, and explore some characteristic ways in which Israeli writers find themselves, and readers find their texts, submerged in its cultural field.

It is necessary, first, to put this study and its hypothesis in the context of another way of looking at literature, in terms of technique and idea. From this point of view, the failure of a novel is, in one way or another, the author's failure. This emphasis on the relationship among *author, form,* and *content* yields different results from my emphasis on *text, context,* and *reading.* The first attempts to identify an instance of literature and then purge it of ideology and politics. My approach looks at a literary text through the prism of the politics of which it is part. In the Israeli case, context cannot be and is not avoided. However, I see context as playing a constitutive role in literary or cultural production rather than as operating as conditions of meaning. It seems to me that the latter cannot show how a given text is an instance of history.

If we take such a denial of history to be symptomatically intentional, we can ask what this intention is and how it is reflected in critical commentary. Without arguing the point further, the emphasis on author, form, and content evades the connection of meaning to experience, therefore the relevance of culture to society. The dilemma of Israeli criticism is that it cannot acknowledge the problem "Arabness" poses for Zionism without undermining Zionism, therefore it tends to evade the problem even where it is found, in order to police the cultural boundaries of the Jewish state and Zionist exclusivist consciousness. But a Jewish people is conceivable, like any other, only on cultural grounds, as an intentional collectivity whose history cannot be separated from the play of differences that determine its "voices" and the limitations of those consciousnesses that speak in the form of voice. To admit this is to admit context and ideology to analysis and interpretation.

On the other hand, there are several criticisms of Kaniuk from which I wish to distinguish my own, criticisms that seem to ignore the rhetoric by which literary texts such as Kaniuk's insinuate the moral/political and, by doing so, beg the question of how such texts in general attempt to challenge, and whether they can succeed in challenging, the constraining power of Zionist ideology. That is, some critics have argued that *A Good Arab,* appears only because of the pseudonym to be a novel written from the point of view of "the Arab," that Kaniuk has disguised his own ethnicity in order to avoid the obvious, that a novel by a Jew is not likely, in practice, to be able to represent an Arab point of view. In some sense this is probably true. But what is at issue is how such a critique makes its point, namely, by identifying instances of lapse, such as incorrect language and stereotyping, cast as unintentional technical failures constituting evidence that the author contrived a pseudonym in order to convince his audience of something he could not otherwise do.[14] This seems far too convenient a criticism. What appear to be sloppiness and stereotyping are better understood as strategies of the text. This interpretation is valid only if the book is taken in context so that ironies of it as text, beyond the ironies within its own discourse, are made visible as evidence of a far more critical intention than the critics of disguise are willing to admit. The apparent arbitrariness of syntax, the curious spacing of words on pages, the abruptness with which sentences begin and end, as if wrenched from their own context and later allowed to proceed according to a different logic from which they began, are not themselves symptomatic of a failed perspective. They are, as I will try to show, deliberate reflections within language on the foibles of language, and on the subtle controls it exercises on consciousness.[15]

If this interpretation is correct, the syntax, spelling, and the rest are part of Kaniuk's attempt to build into his novel a Jewish self-criticism rather than merely helpless expressions of prejudice. They can be seen within this greater irony to be part of the same irony on which the protagonist, Yosef, reflects—that he lives in a society that demands he constantly affirm and prove his ethnic identity but that cannot abide his simultaneous claims to both Arabness

and Jewishness. This is Kaniuk's critique of the moral limitations and paradoxes of Zionism's exclusivist emphasis on the moral presence of Jewish
identity.

This interpretation of irony upon irony is substantiated further by a poetics
of dispersion in which what is written so swiftly outpaces the momentary
promise of unity and reconciliation that it makes of such promise at a least a
joke and at most an embarrassment. Short, abrupt, detached, staccato sentences, oxymoron, and typographical interpenetration of lines violate the
condition of linearity typically associated with writing to be read as narrative.
For example, we read, on page 9 of the Hebrew version:

> *She* stood up again, dialed and shouted hahahaha, banged the phone, and
> returned to drink more champagne. *Rammy* was wearing a brown pullover
> which in the crossing light in the rain seemed violet, his hair looked as if it
> were burnt. The phone woke up *Hetzkel* who while sleeping said: we have
> stomach and grist soup lowered his head and waited for *Marcel*, his waiter, to
> answer the phone. *Nissan* said to *me*, everyone knows everyone else. Perhaps
> because I said that *he* looked familiar to me. *An old chase player* was sitting there
> which *Franz* and *I* used to meet at night and *who* would always ask about *Kathe*,
> and *Franz* used to say to *him*, there is no *Kathe*, *Kathe* kaput, and *the man who
> Franz* said was once a genius in mathematics used to cry for *her*. And then
> *Franz* used to look at *me*, *how we were all crossing each other*, I being the son of
> *that who* desired *Kathe* most and *Franz* felt the emptiness and *he* would embrace
> *me* with a totally defeated but arrogant look. (emphasis added)[16]

In this contrariness between the display of signs and their use yields an
irony poised against itself, constituting a trope of self-reflection in which the
ironic subject becomes itself the object of an irony. If this were all that the
novel did, its value for the critique of moral and political discourse, that otherwise calm subjectivity, could not be denied. In *A Good Arab*, the Jewish self
does indeed confront the other within the self; and this is indeed a confrontation that subverts language every bit as much as it disturbs moral complacency.

But, as I shall try to show, the real other, in the world beyond the text *to
which the text appeals*, which is "the Arab," is finally suppressed. The suppression leaves in its place an abstract morality of ungrounded self-doubt where
one might have expected a far more catastrophic moment of recognition of
self and/or other. This criticism nevertheless sees Kaniuk as having carried the
moral predicament of the biblical Israeli Jew to its very limits, beyond which
the history of Israel and the history of "the Jewish people" must be thought
apart from their traditional allegory of self-realization, reinforced by Zionism,

therefore apart from the mix of secular and theocratic elements that constitute the militarized statism of present-day Israeli politics and Israeli law.

Upon announcing his identity as the author of *A Good Arab,* in his weekly newspaper column, Yoram Kaniuk responded in an "open letter" to some of his critics' concerns. There he justified his writing and reflected critically upon it: "I have tried the method of camouflage: writing Arabic names as a Jew who had discovered his Arabness following graduation from Hebrew school; but it didn't work, and it aroused suspicion."[17] Regarding his choice of a name for the author-protagonist, Kaniuk said, somewhat curiously:

> I erred badly in one thing. I called the author Yosef Sherara. I should have
> called him Yosef Galili. By giving the author a half Jewish and a half Arab
> name I sinned to myself and to Yosef. I had brought curiosity to its limit. . . . If
> I had signed the book with a Hebrew name I probably would have succeeded in
> remaining unknown for a long time.[18]

Is this all it was so far as Kaniuk is concerned? A matter of provoking a mystery about the identity of an author? Or is he saying that a name made up of incompatible parts must be seen as doing something semiotically powerful in *its* context, and that the misspellings inherent in misidentification or ambivalent identification are, after all, about identification? If so, his comments reinforce what I am suggesting is evident in any case in the text, situating it firmly within the context of the overriding moral predicament constituted politically as one crucial feature of Israeli Jewish culture.

Of course, Kaniuk's late apology cannot be taken unequivocally as evidence of an underlying intention of the text as a whole, as an instruction to the reader. But that does not mean that it should have no bearing on our attempt to read the novel, or to read our own reading, or to read in regard to a context. Kaniuk's apology creates yet another textualization of the book in which he now emerges as critic, author, and character, a multiplicity with no clear lines of demarcation. *We still do not know the author's "name."*[19] By his letter, Kaniuk redoubles the text's effort to resist disclosing its own limitations and, of course, those of its culture.

One crucial question presented by the new text, "novel plus apology," is what can be meant by declaring that someone who learns Arabic late will misspell, and by the peculiarities of writing that could have escaped editing only intentionally and that therefore must be recognized as part of writing? Clearly, inscription as well as conception have become objects of a complex textualization. Kaniuk's statement about defects in learning must be read as ironic, because an apology for misspelling based on late learning is obviously an excuse for something else, especially in an area as sensitive to casualness and indifference as the representation of the other. Because it is transparent, it fails as an excuse, one might say ludicrously. Therefore, the failure must be read in quotation marks, as an ironic and self-critical notation about excusing and excuses, therefore about something inexpressible or incapable of being represented. In this respect, the apology provides a new and remarkable aspect of the book, its way of excusing bad faith in such a way as to disclose the ease with which we fall into bad faith.

Rather than dispelling the confusion of his critics, Kaniuk adds to it until there can be no further doubt that confusion is the deepest part of this remarkable text of self-doubt, self-defeat, and sacrifice. What appears as a lack of skill is, in the text, a way of rendering a morally significant interior division of the self. The student from Hebrew school is said to have learned to disattend to the signs (names) of what Erving Goffman calls "*personal*" identity (what identifies the particular person), yet to use types of names adequately for them to serve as markers of "*social*" identity (what identifies the person as an instance of a type).[20] That is, this student sees a radical opposition of persons (named) and relationships (in part constituted by social types indicated by types of names). The Arab, either purely concrete or purely abstract, would appear in this program as an agent without principal or reason, and as an individual without context. Kaniuk's apology must be seen, then, as adding nothing to our interpretation of the *novel*, though our interpretation of the *text* must be responsive to its insertion in the *book*. The misspellings are, then, neither mistakes nor evidence of indifference, but a *show* of indifference, and not merely to persons and names but to language itself. In this way all that could be Arabic in the identity of "Arab" is systematically "spoiled."

Kaniuk is therefore holding bad faith up to the "good face" of an Israeli consciousness that can find no room in its "goodness" for the subjectivity of its other, and therefore for even its own moral significance beyond the most immediate self-affirmation. Ultimately, as Kaniuk knows but cannot quite demonstrate, this other-denying Jewish self collapses, the spontaneousness of its morality exposed as pretense, the authority of its goodwill little more than the desire of the self to congratulate itself for its tolerance, forbearance, and idealism.

But what makes Kaniuk's novel brilliant is its capacity to extend this moral dilemma, to draw it out agonizingly and in detail until the reader is on the verge of discovering it in him- or herself—as a choice between a radical break with the racialism of Zionist morality, or a compliant acknowledgment of the dilemma in a text seen merely as "literature." Kaniuk's failure is to have given the reader an easy way out within a text that initially promised no way out at all. Ultimately, Kaniuk's reader feels welcome in a world whose dilemmas determine what counts as morality but do not raise embarrassing questions about the determination itself. By acknowledging that Arab-Jewish relations pose a dilemma for identity as such, in the abstract, the reader is restored to the status quo as a utopian unity at the expense of both the other and the self. How does Kaniuk restore the reader's sense of self-righteousness, having demolished it at the outset? How does the ideological context of this self-critical Israeli Hebrew novel come to reassert its dominion over the self-criticism the novel attempts to institute? We will see that the answer lies in a trick played on Kaniuk by that context at the moment he begins to write.

To establish the basis of a liberal moral critique of Jewish-Arab affairs, Kaniuk begins with a politics of identity from which escape is impossible, the self-limiting framework of self and history fixed from the outset. However, the desire of Israeli Jewish liberalism to go in this way beyond Zionism is ultimately defeated by the inability of the liberal to admit that the division signified by Arab and Jew lies within his or her own self. But this inability is not merely psychological. It is enforced through a culture-based poetics of identity that is also an irresponsible rhetoric of exclusion embedded deep within prevailing discourses of morality and politics. The politics of identity rationalizes itself, by the projection of a higher, transcendent, identity that, for Kaniuk as for most Israeli Hebrew writers, can only be seen as, read as, the higher Jew of the highest morality.

3

Dual Identity: "To Be My Own Enemy"

Limited Recognition of the Arab

Before the narrative begins, in the introduction, Yosef presents himself as a symptom of a disease that encompasses the self. Because such a disorder can only be indicated, the best he can hope for is that others might learn about this condition.

> I am speaking of a tax of grief because it is hard for me to experience regret since I was denied the possibility of being born someone else. Between two righteousnesses, in the midst of a tragedy from which I do not see a way out, I am not an accidental, insignificant victim; in my room I live alone, and my mirror is not scored by objective principles.

Nevertheless, Yosef puts himself beyond this condition, this betweenness, by reflecting on an aspiration that seems to be part of a different history, the history of literature and its eternal standards of value:

> Once, when I had read "An American Tragedy" by Dreiser I thought that perhaps one day I would be able to write "An Israeli Tragedy"; but on second thought, I'll leave it to someone else, more capable than myself.

In this elevated reflection on talent, Yosef's "second thought," already governed by a first autobiographical reflection on reading and writing, dissects his feeling from loneliness, drawing the reader analytically into a narrative paradoxically freed of tragedy, and into a perspective with which literature ultimately cannot compete:

> What came out is the flower of the wound. I'm not Dreiser, I look at the world from a perspective of a hostile person, screwed up, and wasted; that is why I am able to deride myself with such indifferent satisfaction.[1]

Yosef's condition is now a limitation of writing, and a virtue. Rather than take the stance of a "metaphysical rebel," rather than confront his putative Israeli Hebrew readers with a flagrant Arabness, he writes in Hebrew. For those readers, however, this both invokes an untoward intimacy and prepares a foundation for pity through which is laid the foundation for a limited—that is, abstract—recognition of the Arab.

> Because of my emotional handicap I am capable of writing this book only in Hebrew. My anger is bilingual; when I translate myself into myself I have to shoot the mirror rather than let it shoot me. (Heb. 5–6; Eng. 1–2)[2]

This appeal is insidious, far more effective than a direct confrontation, for the abjectness Yosef expresses is a con. In the name of an appeal to empathy, it insinuates a culture of stereotypes, a range of response that includes only the possibilities of pity and disgust, which lend themselves, in terms of reception, to a corresponding antitragic sense of righteousness. Thus, at the outset, Yosef displays his duality as something outside of the reader's practical subjectivity. In other words, it can be recognized, but only clinically. The only empathy the reader can experience at that point is that of the professional diagnostician. More is possible only when Yosef meditates on the Jewishness of his experience, a mediation that ultimately, and fatally for the critical project, displaces the original duality.

On the other hand, the Jewish reader can take the point of view of an Arab, but only in the context of the confluence of unequal and absolute Arab and Jewish identities in a single character; and that is a point of view framed entirely by the Jewish conception of the perspective of the other. Kaniuk believes that the limitation of Zionism, its dedicated exclusionism, can be breached only by compassion. He hopes to inculcate compassion through the literary device of doubling identity, on the assumption that the unavoidability of Arabness is, by itself, sufficient to establish it.

But the dilemma that Yosef presents to the liberal Israeli Jew is how to be compassionate to one who seems to deserve at most only pity. The duality of Yosef's identity is ultimately all the novel provides as context for compassion, and therefore Jewish entry into a Jewish-Arab dialogue.

Indeed, Kaniuk reveals something of this intention in his open letter:

> I was so close to Yosef that I did not know who was I and who was
> he. . . . Because of my close identification with Yosef, the son of an Arab father
> and a Jewish mother, I went to Acre to look for Yosef's [my] father's house.[3] . . .
> I felt for Yosef that the Jewish-Palestinian tragedy was slicing through his
> flesh.[4] . . . It was difficult to be Kaniuk while I was writing about what it was
> like being a Jew of Jews.[5]

Yosef himself finds just the language needed to complete the conversion of the
Jewish reader of difference to a Jewish reader of unity:

> No, I couldn't go into all kinds of explanation. I simply wanted to belong, to
> insert myself into the seam between the lonelinesses, between the strangeness-
> es, to find a hiding place in their tired rituals. I couldn't tell them about Franz
> or Azouri or Gertrude. I was frightened. I didn't want to confront their amaze-
> ment. My old urge awoke to be a sort of Rammy. He was my idol long before I
> met him. His look divulged intelligence, friendship, pain, and power. (Heb. 12;
> Eng. 9)

The Arab of Yosef's dual identity finds his role model in the Jew, Rammy.
It is the search for virtue that is compelling in this passage. The Arab longs to
be a Jew, a moral being, and it is through this longing that the Jewish reader
finds it possible to identify with the Arab. This is Kaniuk's predicament: if the
Arab is to achieve a subjectivity capable of engaging the reader's capacity for
identification, he must assert the moral vitality of Arabness. But he can assert
such vitality only in the form of a desire to be not an Arab but a Jew.
Moreover, if the Jewish reader is to be capable of compassion, he or she must
recognize the Arab as morally vital in his own right, and acknowledge that
vitality as a point of view from which the Jew might be judged. But because
the categories, Jew and Arab, are defined at the outset as exclusive of one
another, the Arab can be morally vital only from the perspective of the Jew,
that is, if he is sufficiently Jewish. Given that exclusiveness, any other vitality
could only be that of an enemy, for whom compassion would be impossible.
Thus, the failure of the novel, if it is a failure, lies not in its withdrawal from its
own design, but in its initial premise. To begin with an *absolute* difference in
order to teach compassion makes it impossible to teach the *necessity* of compassion. It is the Zionist presumption of absolute difference that leads to the
Jewish part of Yosef's character being the only active moral agent possible.

There is another feature of the above passage that speaks to this paradox.
Yosef says that he wants "to insert myself into the seam . . . to find a hiding
place in their tired rituals." However, nothing reinvigorates a "tired ritual"

more than such an insertion, if only because a "seam" is a site of tension, where contradictory impulses meet at the point of greatest strain. To aspire to insert himself in the seam is for Yosef already to have confronted that tension, already to have become the creature of an opposition. To insert himself at that precarious point of crisis is both to highlight it and to constitute yet another opposition—between an agent who inserts himself and the place of insertion that remains in equilibrium only on condition that it remain unoccupied.

Yosef cannot hide and he cannot run. His attempt to hide in the folds of the seam is his only possible strategy, but it cannot succeed any more than Kaniuk's choice of an Arab *nom de plume* can elude the antagonistic difference that he wishes, as a writer in the interest of compassion, at least momentarily to neutralize. Indeed, the *effort* to hide exposes even more the *desire* that motivates the attempt to hide. And it is, above all, *desire* beyond even the notion of fulfillment that is dramatized in A Good Arab,.

This is the point of entry for the reader who is open to compassion. The moral persuasiveness of the novel depends on whether or not it supports the identification of the reader with a *desire* to neutralize and thereby avoid—not overcome—difference. I will argue that the novel fails to do this. It fails to acknowledge and give foundation for such desire, and this lies in its inability to address the foundation of the difference in the first place, that is, the confluence of the exclusionist idea—Zionism—and a practice—of exclusion through conquest. Thus, the unity of identity achieved for the reader by avoiding difference is predicated on a militant utopia geared to denying self-critical compassion.

Kaniuk's method of giving moral subjectivity to his protagonist, by ascribing to him two separate identities only one of which is capable of such subjectivity, poses the moral question and then withdraws it. The Arab identity is certainly available to the Jewish reader who identifies with Yosef. But it is the aspect of Yosef's identity that is problematic to what is Jewish in Yosef. The Jew in Yosef is only occasionally a problem for the Arab, and never a moral problem.

In his "confessions," Yosef is not satisfied with expressing this predicament. He perceives himself destined from birth to embody the Israeli-Palestinian "condition." This is something he cannot overcome. It is his contradictory, and therefore unstable, essence. He is, in other words, an instance of the historical, but not of the making of history. In order to avoid the stereotype Jews have of the half of him that is Arab, he has to become the entire Israeli-Zionist ethos, with its intractable opposition of Jew and Arab. When he defines his Arab aspect, he defines it as a Jew would, which poses a difficulty for this contradictory totality because he must, at the same time, be able to claim the most important attributes required of its subjects by that ethos: (1) a "credible" Israeli Jew must be a descendant of Holocaust survivors; (2) he or she must reflect the history of Zionist pioneering and heroism, particularly its emotional terror in the struggle against the Arab; and (3) he or she must have served willingly and as a matter of principle in the Israeli military, in defense of Jewish Israel and in the conquest of Arab land.

It is no wonder that Yosef narrates these traits as if they are for him contradictory:

> What remains is therefore my own irrational theory; I was there as potential. A good Arab is a dead Arab for Nissan and his friends. I had to be born so as not to grant Bunim and Nissan such liberty, but to understand them with the part of me that was supposed to be expropriated from the ordinary stereotyping, and to appear under the pronoun as "a descendant of Holocaust survivors," [here, following the comma, Yosef adds *his* version of the "rational"] Franz was not a Holocaust survivor. He ran before it. But . . . they forced Judaism on him with the yellow patch, made of him a refugee. (Heb. 30; Eng. 37–38)[6]

In this passage, Yosef draws a distinction that is, for him, necessary if he is to be eligible as a moral subject. Nissan and Bunim "and their friends" are Israeli Jewish nationalists. Yosef represents them as "maximalists." Bunim is an officer in the Mossad directly in charge of Yosef, and Nissan works as an informer for the Mossad and had "informed" on Yosef to Bunim. Thus, when Yosef says that "a good Arab is a dead Arab is true *for them*" (emphasis added), he implies a distinction between "them" and Israeli liberals, who Yosef believes do not "expect" an Arab to be dead before he or she can be "good." What Yosef seems to mean is that, from the point of view of an Israeli Jewish liberal, if an Arab is good, he or she could be tolerated if not beloved.

It is clear to Yosef that "Israel was the necessary response to the Holocaust," even if another people had to pay the price. "All around him" he says, "there were the parents of friends who came from there," and their stories of suffering affected him much more strongly than those of his friends who "wanted to be normal Israelis." The latter, he says, did not want "to think of *aktions*, of the dismantled skeletons sent by Eichmann to the Institute of Racial Research." He read all he could lay his hands on; he established a total identification with them; he received their suffering as his own, more than he could Azouri's. Parents of friends "were talking about the cruelty of Arabs in the '48 war, about slaughtering and tortures, about Jews' heads stuck up on poles."

Clearly, Yosef is trying to square the circle, and although his two identities may seem equally distorted, the distortions are not quite symmetrical. It is the

Arab half in him that has to be neutralized or erased. As the "exile" Jew did in the past, Yosef wants to appear more Jewish than the "pure," undivided, Jew.

> Azouri tried from time to time to tell his side of the story, but it seemed that he was not sure of himself anymore. He spoke of "the expulsion." He spoke of Jews "assisting" in the expulsion of Arabs, of "Present Absentees,"[7] of the disgrace of Deir Yassin,[8] and of house arrests, beatings and tortures. (Heb. 123; Eng. 176)

But Yosef "couldn't feel complete identification" with him:

> I understood that he was speaking of pain, but the real pain was that which was avoided from Hava my mother on Franz's side, the pain and humiliation of a people that found itself in a world of locked doors, where everyone shuts their eyes and allows others to die in a slaughterhouse. (Heb. 123; Eng. 176)

There is an analogous asymmetry in the language of the narrative. Whereas the suffering and torture of Jews, either under the Nazis or in the " '48 war," are relayed by means of plastic, descriptive, concrete images, the suffering and torture of Palestinian Arabs caused by Zionists or by Israeli Jews are presented in abstractly neutralizing and general terms. Every Israeli Jewish schoolchild, from the age of six, learns the history of the Holocaust. Thus, as a reader of Israeli Hebrew literature, every Jewish Israeli would be moved by the use of the German term *aktions*. At the same time, he or she would remain indifferent to the use of such terms as "present absentee," or even "Deir Yassin." These are not mentioned in the Israeli Jewish school curriculum. Moreover, Israeli atrocities committed against Arabs are immunized against moral judgment by the standard of the Holocaust. It was not the pain of which Azouri spoke, as Yosef says, but rather "the real pain" of his mother Hava. In the final analysis, it is not pain compared with pain, but rather "pain" with "real pain." Thus, Yosef recounts his feelings about Anne Frank: "I loved Anne Frank, I fell in love with her, I wanted to dream about her at night" (Heb. 123; Eng. 176). And he writes of Azouri's reference to "pain that became abstract." What is meant by the fact that his grandfather, Franz, "was trying to balance" the concrete experience of his own pain with suffering in general? Did Franz, too, tell stories of the suffering of the Jews? Did he say that it was not "all that bad"?

Franz was a second-generation assimilated Jew who had converted to Zionism through the persuasion of a Palestinian Arab named Azouri. Franz had never quite fit the Zionist mold in Palestine despite his efforts to seek his "roots" there by collecting, on private archaeological excursions, pieces of broken glass and terra-cotta. If that is the balancing of the concrete and the abstract of which Franz was capable, it is one more example of Kaniuk's irony.

It is an asymmetry that mirrors that of Yosef's identity. In both cases, balance is an illusion and a hopeless reflection of intractable dualities. Giora (one of Yosef's closest Jewish friends) spoke with him "about the Macabbees, about the Palmach, about haShomer. I was proud of them. I was trapped by the myth," he says (Heb. 123; Eng. 176).[9] Azouri knew that he was losing his son, Yosef, to an identity he could not share. But "it was part of the risk he took" in encouraging Yosef to assert himself in one way or another, though he may have actually believed that, "in the end," Yosef would come back to him, and that Yosef "didn't have an alternative but to be burnt and then to choose for himself."

In fact, Yosef never chose for himself. He had to end up a "Jewish" refugee, an overdetermined result of an overdetermined cause. The identity he chose was already implicit in his duality. The only legitimate choice was the Jewish part. "The great and fearful justice was still on my side," says Yosef—meaning on his Jewish side (Heb. 123; Eng. 176). Thus, he reacted to Nachie's (Giora's father) participation in demonstrations against Arab dispossession, and to Azouri's house arrest and beating, with the tragic but lame reflection of the absurdist:

> But I said to myself, nobody is putting him in a gas truck; nobody has humiliated him completely; nobody closed any doors to him, the world was filled with Arabs, full of Arab states; he had family relatives there; he was a son of the great Arab nation, one hundred million; he had somewhere to go. Nachie didn't. I identified with him, "the poor man's lamb." I didn't think of the absurdity of my situation. (Heb. 122–23; Eng. 175–76)

These are words most Israeli Jews would use. Again and again the "gas truck" and "complete humiliation" become the standards used to deny that Palestinian resistance can be justified as resistance to oppression. Thus, for Yosef to avail himself of this kind of self-negating rationalization is, as he says, an "absurdity." But like any absurdity, this too is unavoidable, given, as he says, "my situation."

Of Absurdity, Balance, and Symmetry

Within a single year, between Yosef's tenth and eleventh years, both his mother and grandmother died of extreme hysteria. During the months prior to his mother's death, his family moved back and forth between Tel Aviv and Acre. Yosef was taken out of one school and put into another. It was, he says, a year "misty" in his memory. For a while, he went to a Christian school in

Haifa. Apparently during the same year, he attended the fifth grade of primary school in Tel Aviv, where he wrote an essay about "drying the wilderness."[10]

> I wrote about how we came to a desolate country. There were swamps all over. We were sick with malaria. We wanted to civilize the only country we ever had and of which we were robbed, the homeland no people attended to since we were exiled from it. I wrote about the wicked Arabs who came at night to burn the haystacks, about Mordechi Halpern,[11] about Bilu.[12] About the pioneers. I wrote a very florid essay, but the teacher wouldn't let me read it in class.[13] (Heb. 112; Eng. 160–61)

When Yosef "read it to Azouri, he burst out laughing" that "I wanted to avenge myself on the wicked Arabs. I said *be-tu tu tu tu tu ha-Aravim yamutu*.[14] He said, *Yahudi fil surmaya*, which means Jews under my sole" (Heb. 112; Eng. 161).

This exchange is said to "straighten the balance"—children on both sides cursing each other's nationality as if each curse carries the same sting. But in the same sentence, Yosef again finds balancing absurd, but now in its denial of the priority of Jewish suffering:

> As the Arabs used to say when the Turks revoked the foreign consulates' protection of Jews and let their blood in the First World War. Listen, I know this story in the fissures of my blood; I know it, and I'm sick of it. (Heb. 112–13; Eng. 161)

The last sentence seems to be directed to the reader, not to Yosef's father, and it is clarified in the following passage from Yosef's "confessions":

> For two thousand years a country stood empty. There were Arabs but they did not have a Palestine. The Jews could have come but they didn't. The tragedy began the moment the Jews remembered too late, and the Arabs suddenly realized they were a separate nation. One nationalism fed the other. Justice belongs to God alone. (Heb. 113; Eng. 161)

In what sense did the Jews remember "too late" and the Arabs "suddenly realize"? These too are only apparently symmetrical predicaments. But it is an appearance that shapes Yosef's sense of the Zionist-Palestinian "tragedy," one that denies historical significance to the Arab/Palestinian experience. Yosef's endorsement of this perspective is liberal and it is Jewish. In its self-deception, in its denial of what Yosef cannot help but be for others, it too is absurd.

Yosef's rationale for the suffering of the Palestinians is the conventional one. But its cost is the significance of Yosef's dual identity, and therefore of Kaniuk's intention; given that duality, Yosef's statement is absurd and must be read ironically if the two identities are not prematurely to dissolve into one. Even then, Kaniuk could not have succeeded in completing this particular irony because Yosef's rationale for Palestinian suffering is the only one possible given that Yosef's identity is originally presented as divided, hierarchical, exclusionist. Because of this, it is only too easy to read Yosef's sense of the "tragedy" in the context of Zionism's own declarations about the relation of Jew to Arab, in which case the novel reproduces the irrepressibility of the uncompassionate division it had hoped to use in order to inculcate compassion. It is, finally, too much an instance of the trope it had hoped to challenge—the commensurability of sufferings.

Yet Yosef's statement remains, for analysis if not for reading, absurd as a reflection on the duality that constitutes A Good Arab, a sense of absurdity Kaniuk does not permit his Jewish readers. He forces them above duality, finally allowing only for the inclusive and elevated voice of analysis. Who can recognize, who can speak to the absurdity of a Jewish definition of the Zionist-Palestinian conflict as tragedy? If analysis has its own voice, it can only be outside of the Arab in regard to which the subletting object of analysis—difference itself, therefore difference as given—has its concreteness. If so, then analysis is altogether abstract, a mystical realization of a truth incapable of communication and unable to support compassion, as matter of practice.

If, on the other hand, it is Kaniuk himself who speaks of absurdity, one must ask, Who are his community? What capacity to appreciate absurdity allows Kaniuk to write and expect his writing to get a hearing? If the community that can hear that voice is not the community of Zionists, to whom does he speak of absurdity? Either Kaniuk, if the voice of absurdity is indeed his, had no need to speak for the absurdist, or he is doing little else than teaching those non-Arabs whose sensibility is irrelevant to the difference that is absurdly portrayed as tragic. It is at this point that Kaniuk's novel loses itself to the context in which it can only be literature, reconstituting itself in that context as a, the, voice of moral reason.

The failure to begin with the basis of difference, the coerced unity within which the Arab is, relative to the Jew, an inessential subjectivity, marks Kaniuk's novel with its own "tragic" inability to avoid reproducing what it had hoped to make no longer possible. What is left? Yosef's duality becomes intractable according to its own internal hierarchy; and, as we will see, it becomes the foundation for a new emancipation—not freedom from antagonism but rather from the obligation to recognize the Arab. The difference of Arab and Jew becomes the basis once again for Jewish self-recognition, and for a

58   Dual Identity

paradoxical compassion for an other that has no substantiality that can or needs to be recognized as such.

Absurd and Asymmetry as Childhood Experience

In 1963, when Yosef turned thirteen, he demanded that his grandfather, Franz, give him a bar mitzvah.

> Friends and a few relatives came to the bar mitzvah. Azouri also came and stood at the side. I was called to read the portion of the Torah, and in hindsight it was superfluous but necessary. The Rabbi taught me the Law and the concluding chapter from the Prophets. He didn't know a thing about me besides my name. The Office of the Interior had not yet compiled these black lists.[15] The Rabbi didn't know that my father was an Arab, and even if he knew he could not refuse. From the point of view of Halacha, I was Jewish. (Heb. 122; Eng. 174–75)[16]

But only from a "point of view." Even his bar mitzvah dramatizes the asymmetry of Yosef's dual identity. Again, Kaniuk has been able to create in Yosef the sense of a predicament based on the arbitrariness of designation, but only as a point of view. Kaniuk cannot make explicit the real, implacable asymmetry that accounts for Yosef's sense that his "situation" is absurd because *A Good Arab,* is predicated on it, and therefore depends on the premise that only a Jew can express and manifest the fullness of moral agency.

Yet Kaniuk still pushes that premise to its limit. Yosef lives vividly and with an incredible ruthlessness of self-reflection through and against absurdity. He considers his father, Azouri, "responsible" for his being half Arab. Indeed, he rarely uses the term *father,* but almost always speaks of Azouri, which is not an Arabic but a Hebrew name. Yosef blames Azouri for attempting to kill his mother in a battle during the 1948 war, and for her death, later, in a car accident. His father serves as a metaphor for Yosef's own absurd and unreliable life: Azouri is a mechanism rather than a character, there only to move Yosef. Yosef rarely engages him as a subject.

And yet it happens once at a very critical moment, the death of Kathe, his grandmother. The family gathers under an old fig tree; in keeping with her wish, they scatter her ashes in Acre, at a spot chosen by Azouri. At the end of this wrenching experience, Yosef's mother, Hava, "entered Azouri's arms" and said to him: "Even if everything is already over, you're all I have; the only question is for how long." In retrospect, Yosef reflects on this moment:

> I said to her, Mother, and what about me, and suddenly she looked at me with Kathe's eyes, trying to understand. She blinked her eyes, and I saw that she

couldn't remember who I was. And Azouri took me by the hand and said, look, have you ever seen a sunset like this anywhere else? ha? And he tried to smile, and Franz scattered more leaves to protect his beloved. (Heb. 116; Eng. 164–65)

Here is what makes poignant Yosef's sense of absurdity—the fact that he cares for each part of what as a whole he finds absurd. It is this caring that makes his sense of absurdity compelling and not merely glib or clinical. This is the source of a desire that could have engaged the reader's capacity for identification, and therefore compassion, if that had not already been made impossible by the terms with which the novel posits duality. Whatever possibility of identification exists, it is not connected with the duality of Yosef's identity, therefore with the telos of the text. Indeed, the latter has now become more an element of plot than a stage onto which Kaniuk can draw his reader and then teach him or her compassion.

Yosef feels that his mother never loved him. Perhaps, from his point view, she too is to blame that he was born half Arab; and perhaps in his hidden, unspoken fears she has betrayed her own nation by having married an Arab. All these suspicions are implied in many different ways throughout the narrative. Yosef's grandmother was always alienated from him. She could not even identify him by name. He has an Arab aunt, "Aunt Khuri," whose relationship to him is mysterious. The only person who loves him who recognizes him, who is close to him and concerned for him, is his grandfather, Franz. But Franz was never a real Zionist. In a hidden corner of his being he remained a Jew, but was an internationalist and, at times, appeared even to be a ridiculous cosmopolitan. Yet, Yosef never uses the word *Grandpa* or speaks of Franz as "grandfather." Perhaps he suspects that Franz's affection toward him was never quite honest, that it stemmed from his greater love for the one he had loved long ago, Azouri.

Yosef is sure of very little, but he is most sure of what he does not like. He cares, and because of that he reflects credibly on the absurdity of caring. Similarly, Kaniuk, the author possessed of a different sort of dual identity, cares about Yosef and his divided self. But, as Yosef cannot redeem an identity adequate to being a self-recognizing moral agent, so Kaniuk cannot redeem the Arab past of the duality he has created as the basis for compassion, except as a redemption that cannot bear the practical freedom and weight of moral agency. Yosef's life, his freedom to reflect, is based on missing the real point of his predicament. The righteousness of Kaniuk's authorial voice is based on missing the point of Yosef's missing the point.

Predicating Morality on an Absolute

The question is, then, who can identify with a character such as Yosef? And if identification is possible, with what does one identify? And if that identification can be said to occur, who could be its agent and what could be gained? We have seen that the reader does get caught up in Yosef's predicament, but that only the Jewish part of his identity can be the subject of identification. Because the problem of identification was initially set by Kaniuk's desire to teach a recognition of the Arab, identification with the Jewish part can only leave the reader in a moral state of mind prior to any identification with Yosef as he is.

In this sense, for all its striving to mediate and make use of the difference of Arab and Jew, the novel is irrelevant to its project. But if the novel had succeeded in turning the tables, in imposing an Arab subjectivity on what was the exclusively Jewish province of moral agency, who would this enlightenment benefit? I have argued that this could only be *analysis* itself, therefore a "subjectivity" for which the problem of identification can only be of idle or professional concern, not at all a critical matter. In this case the novel can only be said to have produced a theoretical rather than and in opposition to a practical community of readers. Even if it could have produced the latter, it would be a community for whom the writing of such things, of duality and the need for compassion, would in the face of the reality have been absurd.

There is a related problem having to do with the logic of dual identity. The personal foundation of Yosef's moral agency is Jewish. But what allows for the possibility of that agency is its antithesis, the Arab. Jewish compassion, like compassion in general, needs a greater object than that of any momentary expression. Thus, it requires that particular non-Jew, the other against which the Zionist subjectivity asserts itself positively, for its object. Because compassion without recognition can have its *object* only in the form of its abstract opposite, it can hold to its possibility only by negating that universal other, in this case the abstract Arab. In other words, Yosef cannot choose one identity without affirming its negation of the other, as it is only in terms of that very other that choice itself could have been envisioned. If he were to identify himself as Arab, there would be nothing practical, historical, about him with which to identify. If, on the other hand, he were to identify himself as a Jew, even if he could get away with it, there would be nothing about him that would need compassion. If he were to sustain his dual identity, it could still be only as one or the other in an internal alternation that neither Jew nor Arab could know as such. In other words, what Yosef truly *is* cannot be represented by anything that has to do with morality. Therefore, when Yosef speaks of his "sickness," it is as a malady of language itself, and because of that, one that operates under historical conditions that include the politics of moral thought and the inevitably "fictional truths" that dominate such thought.

Yosef's "emotional sickness" is not merely something suffered by an individual character. It is a literary reflection of the greater dilemma faced by the Israeli Jew. The Jew can act morally toward the Arab only in the context in which the Arab is already recognized as a moral being. This is impossible where the difference between Arab and Jew is, from the outset, represented as absolute. In that case, all that is possible is to acknowledge the Arab as a *fact* in contrast to a *subject*. For this logic, the morality of the Jew *implies* the amoral objectivity of the Arab. A *Good Arab*, exemplifies this even within its liberalist Zionist project, and by doing so it shows how Zionism operates culturally, predicating the full range of its moral responsiveness on an absolute, hence militarized, difference. It is this predication that reappears, even at the end of Kaniuk's critique of Zionism, as an affirmation of the stratified order of that difference: the Jew as moral subject, the Arab as merely juridical subject; the Jew as the foundation of the law, the Arab as the law's object. The moment at which the Arab is acknowledged as the source of problems is the moment at which the Jew rediscovers his or her capacity to acknowledge (but not recognize), to confer identity upon (but not to identify with), and to feel for the other (but not with the other) without having to subject him- or herself to that other's judgment.

As I argued in chapter 2, contrary to what Navot claims, Yoram Kaniuk had in fact found a way of momentarily transcending the absolute intransigence of the difference forced by the Arab on Zionism, and through that on the Jew. To the extent to which Yosef's duality succeeds in engulfing the Israeli Jewish reader, even for the moment, it succeeds in challenging the convenience of Zionism's version of that difference. Where the narrative of that duality fails is at the point at which it needs the Arab's subjectivity as much as it needs the Jew's. By casting the Arab as an object of Jewish moral subjectivity, it restores the reader to his or her originally presumed condition as the exclusive subject of moral reference and moral judgment. Each reader is able momentarily to be compassionate to some extent; but no reader can experience community with an *object* of moral judgment, much less allow him- or herself to be subjected to the judgment of that object as if before another, alternative, subjectivity.

Yosef endlessly resists the implications of his duality but fails to relieve himself or the reader of the force of those implications. Unlike his Jewish friends, Yosef is rejected by the army. His credentials as a Jew were secure, yet, in his introduction to this episode, he reiterates what one has to assume is his view of what are the most important characteristics of the Jewish self. There, he reminds us that in his mind he is the son of a Holocaust survivor.[17] He explains that he was healthy and physically fit; that his average grade in school was ninety; that he majored in science and knew Hebrew, Arabic, and French; that he could read and speak English; and that his German was passable. Yosef had read "the protocols of the Eichmann trials in the original."[18] This was "when the desire to be Jewish was so strong" that he had invented a past for himself in which (the paternity of) "Azouri was erased"; he had called him, then, "Uncle Azouri." Because Acre was a "mixed city," Yosef avoided going there. In other words, as far as he was concerned, in all respects he was fit, *as a Jew*, to serve in the Israeli army; yet, "the call-up papers came, [but] none came for him" (Heb. 125; Eng. 179).

With the help of Franz, and through the connections Giora's father, Nachie, had with some army officials, an appointment was arranged for Yosef to appeal his rejection to a committee composed of three officers in charge of recruitment. In an excruciatingly humiliating interview, Yosef adamantly sticks to his argument that he "was a Jew and therefore had to be drafted." One of the officers replies: "Are you trying to tell me that you know better than me what you have to do? Maybe the army knows better?" (Heb. 126; Eng. 181). Yosef looked at them and said:

> I was born in the country,[19] I was born to a Jewish mother, my grandfather is a Holocaust survivor (here I gave Franz a title which he wouldn't exactly have dreamt of); by law I have to be drafted and you have to draft me. (Heb. 126; Eng. 181)

The officer sitting on the right said, "as if he was squashing a mosquito and at the same time contemplating some profound philosophical theory,"

> Your father is an Arab called Azouri! He has been detained four times as a member of an anti-Zionist party.[20] He worked for years on a research project that has caused great damage to the state.[21] These are the facts. Your father has relatives in Jordan, on the West Bank, in Lebanon. (Heb. 127; Eng. 182)

Yosef admits these "liabilities" but argues that he has "another side," his mother's: "I am Yosef Rosenzweig, an Israeli, studying in an Israeli high school,[22] living here. Who gave you the right to deprive me of my duty?" He continues:

> The officer shouted, "the privilege!" and I repeated, "the duty," it's my duty. I could have been made into soup for the Germans if Azouri hadn't saved my

grandfather. . . . I want to serve. I have no problems with my conscience. . . . If I want to serve that's because it is my duty. (Heb. 127; Eng. 182)

The argument goes back and forth until the officer says:

There are some Arabs (he almost said "good Arabs" but he caught himself in time) serving in the IDF, but they are *Arabs* who serve in the IDF. You're not exactly that sort of an Arab. . . . What exactly do you want? (Heb. 127; Eng. 182–83)

Yosef told him that if they called him, he could appeal if he had any fear; but who gave them the right to appeal for him?

One of the officers said, what gives me the right is that I'm a Jew fighting here for his homeland. That is a right. And me? I asked. He said with a little sneer in his voice, You? You? What are you, exactly? (Heb. 127; Eng. 183)

Yosef realized that his struggle was already lost before it began, and "under this officer's contemptuous eyes" he began "to gnash [his] teeth of an *Arabush*, of *Arab work*, of that of a good Arab is a dead Arab."[23] The other officer said:

Don't you understand that you're not wanted, Yosef? It's nothing personal, this is a matter of significance! Why do you struggle to push in where you're not wanted? (Heb. 127–28; Eng. 183)

Yosef screamed, "Don't you talk to me like that. My mother was as Jewish as you are. I am a Jew. I wanted to be one. I learned to be one. What do you mean "'you're not wanted.'" And then the officer said, "in words that hardly touched one another, what did your mother have to marry an Arab for?" (Heb. 128; Eng. 183)

Yosef's desire is not so much to serve in the Israeli army as an Israeli citizen, Arab or Jew, but to be recognized as a Jew, and only as such to have the right to serve in the Israeli army. This is not a confrontation of a citizen with the state over civil rights, but rather one between an individual's desire to define himself as a moral subject and the absolute authority of the military to define all individuals based on prior definitions. Yet Yosef's desire to dissolve the impossible duality of his identity into an authentic unified subjectivity is itself an expression of his acceptance of the legitimacy of his having been denied as a Jew. Yosef's own self-justification is inconsistent with his claim to be a moral subject.

The . . . officer yelled; I came here from "there." Boy, I had it stuffed into me. I walked between corpses and took shit out of dead men's backsides. They used to beat me. You won't teach me what reason is and what is the word. I do not

want Arabs in my army. I am in charge of drafting soldiers and you won't fight
anyone. You'll put your tail between your legs like all Arabs do and you'll curse;
maybe you'll take a pot shot at me in the dark. I know your kind. (Heb. 128;
Eng. 184)

Once again, the Holocaust is the standard of morality and provides the
only legitimate basis of mutual recognition among moral subjects and objec-
tification of the Arab as other. The only thing left for Yosef to remember and
learn is that he is human only to the extent to which he is not eligible for
recognition as a subject. This is clear when he is told that his friends are

getting their call-up papers now. In less than a year they'll be soldiers. It would
be better if you do not ask them too many questions; do not try to find out
where they serve and what they're doing. . . . Try to learn how to be one of
those who do not hear and do not see, okay? (Heb. 129; Eng. 185)

That even more is at stake than recognition is made explicit to Yosef when the
officer continues:

If the situation were reversed and your Arabs had won, you wouldn't have
dared talk like that. You'd be hanging from a tree, with your feet up and your
balls being picked, slowly. Some friendly advice, he added. Do not ask questions. If you have any friends who fancy the idea of marrying Arab women, or
the other way around, tell them that every lechery has its price. And then he
yelled, who is next? (Heb. 129; Eng. 185)

For the officer, for what he symbolizes, Yosef is neither subject to nor capable
of moral impulse. His otherness is complete and incorrigible.

Intimacy as Weakness and Self-Pity

To the best of my knowledge this is as close as any important literary text has
come to depicting the intensity and prevalence of racism toward Arabs in
Israel. It is, in the extreme and vivid revulsion with which the soldier condemns Yosef, also close, through the clarification of racism, to acknowledging
the subjectivity of the Arab. But, even then, because the acknowledgment is
rhetorical rather than a matter of content, it leaves intact the Israeli Jewish
perspective. It represents that other subjectivity as only a possible one, and
defined only by anguish. For it, the Arab is, to the reader beyond the text in
any case, an object of pity. Yosef's duality permits the reader a moment of
reflection that in the next moment gives way, in the relief that pity gives, to
self-righteousness. It is, however, admittedly a relief tempered by the fire of a
certain revelation that suggests—but only suggests—an Arab subjectivity

beyond this object of pity. Yosef's duality is not merely Jewishness contaminated by Arabness. It is Jewishness that has in it at least some of the pain, if not the knowledge, of the other. That it can only remain the pain of an other is a limitation of the novel as it is of the liberal consciousness to which Kaniuk appeals. The externality of the difference between Arab and Jew remains in its fictional depiction as two sides of the same personality. The conflict is not one within a single soul, but between souls as separate in Yosef as they are in the militarized unity posited by Zionism's utopian vision of the Jewish experience.

As a result of his rejection by the military, Yosef prepares "to avenge himself on the Jews," though his method is, on the surface, contrary. First, on the level of social action, he goes to work "for Bunim"—that is, for the Israeli Mossad—becoming a *shtinker* (Yiddish for "stinker"), "spying on his own people." In this he flaunts the traits for which the military rejected him. He becomes *their* Arab with a vengeance. On the personal level, in a liaison with a lover, he does "what every Arab boy dreams of, to fuck a Jewish soldier, to fuck her uniform."

> Afterwards she said . . . you probably enjoyed fucking my uniform more than
> fucking me. . . . the light fell on my half-closed eyes and I couldn't resist saying,
> yes, your uniform was sexier! She said, that's what every Arab boy dreams of,
> fucking a Jewish soldier, fucking her uniform. . . . I closed my eyes furiously, for
> a moment I wanted to hit her but then I had a thought, as if I actually went a
> few moments backwards and I knew that she was right. (for the whole passage,
> see Heb. 96–97; Eng. 137–39)

This passage provides another instance of Kaniuk at his most relentless. However, Israeli literary critics tended to trivialize all such devastating revelations as too "controversial," "exceptional," "sensational," "traumatic," "opportunist," and "gimmicky." Their point was to evade by all means the political implications of Kaniuk's savage iconoclasm. In *Iton 77*, a well-known liberal literary magazine in which one would expect at least an acknowledgment of what Kaniuk is attempting in such passages, Neli Milo states, "In regard to such an intricate web [the novel] and in a forum for artistic discourse [the magazine], it would be a waste of time to deal with political implications, to deal with national identities or with self-identity rather than with the artistic work." Milo concludes that Kaniuk's content limits appreciation of the art of his novel:

> [The author's] engagement with traumatic materials which also have social and
> political implications hinders us from joining Yosef in concluding that "perhaps

this was all just one great joke." I prefer Yosef's opening words: "I wanted to weep, a story came out," to which I would add "and almost a poem."[24]

Amnon Navot, who refers to such trying passages as "external layers," seems to be similarly preoccupied primarily with damage control:

> Exceptional cases like this call for a thorough examination. The "materia" of an Arab having intercourse with a female cadet, confessing to himself . . . that he is actually having sex with the uniform's cloth and what this cloth represents, is equivocal. It echoes distress and estrangement, and even hostility toward the "automatic symbols" of our existence in this country. But in vignettes of this kind the author has failed by showing insufficient sensitivity to the possibly ambivalent and sensational aspects of the materia.[25]

These comments provide evidence of how many important Israeli critics deny A Good Arab, political significance by reducing its art to a type of work that could only be foreign to society, by suggesting that the text fails to achieve moral profundity because of its selection of "materia," and that the failure lies exclusively with the author. It is as if these critics hope to control further the tension implicit in Yosef's duality by constituting the author himself as both (and neither) poet and vulgar politician. This doubling of a moral division effectively eliminates all perspectives from which any real division can be criticized. It is, in effect, an instance of the same trope by which Zionist ideology anticipates and then preempts even a modicum of compassion. But where the novelist's failure is one dictated by culture, the critics' reflects only their own bad faith, a refusal to take the opportunity for moral reflection that Kaniuk provides despite himself and in the midst of failure. This reveals one function criticism serves for Zionism, policing the reception of texts in order to make culture at all times explicit and therefore its instances fully accountable.

Yosef's humiliation occurs not only in the military recruiting station, where the Israeli Jewish liberal might sympathize with the Arab who has been denied his civil rights, but even in the most intimate of situations. Yet, even in these, Kaniuk cannot help but undermine his own project by having Yosef constantly resort to self-pity, and, at the end of every moment of strength, having him retreat to self-bashing. For example, rather than relishing the subversive affirmation he felt in the act of "fucking" Dina's uniform, Yosef immediately falls back into the stereotypical role of one who needs sympathy, one who needs to be an object of virtue but has no virtues to offer others. He reconsiders his relationship with Dina as one predicated weakly on his own personal need rather than on mutual attraction. Thus, he muses, "When I had been with her, perhaps because I was rejected, perhaps because of things that went much deeper which only Bunim knew how to set before me in simple and cruel formulas" (Heb. 97; Eng. 139).

Whatever power as subject that he attributes to himself is derived from another. This analogy between Yosef's self-reflection and the type of reaction he experiences at the recruitment office is clarified in the following passage:

> From the moment she put on that fucking uniform she was ten times more powerful than Azouri, and I thought that perhaps just because of it Azouri inherited Franz and she inherited Azouri, and that's why he will become stronger than her, and through him I too become stronger just because I do not have that uniform (Heb. 97–98; Eng. 139)

This freedom of the signifier, its capacity to incite, also reflects the intricate confusion of a dual identity derived from an absolute difference predicated, as a practical matter, on power. In the final analysis, the site of power is the Israeli Jew, male or female, concrete or abstract. And because of that, the love scene with Dina turns into a nightmare, as it must since, as the Israeli officer in the recruiting station reminds Yosef, "every lechery has a price." Thus:

> When I was with her, I really enjoyed myself more than usual. It was a moment of happiness to fuck not only Dina, whom I loved so much, but a Jewish soldier: a fantasy of toughness, a woman with an Uzi glued to her body, who could walk into my house to expel Azouri whenever she felt like it and arrest me. (Heb. 97; Eng. 133)

Expulsion and Estrangement from Self

The expulsion of the Arab—as metaphor and in reality—is the ultimate manifestation within Zionist consciousness of the relation of Jew to Arab. Here, it expresses Yosef's failure to *achieve* moral identity—he cannot merely *have* it. Indeed, Yosef's failure is predicated on his having too much identity, too much about him that demands further and further explication. As such, he can be only a resource for another's more limited identity. What does expulsion mean for Yosef, as a practical matter? Only, he tells us, distance and defeat.

> And if Azouri's cousins in Jordan or in the West Bank have uniforms and they shoot and throw shells, then from all of this and from her, I become stronger; but of course I am also totally defeated; I have no way to retreat; I had to fuck my mother's uniform to kill my father.[26]
> I told her, ha! you'll be standing on the border with my sperm and guard your state against me! (Heb. 98; Eng. 139)

It is tempting to see this version of expulsion, which is also an estrangement from self, as an "identification with the aggressor," except that in this
case the failure of gratification remains on the surface of, rather than beneath,
Yosef's consciousness. He considers this, or is forced to consider it, throughout
the novel. For example, when we turn to the 1948 war, both Yosef, the half
Arab, and his father Azouri, who is a "complete" Arab, find it morally justified
for the Jews to have conquered "their" towns and villages, to have removed
"them" from their land, to have expelled "them" from their country, to have
turned "them" into refugees, to have taken over their homes and settled
Jewish refugees in these same homes not "two days later." Azouri continues:

> Although I did not fight in the war I was full of its pain. We returned to
> Acre. . . . Jews were living in my uncle's house and in the houses of my cousins
> who were in refugee camps in Lebanon. The Jews uprooted the lemon trees to
> fuel their stoves during the terrible winter of 1949. I understood what my
> brothers did not understand, where they had come from, their distress. I knew
> that this was no reason to exile me, to insult me, to turn me out of my home;
> but there were no more laws as before. (Heb. 63; Eng. 90)

This acceptance, this precritical stoicism, appears in the narrative to be
coupled with one type of goodness Arabs might attain—unqualified sympathy
with the European Jews during and after the Holocaust. However, Kaniuk
acknowledges what his characters do not: that Zionism had already begun to
dispossess Palestinians at least six decades before. In other words, Azouri has
feeling for a history, in this case another's, at the expense of more inclusive,
concrete, History. Kaniuk must be read as having intended to raise this issue of
the cost to Arab self-recognition of being "good." The denial of the historical-
ness of one's own history, implicit in the elevation of a particular history to
the status of a definitive referent, is perhaps typical of all true victims. Kaniuk
can therefore be read as acknowledging the Arab's victimization by the Jew,
but only within the framework, of acknowledging but not recognizing the
other, that is constructed within the novel as a rejection of politics in principle.
The Arab's admission of Jewish suffering and Jewish right is both an instance
of self-denial (in the narrative) and a textual device for confronting the reader with the Arab experience through its very denial. When the admission of
politics finally comes, it is by then merely the exception that proves the rule.
Kaniuk builds political exceptionalism into the fabric of the novel, as internal
to the reading of it. The rejection, and evasion, of politics is part of the poetics of the text, as what one might call its strategy. What makes the rejection

an evasion is the way in which Kaniuk surrounds every political moment with confusion, suspicion, and irony.

Thus, the uncertainty at any given moment as to whether the speaker is a particular character or the narrator himself; whether what is written was spoken in the past, is said in the present, or occurs in the future; whether something has been told to the narrator or is the narrator's recollection; all these ambiguities and more are rhetorically integral to the narrative's "fictional truth." Yosef says: "My earlier is not your earlier; I live in linear time; time is like space; there's no past or future. But I knew that I wasn't explaining properly" (Heb. 9, 11; Eng. 5, 9).

To assert and then take back, this too is part of the "tropics" of Yosef's discourse, what casts the novel as discourse such that reading it becomes a practice caught in conditions rather than an act of consumption, or even of criticism. Indeed, this intricacy duplicates Yosef's psyche. Thus we cannot blame Kaniuk for undermining the defenses of the reader who follows the course of this surplus-ridden text of escalating deprivation. The excesses of the text and the excesses of Yosef are mutually reinforcing. The duplication is the means by which Kaniuk leads the reader toward Yosef's predicament, to enter it only for a soon-to-be-lost moment. The reader has no need to suspend disbelief to enter deliberately Yosef's consciousness. The entering is done on behalf of and to the reader. Thus, Yosef says that Azouri "had already begun to understand the destroyers; and he said that in a war for life and death, in which each side is persuaded of its own justice, destruction is inevitable" (Heb. 63; Eng. 89). Here Yosef speaks *for* the subjectivity of a reader who stands above duality as its witness but is not subject to it. This abstract and ultimately abject appreciation of one's "destroyers" is all that the Israeli Jewish reader can see as the moral courage of an Arab—to admit the legitimacy of the point of view of one's destroyer. The best the Arab can be is a relativist, and given that relativism is denied to all moral subjects by virtue of the Holocaust, whatever the Arab "best" is, it is not once again on the order of moral subjectivity. It is the goodness of the good inmate, the good patient, the good victim.

Azouri's statement that "in a war for life and death, in which each side is persuaded of its own justice, destruction is inevitable" finds its limited truth in the context of liberal Zionism. There, one can recognize the other only after denying the other's right to recognize one. The solution is a parity of suffering, but not a parity of wrongs. No distinction is made between victim and destroyer. In this way, liberalism preserves morality at the expense of experience, historical effect at the expense of history. The liberal Zionist admits to Arab suffering, therefore allowing an Arab also to admit it; but it cannot admit the

wrong involved. Therefore, the Arab can dwell on his own suffering only vic-
ariously—through the Jew's suffering and as if his or her own is really someone
else's. Thus, Azouri's wisdom lies in his lack of presumptuousness. In affirming
the parity of suffering without a parity of wrongs, he asserts a one-sided truth at
the expense of an Arab history that could be truly historical.

Yet a type of Arab historical thinking is permissible, if only it does not
include the Jews or contain any possible reference to Jews: "We" (the Palestinians), says Azouri Sherara, "should have persuaded our leaders to accept
the U.N. resolution and establish two states; we did not do that" (Heb. 63–64;
Eng. 88–89). Here is the sort of regretful historical reflection required of the
good Arab—regret not for what he, Azouri, may have lost, but regret for having attempted to oppose that loss. In this subtle reversal, in which an Arab
reflection on history withdraws from attributing any significant role to the
Israeli Jew, it is the Jews who were paradigmatic victims, the Arabs only victims of themselves. Now, it is as if the claim of that Jewish minority over the
whole territory was founded in a right greater than any rights of its majority
non-Jewish inhabitants, who now appear to have suffered without being able
to claim that their suffering was a wrong done to them, that it was a product of
a history of which the Jews were a part.

Azouri's regretfulness is at the same time a totalization of himself, and
through that the Arab in his son, and through that the Arab as such. The
space and time of Azouri's catastrophic reflection is Palestine in 1948. It provides the chronotype of a moral universe, therefore a total and persistent
frame of reference for the reader. This is also clear in other respects from the
rhetorical constitution of the passage quoted above. Yosef is the narrator, but
the actual speaker is Azouri. He begins with the pronoun "we," purporting to
represent Palestinian consciousness as such and a putative body politic: "We
should have persuaded our leaders." He proceeds, "Bleeding refugees wanted a
state of their own, and it had to come at my expense because my people
grasped neither the moment nor the intensity of the insult incurred by the
refugees from Europe" (Heb. 63; Eng. 89).

It is the relativism of the last phrase that allows reading to proceed through
and past this Arab reflection on suffering. Arab suffering is relative; that of
Jews is absolute. Azouri's expression of compassion for the Jews is a necessary
condition of his being recognized by a moral subject, though not recognized as
a moral subject. Despite this limitation, the passage comes close to a greater
moment of critical truth. The expression "my expense," conjoined with "my
people" and governed by "we," yields a voice that is both personal—of *this*
Arab—and general—of *the* Arab. This voice, at once concrete and general-

ized, brings Arab experience close to being recognizable by the reader. But the Arab in general, denied politics, can speak neither with nor for moral authority, and without that, the concrete Arab has voice but not authority. Thus, Azouri's acknowledgment of the Jews is without any autonomous authority that could stand equal to or even occasionally above the moral authority asserted by the Jew in the name of the Holocaust. This is why Yosef can only follow Azouri by speaking always of his own failure of moral authority. In no sense will an Arab voice of moral reflection ever judge the Jew.

At the same time, the singular possessive "my" separates Azouri from his people and from their leaders. An Arab can speak against the Arabs as no Jew can speak against Jews. Azouri's salvation as a "good Arab" lies in his willingness to speak against politics, against the legitimacy of Arabs' deciding their own fate, against the possibility of an Arab right at all commensurate with the right of the Jews victimized in Europe and throughout history. The latter can be shared with no one, but above all not with the Arab other who insistently occupies a space Zionism wishes to and must purify. Azouri stands, in this passage, for the Arab outside of history, therefore for a moral reflection that is moral only in its acceptance of the existing fact, the conquest of Palestine by the Jews. Thus, when Azouri laments the treatment to which the Arabs were subject, even when he gives vent to the experience of Arab suffering, the implications of this are muted in his acknowledgment of a Jewish right beyond any law that could conceivably be shared by Jew and Arab.

When an Israeli Arab says, in a text written for an Israeli Jewish audience by an Israeli Jewish author, that he did not fight in the (1948) war, as Azouri does at the opening of the quoted passage, he is cleansing himself—but only in the eyes of Jews. At the same time, he is estranging himself from his own history, allowing the Jewish reader to hear him only as an individual and in so doing not to hear the greater voice of those who had both suffered and fought, that historical voice of what the conquest of Israel has constituted as "the Arabs."

But Azouri is, for Kaniuk, more than an Arab. His voice is doubly authentic. It is the voice of one who accepts the mastery of Jew over Arab and therefore wills himself to be abject in order to be good. But it is also the voice of knowledge. In this duality, Azouri's truth is both moral and historical, though only in its endorsement of Zionist history. He is in a sense the final and most complete witness of the Jewish experience and the special right derived from it—both as an outsider who admits that right over any he might himself declare and as an expert who can certify as valid the Jewish claim to history. Azouri is after all an important professional Arab historian with, as the narrator tells us, five doctorates (Heb. 61; Eng. 85),[27] and he is an acknowledged expert on the Arab-Jewish conflict (Heb. 12; Eng. 10).

If a man who experienced "the humiliation [and] the plunder," who was among those "who stood on the Acre beach for two days and two nights," who "never fired a shot, who was pushed by Israeli soldiers into the water and forced to stand in the surf as if he should swim to some Arab limbo in the sea" (Heb. 66; Eng. 92), if such an Arab can feel and think and say all that he does about the possibility of all that, Azouri is beyond question a "good Arab." If, in addition, he can speak from a position of expertise and as a recognized authority, he is someone even beyond Jew and Arab, whose assertion of the rights of the one sufferer over the other must be true. In this, Azouri is the reader's own surrogate within the text. It is not Yosef who is supposed to enlighten the reader; his duality is only a condition of enlightenment. It is Azouri, his reflections and his credentials, who speaks with the light of finality. He reflects on duality from above, and from the only position from which compassion can be defined and delimited—that of the Zionist.

Finally, if Azouri could bear witness to the terrible winter of 1949, to the destruction of the homes and families of his people, watch them being marched through their own abandoned orange groves and forced to leave behind their flocks, cattle, and beasts of burden, see them forced to flee into exile through pastures and valleys of lands they had sown, and even then he could justify that devastation by another people's history and require that it be accepted as justified, then he is not only good, he is truthful. For the moment, he speaks of Arab life, even if only for, if not from, the point of view of the Jew.

The grandeur of what Azouri represents as an Arab, the stoicism so essential to the truth he represents, requires, for his completion as a "good Arab," the additional element of *life*. This newly recognizable Arab for Jewish history must be formed in life (praxis) as well as in speech. There must be moments, typically more private affections, in which the vitality and beauty of the Arab is made manifest. Thus, Azouri tells Yosef:

> I didn't want the obligation I had to guard Acre, the town which is my heaven and my historical land. After you have already taken the beautiful houses and the orchards, Kafur's garden and his seashore and the lands of Galilee, I didn't want what I'm doing here in Acre to be directed against Franz and Kathe.
> (Heb. 64; Eng. 90)

Azouri addresses his son in this passage as if he, Azouri, were the Arab compromised by Jewishness. He speaks as if he had somehow benefited from his own father's misfortune and that of the entire Palestinian people. This moment of hostility by a son toward his father, this momentary intimacy of what had just been presented on a grander scale, gives leeway to what is taken for a specifically Arab complaint; but again it is one that abjures politics and expects true reconciliation (between parent and child), if only a reconciliation in anger; thus Azouri can remain an Arab in detail even as he sets himself above that history. He tells Yosef:

> I wanted to protect Acre for my grandchildren. I couldn't have known that if I ever had a grandson it would be a dead fetus aborted by a Jewish girl called Dina, from the boiling sperm, ejaculated and red, of a Jewish son who is the fruit of my loins. (Heb. 65; Eng. 90–91)

The premise of the trope of Yosef's dual identity is that the Jewish reader is already mired in an unavoidable dilemma predicated on an essentially militarized difference. This, among his readers, in their terms, is where Kaniuk begins, but it is also where he ends. The tables are never turned, nor could they be by so minimal moral vitalization of the other (the Arab) in so dedicated a culture. The Arab does finally emerge, but only as an object of the reader's pity and in order to demonstrate the righteousness of that reader's sense of Jewish-Arab relations, a righteousness already present in Zionist liberalism. What Kaniuk has added is a willingness to listen to an Arab. This is a critical gain even though it is one that speaks fundamentally for the Jew.

The novel conveys the greater culture of which it is part, but, surprisingly, it reinstates what its author intended to challenge, the otherness of the Arab. Not only is culture saved, but even ideology is salvaged; there is a cost, however, and this is what is most interesting about A Good Arab,. In Yosef's dual identity, the unavoidable conversation within the self, the Jewish reader is forced to encounter Arabness as at least a moral possibility. But the standard of the Holocaust and the Zionist rejection of the Diaspora remain the contexts of meaning for this possibility. The resulting depiction of Arabness denies moral subjectivity to the Arab in a way that leaves intact the very division on which Zionism rests, between the moral and the juridical self.

A Good Arab, aims to embody the possibility of a greater moral universe. On the other hand, it addresses readers for whom this moral universe is already complete and exclusive. And so the dilemma posed by the other for a self that wishes the other to remain external cannot be overcome; it can only be restated endlessly. My reading of A Good Arab, attempts to respect the desire in the text to overcome this dilemma under conditions that make its resolution, its transcendence, impossible.

4

The Palestinian "Extremist"

The Significance of the Goodness *of the* "Good Arab"

A *Good Arab*, is not merely the invention of its author, nor is it a self-contained text operating solely as a vehicle for "fictional truth." Like all literary works, it is, first of all, a complex product of operations mediated in all respects by the culture of which it is a part, and its intercultural aspects, as a "moment" of that culture. That is, it embodies practices that articulate the intersection of interests, identities, and social organization, according to a historical project itself defined by an absolute and morally constitutive antagonism drawn along racialist lines. The most definite antifigure of this project is "the Arab," against which all of Jewish experience is delineated as a synchronicity and given status within a universal historical narrative, an allegory of identity and the Law, as the enactment of a fundamental truth.

It is in this context that the significance of the *goodness* of "the good Arab" must be understood and its paradoxes explained. This is, of course, a familiar problem. Every racialist project situates the individual instances of what it categorizes in a dimensionlike space that yields a variety of exemplary and interchangeable figures or types.[1] In this way, the culture provides a sufficient range of moral, aesthetic, and political response to ensure that the hegemony of any particular categorization operates across society and is made subtle, varied, and capable of regulating argument among people of good faith. This, in turn, confirms an essential decency within the racialist culture, cohesiveness and mutual recognition and respect among the denigrators, and the constant illusion that there are ways out of the social problems that accompany racialism by identifying a subcategory of acceptable others whose exceptional qualities justify both compassion and the rule that ultimately prohibits it.

How, then, or in what sense, can there be a "good Arab" for Israeli Jewish culture? Jewish children regularly encounter Arabs as janitors or gardeners, construction workers, garbage collectors, street sweepers, cleaning women, gas station attendants, and others who perform such apparently artless tasks of service and maintenance.[2] The unthreatening and politically empty presence of such Arabs, given the larger significance of "the Arab" in Israeli society, has to be rationalized within the racialist discourse.

The rationalization of this extraordinary Arab, defined vocationally and in relations of subservience to Jewish consumers, is a practical moment of Israeli Jewish self-reflection. It is usually made explicit by a sensitive parent, who gently explains that "not all Arabs are the same," that "there are Arabs and there are "'Arabs,'" as the officer at the recruiting station told Yosef. "This," says the parent pointing to an Arab at work, "is, as you can see, a good Arab."

Thus, a distinction is not only implied, it is made self-evident: "this" individual is different from most of *them*; that is, he or she is not typical of their kind, not what we mean by "Arab." And what *we mean* turns out in political terms to be at the extreme of the category, "extremist" or a terrorist. In cultural terms, it is "them." The result is that there is no "typical" Arab who is a subject, and no exceptional—"good"—Arab who is an agent. The latter is exceptional, good, precisely by virtue of being defined functionally. The former is obsessed and lacks the capacity for moral reflection; which is to say, the "typical" Arab is a monster. The exceptional, good Arab is a functionary. He or she can perform duties virtuously, but cannot address the question "Why?" or reflect on matters of substantive value.[3] The Arab as such, the true Arab, the monster, is human without capacity for moral reflection. Therefore one has an obligation to respect the incipient soul of such a creature, but one must never confuse *that* soul with one of a moral subject. *The Arab* cannot constitute the subject position from which another can be judged. In this Arab, the range from functionary to monster, Zionism creates its perfect foil—one who can be judged without fear that the tables will be turned or that the judge will be held accountable. The Arab, good or bad, is one in relation to whom "we" can never be object.

The distinction between the inconsequential "good Arab" and the monstrously dangerous "real Arab" is reproduced incessantly in Israeli Hebrew lit-

erature. It is manifest there from the early days of the Zionist colonial settlement in Palestine. One finds it later in explicitly denigrative forms and with a
greater degree of sophistication. The same polarized construct of "good" particular and monstrous universal appears already in its most vulgar simplicity in
Hebrew children's literature of the 1930s.[4]

In *A Good Arab,* the quintessential "real" or "typical" Arab is represented
by the character abu-al-Misk Kafur Sherara. It should be noted that the "bad"
features of this character are so exaggerated that one can suspect it of being a
parody of a stereotype, therefore an attempt on Kaniuk's part to ridicule just
such a characterization. On the other hand, all the Arab characters in this
novel, including Yosef and Azouri, appear in ways that make it difficult if not
impossible to determine the boundary between irony (self-criticism) and
abuse (the denigration of the other).

We are introduced to abu-al-Misk Kafur Sherara via Franz Rosenzweig,
Yosef's grandfather, who, as a young German officer, was sent to assist the
Turkish army in the construction of a second fortification line on Mt. Carmel.
Franz was sickened by what he saw, and by the people of that backward coun-
try. But he once found himself in "an enchanting garden of a kind he never
saw before in his life" (Heb. 26; Eng. 32).

It was enormous, stretching from the middle reaches of the mountain to the
sea below. Following a detailed description of the garden's marvels, which all
constituted "a wonderful arabesque," we are told that "the gardener who had
planned it came from the Haifa German Colony" (Heb. 26; Eng. 32). Such a
creator of so perfect an arabesque—something so *Arab-like*—would not have
been, for the Germans, an Arab. Thus, we have a vision in which the arabesque is the product of the European imagination, its perfection that of the
essentially "Oriental." In this fantasy there are no lives to enjoy the garden as
part of its appropriation.

Looking through the entrance gate, beyond the growth of foliage and
creepers, Franz saw an enormous house embellished with arches and vaults. He
entered and met "Abu Misk Kafur Sherara."[5]

> Kafur was sitting in the inner courtyard with Franz's Turkish friend, who said,
> here is Rosenzweig Franz [the last name comes first in the original], and Kafur
> nodded his head. He was holding a sword which he claimed had once belonged
> to Salah Addin, and was wearing a silk suit. And at a short distance, adorned
> ladies were sitting smelling of perfume and drinking blood from tall goblets.
> They looked at him through the . . . dusky dimness of the light, and afterwards
> they laid romantic traps for him from which he was forever escaping. (Heb. 26;
> Eng. 32)

This account comes close to imitating classical European orientalist literature of the kind discussed by Edward W. Said in his book *Orientalism*.[6] It also has, however, at least one Israeli peculiarity worthy of notice, the ridiculing of Salah-al-Din. This is traditional in Israeli Hebrew discourse on the Arab, and it is in many ways especially revealing of its racialism.

Salah-al-Din versus the Crusader in Art and Politics

It is difficult to determine exactly when reference to Salah-al-Din became prevalent in Israeli Hebrew literature. It is reasonable to set the date soon after the October 1956 invasion of Egypt by Britain, France, and Israel aimed at reversing the nationalization of the Suez Canal, defeating Egypt once more in a colonial war, and humiliating Jamal 'Abd al-Nasir. The joining of forces with Britain and France culminated four years of aggressive anti-Egyptian foreign policy by the Israeli government. After the war, hostility was focused on Jamal 'Abd al-Nasir, who had, in 1956, assumed the office of the Egyptian presidency.

In *A Previous Chapter* (1985), Nissim Calderon, an Israeli literary critic, is concerned with Israeli Hebrew poetry and politics during the 1950s and 1960s. The second part of his book is titled: "Moshe Dayan, 1956." In it, Calderon quotes a section from the diaries of Moshe Sharet, at that time Israel's foreign affairs minister, and writes the following preamble to the quotation:

> Moshe Sharet was forced to resign from the post of prime minister in consequence of his objection to the policies that led to the Sinai War. Israel attacked on 29 October 1956. About a month earlier, Moshe Sharet went on a diplomatic tour of Asia. He did not know of the decision to go to war, either because it was concealed from him or because he was ignored. On 2 December, while in Cambodia, he received Israeli newspapers, and he writes in his . . . diary:[7]

Sharet's discussion, as quoted by Calderon, opens as follows:

> As usual, when a great event takes place, Nathan's mind thrust into it like a dagger. He produced a . . . column which was the most arduous and piercing political essay of all those which appeared or could have appeared in our press on this topic [the Sinai march].[8]

Calderon presents Sharet's critique of the poet, Alterman, in which Sharet argues that Alterman had written politically in a way that was inconsistent with the government's promise never to engage in a preventive war. What disturbed Sharet so much was not Alterman's view, but that he had used his authority as a nationally prominent poet to "take sides" in a political dispute. This intertwining of art and politics, I argue, is not a genre. It is characteristic of Israeli critical writing.

There are many similar instances where literature is the site of a political debate. I chose this one as exemplary because of the involvement of a politician and because of a particular quality of the representations employed by the parties. Here is heroic writing in reference to a heroic episode, an epic treatment of the depiction of a military event that is itself militarylike and that aspires to a limitless magnitude of moral persuasiveness. This epic historical consciousness dwells simultaneously in past, present, and future; it is by no means peculiar to Zionism, though it is characteristic of it.

After the establishment of the state of Israel, the Palestinians and nationalist Arabs elsewhere made an analogy in their literary and political discourses between the "Zionist state" and the Crusaders' kingdom in Palestine (the Latin kingdom of Jerusalem). There were in this analogy complex intimations, on the one hand, that the Jewish state was parasitically established by European invaders of a different religion hostile in principle to the native cultures, and, on the other hand, that hope lay exclusively in the Moslem reconquest of the land. These intimations were embodied in the historical figure of Salah-al-Din, who led the battle against the Crusaders and restored Jerusalem to Islam.[9] It is in this regard that Israeli Hebrew literature began to treat Salah-al-Din as an antihero and to ridicule the Arab accounts of his heroism.

After the Egyptian Officers' Revolution of 1952, many Third World countries began to regard Egypt as a leading force in the struggle against colonialism. At the same time, Israel's participation in the invasion seemed to make even clearer than before its annexationist intentions and collaboration with imperialism. Anti-Zionist, anti-Israel sentiment among Palestinians and Arabs grew more intense and intransigent as a new pan-Arab nationalism began to solidify around the figure of Jamal 'Abd al-Nasir. The accumulation of imagery and symbolism in regard to the invasion gave it a universal significance for all parties. Liberal Zionists in Israel, who opposed in some measure the invasion and the politics that led to it, began nevertheless to employ the Crusader image in their own accounts of Israel's history and mission.

Again, it is difficult to determine whether the analogy originated in political discourse strictly defined and was later incorporated into literature or vice versa. In any case, the image of the crusader carried the weight of apprehension about Arab-Israeli relations. This, in turn, reinforced the belief that only aggression toward the Palestinians and the neighboring Arab states could prevent Israel, and therefore Jews, from falling victim to the same fate that befell the Crusaders' state.[10] In Israeli literature, poetry, and literary criticism there are numerous instances of this sentiment, and it is in this context that all contemporary major political Arab figures are represented as analogous to Salah-al-Din, as potential agents of Pan-Arabism and vengeance against Israel.[11]

In a comment on Amos Oz's novella *Late Love*, Gershon Shaked says:

> From the speaker's words . . . we learn that the source of national aggression is anxiety, as we also learn that the source of anti-Semitism is society's need to have scapegoats for its frustrations. Distress causes frustration and frustration needs a victim. In sacrificing, the sacrificer hastens his own end, since he is "wasting" as it were his best energy and vigor on destruction, so that there is no vitality left in him. This ambiguous process could be used to describe anti-Semitism, but it could also serve as a basis for describing the forces that are active in our own day's Crusaders' soul. And, perhaps, it also implies Israel's survivalist philosophy of history.[12]

Right-wing nationalist writers, using the same analogy, took an inverted perspective, praising the Crusaders' valor, their relatively advanced technology, and their efficient methods of using power for political ends, and emphasizing the need to learn from the Crusaders' defeat so that it would not be repeated by modern Israel.[13] But what is of greatest interest is the liberal, self-critical Zionist use of the analogy. Its equivocality and the ambiguity of its articulations create the sort of intertextuality that makes any writing intrinsically cultural and therefore knowable only through a critical hermeneutics of difference. These "symptomatic lapses" allow us to observe variations in the analogy according to the Israeli national mood following each national crisis.

A "good Arab" like Yosef would not, then, miss an opportunity to employ the analogy; and indeed, in one of his arguments with his father, Azouri, he says that "they [the Jews] are conquerors, like the crusaders, foreigners, hypocrites, self-righteous; they'll be finished off like the crusaders too; and Azouri said, no, I think you're mistaken Yosef. You'll stay here but we'll stay here too" (Heb. 67; Eng. 95). Here is how Yosef, half Jew and half Arab, presents the question of Arab-Jewish relations to his Arab father, and how Yosef projects the analogy as an allegory of prophetic significance. Azouri appears in this dialogue, Yosef's version of it, as the Arab of the liberal Zionist's most fervent hope: "No, both *you* and *we* are going to stay here." The aspirations of both conqueror and conquered are preserved in this modest—"no, I think you're mistaken"—totalization: the justice of the conquest acknowledged as part of a more general, stoic rather than unhappy, mutuality of rights and obligations. Conquest is now represented as difference, and difference as the occasion for modesty in the promotion of rights. Such modesty, however, can only imply, under the circumstances, the request for decency interpreted as mercy. It is not surprising, then, that Salah-al-Din becomes, for so many Israeli Jewish writers, a figure of ridicule and, as such, part of the reversal of the crusaders' history now to be undertaken as a project by Israeli Jewish society as a whole. Azouri represents a permission granted by the victim to the conqueror to complete the crusade, and then to be merciful.

Thus, the image of a degenerate Kafur holding what he claims to be Salah-al-Din's sword is insulting and intended to be so. Yet, by itself, the episode of the garden tells us little if anything about the overall project of the novel. The text as a whole, with the intertextuality invoked by its passages, attempts to appeal to the Israeli Jewish Hebrew reader's moral sensibilities beyond his or her parochial identification as a Jew. Therefore, this episode must be seen as a momentary turn, in which the presence of an "extremist" Arab, Kafur, operates as a source of moral nuance for the Jewish reader. Extremism stands for a political disposition the total absence of which defines the goodness of good Arabs and the presence of which in any measure allows the Jewish reader to feel free of constraint about prejudice and stereotyping. This way of instituting a negative boundary to the goodness of "the Arab" allows the Jew to remain opposed to prejudice while appreciating what only prejudice can yield. In this way Kaniuk's novel discovers for its readers a total object suitable for a pity that can substitute for compassion, and a capacity to think about that object in terms that disturb neither the sense of moral righteousness nor the prejudice that might otherwise undermine it.

As we have seen, the limited goodness of the good Arab who deserves compassion, indeed to whom it is in some measure owed, lies in the total absence of a political disposition and in the presence of a positive character, that of the juridical citizen who does his or her job, never looks for or feels anything beyond his or her position, and aspires only to be what he or she already is for another. This perfectly unvital, nonsubjective Arab is, for liberal Zionism, the proper object of a compassion that can manifest itself only as pity, that need never risk a turning of the tables.

But it is evident from Yosef's meditations that the Arab part of his subjectivity reflects on the objective politics of division, laments far more than merely material conditions, and in other ways shows itself to be a less comfortable Arab for Jewish readers than most of the other Arabs to whom Yosef refers in his confessional autobiography. A Good Arab, distinguishes between the Arab one individual might or might not be and Arabs "out there," as such. The latter are potential objects of pity disguised as compassion. The former is only one term, ultimately the losing one, of a struggle for the right to be moral, to judge, to demand, to give or withhold compassion, to be the essential subject in the opposition between Arab and Jew.

In A Good Arab, the Jewish reader earns the right to do what he or she is already destined to be able to do—to judge and choose whether or not to be compassionate. Jewish history again provides a context of meaning in which the reality of the Arab is reduced to that of presence without praxis, a type of humanity that lacks the right to claim subjectivity for itself and the extra-juridical rights and identities by which such a right becomes another's duty. The Jewish self is thereby reconciled with a morality that had been momentarily disturbed by the Arab-Israeli conflict. It confirms itself in the small virtue of acknowledging that something is owed, deserved by, the "good Arab" (other than the "dead Arab"), as if the Arab-Israeli struggle could be reduced to an exchange, if only the good Arabs remain good and "bad Arabs"—Arab subjectivity, politics, memory—are vanquished.

Kafur's character plays a key role in the novel's distinction between proper and improper objects of compassion, therefore in its ability to detect error and to identify its source and its margins. But the distinction also evokes a yet more general characterization of the nongoodness of the bad Arab. Not only is the good Arab nonpolitical, abject, and a self-identifying creature of the law, but he or she does not claim an identity of any historical significance. That is, he or she is also a creature of a fixed culture and a context of externalities beyond legitimate dispute. Thus, the total Arab, against which Arab goodness is identified, is the bad Arab whose identity is as clear and irrepressible as his or her politics. There is nothing of the objective and "deserving" in the bad Arab, and nothing of subjectivity in the good Arab. This point is illustrated by Kaniuk's treatment of the Palestinian Arabs' religious life and claims of religious identity. The novel at no point allows for effective and principled religious identity among Palestinian Arabs.

Are There Muslims among the Arabs?

Historically, Muslims have constituted between 80 and 85 percent of the entire Arab population of Palestine. The Christian population has rarely reached 13 percent. In the wake of the 1948 war and the consequent expulsion of Arab inhabitants, the percentage of Christians among the Israeli Arab population rose to its peak of approximately 22 percent in 1955, and then began to decline. Today it is approximately 12 percent.[14]

Yet not one of the Arab characters presented in this novel is identified as

Muslim. On the contrary, all are Christians. On the one hand, it is as if the absence of the Islamic were a necessary condition for representing goodness in the Arab; on the other, the fixed culture that is a source of beauty and of the beauty that redeems the Arab must be, as it were, defanged. The "arabesque" must be external to the Islamic and immune to the historical. Thus, it is a perfect surface, the proper description of which involves survey and inventory rather than analysis intended to yield evidence of structure and the difference it makes as something achieved:

> In the darkening light of the late afternoon the gray eyes of Kafur's brother's son shone like rare precious stones. In the face and eyes of Azouri, hundreds of years of ancient chivalry and glory married the beauty of the northern lakes with the burning desert. The seam between the European indifference which [Crusader] knights brought with them nine hundred years before and the yellow desert-afflicted blazing heat were captured in the man [Azouri]. (Heb. 28; Eng. 35)

Paradoxically, the Christian Arab—the racial rather then ethnic Arab—can manifest the arabesque independent of the danger of history against which the goodness of the "good Arab" can be identified for the Jewish conscience. Yet, in Azouri, the arabesque gives a certain depth to his goodness, a depth that is the miraculous fullness of a surface. In its finest representation, at its most complete and demanding, the "good Arab" is a work of art.

It is an irony that the liberalizing project of Kaniuk's novel is weakened if the good Arab is also real, alive, motivated, an instance of praxis. Kaniuk preserves the allure, to the non-Arab, of the arabesque without situating it in a context by which the alluring traits might be oriented and self-transcending, might be *Arabic*. "European indifference"—the capacity for reflection—makes of Arab passion nothing more than a fixed trait, an accident, a contentless and unreflective presence. Kaniuk could hardly have written otherwise, as he was, presumably, writing in anticipation of his own readers' prejudices and stereotypes. And what better way to dispel these than by using them exhorbitantly. The Arab is "blazing heat" and passion. When contained, it is a beauty that "we" can appreciate; when it is not, it is the threat of a flood, lawless and unpredictable.[15]

Another contrast that concentrates the novel's intention is between the magnificence of Kafur's mansion and garden (definitely European and Christian, yet of orientalistic splendor) and the degraded state of the people who occupy it. This contrast also brings beauty and history together, but this time in a less compelling identification of value and product. Yet, in both cases, the Christianized element of glory appears on the side of the Jews, as a source of Jewish virtue at odds with traditional Jewish historical consciousness. This part of the Zionist "revaluation of values"[16] rejects the image of the passive and lachrymose Jew, but at the cost of identifying with the non-Jew: just as an Arab morality is not possible for the Arab in relation to the Jew, so it appears that a Jewish virtue is not possible for the Jew in relation to "the West."[17]

The need for a unique and absolute moral justification, the need therefore to hold history, as it were, in one's grasp as if it were all one's own, is what most distinguishes Zionism from mere patriotism or nationalism. It frees what Jews do from the standards of all others, including those who have always condemned them. In this way, at least, Zionism transcends its original secular purpose—the Jew imagined as the agent of Right in History, History as the struggle of *that* Right to survive. It is also part of the Zionist identification of self as always categorical, and therefore absolute.

However understandable, this reveals yet another paradox. This universalization *of* the Jew depends on a position external *to* the Jew from which identity is formed. But the categorical nature of the opposition between what the self *is* (for another beyond the self) and what it *does* (for itself against a parallel other), can end only in a double negation: the self that asserts itself against an other can know itself only *in* that negation and *as* negation; that which is in this sense other to the self becomes the source of the self's inevitable opposition to itself, that is, the source of a *need* for what is negated.

Thus, while the poet H. N. Bialik lamented the massacre of Jews by Russian burghers and artisans in the Ukraine,[18] young socialist Zionists in Palestine adopted Russian lyrics of valor and battle, and sang them with the same devotion their parents had once used to pray for mercy.[19] In a very short period of time, young Zionists internalized a hostile Russian culture, and in their metamorphosis from "Zid" to "Hebrew,"[20] they were able to dissociate the "signifier" from its original "signified." Their translation of the lyrics into Hebrew was, at the same time, a reinstituting of war and heroism, and the adding of one culture's sense of sacrifice to another's need to validate sacrifice.

This is just one aspect of the complex sentiment of Zionist admiration of the Christian and revulsion toward the Moslem. Zionism is a fundamentally Western ideology. It combines European secularism and modernist nationalism with an "Eastern" utopian reason in which representation and logic are synthesized aesthetically, and therefore assume an immediately communal form. This is consistent with the fact that Zionism gained its ascendancy among Eastern European Jews at a time when European colonialism and orientalism had come to define a principle of hegemony.

Colonialism and orientalism are not necessarily "Christian," but in the European context they were primarily, and ideologically, directed against Muslims in a Christian way that evoked invidious images of ungoverned sensuality, pride, uncontrollable passion, and narcissism. From such a point of view, the Muslim appears as the exact opposite of modern secularism, nationalism, and civic communitarian virtue. He or she appears therefore without respect for boundaries, indifferent to the disciplines of exchange and compromise, and without a reasoning sense of the importance of universalism. As contradictory as it may seem, Zionism becomes not only a political tool in this offensive, but, because of the Jews' position in the Old and New Testaments, a biblical symbol of its nonsectarian (e.g., Christian) correctness and necessity. At this point Zionism and Christianity find their mutual affection in excluding a shared other. The excluded Oriental constitutes both Christian virtue in the context of imperialism and the Protestant ethic in the context of imposing "order" on what otherwise would be license. One part of that Oriental, the utopian Jew, reappears to justify that very exclusion.

Thus, Zionism, at its most philosophical, endorses the terms by which the Jew was originally condemned. The incorporation of this in hegemonic Hebrew literature is virtually unavoidable in a moral universe that situates the Jew categorically between the Arab and the Holocaust. But for liberals it enforces an imagination inconsistent with the project of liberalizing Zionism through compassion. It is, in other words, their own acceptance of Zionist historiography that traps liberals, including Kaniuk, into reproducing within their own critique of Jewish attitudes toward Arabs the conditions under which Zionism has always reiterated its most fundamental reaction—against the Arab other.

There is a practical aspect to all of this. There is no identifiable point within the history of the Palestinian national movement of absolute conflict between Christians and Muslims, although, throughout the period of British rule in Palestine, British authorities and Zionist functionaries made great efforts to "discover" such "natural" points of opposition.[21] This method of dividing and exploiting the differences among ethnic or religious groups of Palestinian nationalists is still pursued by Israeli authorities in the Occupied Territories and in Israel itself.[22] Thus, when we are told in A Good Arab, that Kafur's "dream of returning to the House of the Ummayad did not appear to contradict the crosses stuck on the fence and the cross suspended between the folds of fat hanging from his neck" (Heb. 27; Eng. 33–34), we are meant to understand that Kafur is a political opportunist and a man with double standards. We will come to realize that opportunism and hypocrisy are Kafur's main traits: "Kafur already then was looking for new friends in his future war for greater Syria and he therefore supported Turkey, winked at the Germans, and supported them. They, on their part, handsomely rewarded him." And just before the final defeat of Turkey: "Abu Misk ibn Kafur courted the land speculators and made deals with them. . . . Kafur saw the houses going up on the ruins of his garden and he ground his teeth and hid his gold in secret places. He was already dreaming of Palestine instead of Greater Syria" (Heb. 26; Eng. 32–33).

This notion of natural differences, exploitable differences, among Arabs is illustrated more generally by a notorious popular conviction, intensified in this case by homophobia, that has prevailed since the early years of the Jewish colonial community in Palestine and later among Jews in Israel, that Turkish (and Arab) men have homosexual proclivities. "Franz could see the Turkish officers in their filthy underpants going in and out of their rooms in the huge corridor as he was captivated by the beauty of the place." Yosef associates his own predicament with the homosexuality implicit in the relationship between Franz and Azouri. When Yosef speaks of them, he tells us that

> their love was bodiless; they missed the opportunity for what might have been a simple but different story. They waited for Kathe [Yosef's grandmother] to arrive. Thus, I missed the chance to be the first boy to be born to a twenty-two-year-old man [his grandfather] and a thirteen-year-old lad [his father]. (Heb. 32; Eng. 40)[23]

This extension of difference clarifies the meaning of the garden scene in which "adorned ladies were sitting at a short distance smelling of perfume and drinking blood from tall goblets." These ladies "looked at [Franz] through the dusky dimness and afterwards they laid romantic traps for him from which he was forever escaping" (Heb. 31; Eng. 38). Yet, when Azouri and Franz returned to the house for dinner, "the women were already giving Franz looks of loathing and contempt." There wasn't a woman there who "didn't lust after the boy" [Azouri], "and Kafur would laugh in his chair and say, he is mine, not yours; he belongs to . . . royalty, not to women. They swallowed the insults in silence" (Heb. 29; Eng. 36).

Childhood Memories and World Politics

This Satyricon-like atmosphere was suffused with sensuality and indulgence: "horses came galloping by, and Franz drank cold grapefruit juice and ate roast chicken served by a giant Sudanese eunuch wearing a white kaftan, who looked like an extra in a German opera." In the meantime, Kafur, who "never got up from his chair," was "the fattest man [Franz] had ever seen in his life" (Heb. 26; Eng. 33).

This decadence predicates a fear in which the the racial is conjoined with the erotic. In this light, the "good" Arab, Arab goodness, is represented by a lack of potency underlying a pretense of it. This false, self-indulgent sensuality, which promises what cannot be delivered, is part of the more general denial of power that allows Arab goodness to be recognized with impunity. Laughter is an essential ingredient of this recognition, part of the denial of mutuality in it. For this, Kaniuk introduces us to the "historical" background of the ludicrous figure represented by Kafur, the historical shadow that gives Kafur his ideological and cultural significance in the novel.

> Kafur was named after a tenth-century Ethiopian, a diseased slave, who was the country's ruler. He lived in Acre, and searched for the caliphs of Abbas and Ummaya among the rocks of a countryside that was then less desolate. He made the earth quake for six months intermittently in order to terrorize his comrades;[24] and to punish the rebellious Egyptians, he stopped the waters of the Nile, refusing to let them overflow their banks for a whole year, bringing famine to the land of the Nile. (Heb. 27; Eng. 33–34)

Out of thirteen hundred years of Islamic history, Kaniuk conjures up a figure whose greatest achievement must be ignored, namely, that he was the first black slave to rise from oppression to wield absolute power. For Kaniuk, what gives the ancient Kafur his connection to the novel's Kafur is power, the one real and the other false. Yet this shadow of the latter Kafur's decadence and unreliability shares with him a certain quality—not of struggle but the manifestation of result, not conditions of possibility but indifference and ruthlessness. To see how this works in A Good Arab, it is necessary to recover the history hidden beneath the appearance invoked by Kaniuk's conceptualization of the old Kafur.[25]

Thus, Azouri says that "Uncle Kafur was a miserable dreamer who lost everything because no dream can ever bring about a reality which will equal it" (Heb. 27–28; Eng. 34). The lesson, that one must not act on desire, that activity must be free of desire, is all the Arab can teach about goodness. Uncle Kafur is a caricature embodying the most prejudicial features of what "is," for Zionist thought, a Palestinian effendi,[26] a nationalist, and most important of all, a national leader. He acts on his dreams, and, although he is doomed to fail, he is nevertheless dangerous. Yosef records Azouri's description in the following passage, as if it is in Azouri's own words:

> Kafur fed people because he wanted to see them fawn. He liked giving so that he could see the shame of a nursed desire played out in front of him. He was shrewd and intelligent and trusted no one. He was so sly and suspicious that he didn't even trust himself. (Heb. 29; Eng. 36–37)

The next occasion on which we encounter Kafur occurs some twenty years later, and it serves a rather different narrative purpose, that of installing hope in the expedient Arab character. Thanks to Azouri's urging, Yosef's forebears, Franz, Kathe, and Hava, have "made Aliyah" (immigrated to Palestine). The year is 1936. They have just settled in Tel Aviv, "the first all Jewish city."[27] Franz travels to Acre in his search for Azouri, despite the ongoing Palestinian armed rebellion against the British. He fails to find him, but

> the sight he saw was perhaps the biggest surprise in a lifetime of surprises. In a somewhat dim alley, in the sunlight that penetrated long eyelets made by the roofs, which looked like the crenellations of an ancient castle, stood a group of little boys in brown uniforms with a man wearing a brown suit and black boots, a swastika on his armband, putting them through military drilling exercises. They held sticks instead of guns. The strange man was Abu Misk Kafur. Franz recognized him from a distance. (Heb. 51; Eng. 69)

When I read this passage, I could not avoid my own memory of a dramatic childhood experience. I was about twelve years old when, with some elementary schoolmates, I joined Betar (the name drawn from the Hebrew acronym for the Revisionist Youth Movement, or, in Hebrew, Brit Trumpeldor). The year must have been 1943. All I remember of our group meetings are the military drills. We were children from poor homes. Our clothing was simple, and some of us did not wear shoes. It may have been summer. We could not afford uniforms, but our "commander," Yehuda Weis, had one. Yehuda was a tall, handsome young man, with gray eyes and blond hair. His family had come from Germany, probably the same year as the Rosenzweigs of Kaniuk's narrative. He wore a brown suit, a black tie, a black service cap, black boots, and a black armband, and we held sticks instead of guns. The room we used was locked and dark. It was the "underground," empty but for the leader's portrait hanging low on the wall, at about eye level. Our most frequent routine involved the commander raising his hand in salute, and in his funny German accent, shouting, "Tel Hai," and we, some twenty children, shouting back, "Tel Hai, Tel Hai, Tel Hai!"[28]

Yosef further narrates his father's memory of that "military" experience:

[Kafur's] enormous stomach had no chair to support it now. There was no Sudanese hovering around serving him cold drinks. There was no cross adorning his halation.[29] He raised his arm in a salute and twenty barefoot children shouted "Heil Hitler!" in a funny accent. Franz stood mesmerized, deliriously looking as if he were watching an utterly ludicrous silent movie. He didn't want Abu Misk to see him. The children shouted "Heil," "Heil." Azouri was nowhere to be seen. The alley thundered with their shouts. Abu Misk looked at the children despairingly. They were his last army, his last hope for reviving the Caliphate Kingdom. The swastika was hand painted, not at all precise, not properly sewn on; the uniform was a cheap imitation; the boots were torn. He felt sorry for the little Fuehrer; then he slipped into a side alley. (Heb. 51; Eng. 66–70)

I remember when, later in the summer, my friends persuaded me to join them in a memorial ceremony for the leader, Zeev Zabotinsky. The memorial was to take place in Metsudat Zeev, in Tel Aviv (the Zeev Fortress, which was and still is to this day the name of the Betar, now Likud, party headquarters). My parents did not know that I had joined Betar, and of course I did not dare to tell them of my plans for that night. I had to snatch a few coins from my mother's purse and sneak out unnoticed. This was for me a very long and dreary night. We stood in a walled courtyard, in formation, for hours. There were speeches in lowered voices, and hushed singing. Aside from a few small kerosene lamps, there was no light. As the hours went by, my panic grew worse and worse. I knew that at the end of this night I would meet my judge.

As I carefully opened the door to our house an hour or so after midnight, my father and mother were sitting there, waiting for me. My father said, "Where have you been?" I said, "At Bracha Gelis's, doing homework." This was a poor lie. My father then went to see the Gelises, who lived just across the street from us. Within three minutes he returned, looking as if he was about to burst like a volcano. He said, "Mr. Gelis told me you were with Bracha at the Zabotinsky memorial in Tel Aviv." I will not speak of the verdict and punishment that followed, except to say that that night was not my only childhood experience with the Zionist Brown Shirts.

The anecdote speaks, beyond its personal significance, to the paradox in Israeli Jewish life discussed earlier: the internalization of one's enemy as an assertion of identity. Yosef was, in the above passages, merely a witness, the voice of another's memory. No such distinction is possible for me.

Depicting Kafur as a "little Fuehrer" in a fascist uniform suggests that this tie of hope to fascism was the most significant feature of the "1936 events . . . [which] the Arabs call the 'Great Revolt' " (Heb. 51; Eng. 69–70). It symbolically links the Palestinian national movement to Nazism and the

Holocaust, thereby reaffirming the boundary between the good Arab individual and the real Arab people. The resemblance to my own Jewish experience
is lost in this identification. All hopes are equal, but some are more equal than
others. The Nazi must remain exterior to the Jew, beyond Jewish potential,
there always to be judged by one who can never legitimately be judged.

Kaniuk explicates the image further in his delineation of the personality
and invocation of the political experience of al-Hajj Muhammad Amin al-
Husayni, who had played a central role in the political contest for control over
Palestine. Al-Husayni was appointed by the British in 1921 as mufti of
Jerusalem. He served in that position until 1937. As the leader of the Muslim
community, not only as mufti of its premier city but also as president of the
Supreme Muslim Council, Husayni was spokesman for the Palestinians to
their British rulers. In this capacity, he was able to articulate Arab grievances
against the Zionist movement and to galvanize support in the Muslim world
for the Palestinian cause.

> From his appointment by the British . . . until 1936, he had pursued a dual poli-
> cy of cooperating with the British while uniting the Palestinians against Zion-
> ism. To his mind, it was the Zionists who were the real threat to Palestinian
> national goals. The British were too strong to evict, but could perhaps be
> induced . . . to alter their pro-Zionist policy.[30]

Charles D. Smith writes about the context of al-Husayni's activity:

> Aware of Zionist tactics and totally opposed to the initial [Peel Commission
> 1937] partition plan, Arab leaders despaired of retaining control of Palestine.
> The ensuing tension led to the second and much more violent stage of the
> Arab Revolt, from September 1937 to January 1939.

For the first time, Smith says,

> British officials became targets, and the acting district commissioner for Galilee
> was murdered. . . . The violence continued, even though the Higher Arab
> Committee had disbanded after al-Hajj Amin al-Husayni's flight to Lebanon
> and then to Iraq, barely escaping British efforts to capture him because he
> opposed partition."[31]

What interests Kaniuk, and every other Zionist, most is Husayni's political
activity in exile, especially his maneuvering in Iraq during the pro-German
coup attempt of 1940–41, his residence in Germany from 1941 to 1945, his
propagandizing on behalf of the Axis, his attempts to organize Arab and
Muslim forces against the British, and his efforts to stop Germany from deport-
ing Jews to Palestine.

Mattar notes that the Allies did not find enough evidence to warrant trying the mufti as a war criminal. In any case, he concludes, the personality of one leader, no matter how prominent, could not have been decisive to the outcome of the Palestinian struggle: "The overriding factors that frustrated Palestinian nationalism have less to do with the policies and actions of a single leader than with the balance of forces. . . . The Palestinians were . . . never a match for the British army, nor, after 1939, for the Zionist forces."[32]

The significance of this history relates directly to the way "Arabs" are represented in Kaniuk's novel, in particular in regard to contacts with the German National Socialist government. There were, of course, similar contacts with Nazis by the leadership of the World Zionist Organization, the leadership of the Zionist Organization in Germany, and the Jewish Agency of the World Zionist Organization in Palestine. The World Zionist Organization, through these affiliates, held negotiations with the German government intermittently between 1933 and 1941, and again in Hungary, in 1944. From the Zionist point of view, these negotiations provided hope under circumstances that seemed to require even the most desperate of strategies. No such indulgence is permitted the Arabs.

But there is also a more invidious interpretation—that those contacts, between Jews and Nazis, looked beyond the immediate urgency of the Jewish people to a different and more protracted conflict with a different enemy. Whatever the truth and whatever critics of Zionism think of those negotiations, and the process of immigrant selection they were intended to secure, the politics of Holocaust is not here at issue. What is significant is the role that the negotiations played in Yosef's autobiography.

Azouri, a Palestinian liberal nationalist, was responsible for Kathe's and Franz's conversion to Zionism. In 1936, he urged them to leave Germany and go to Palestine, because "you are Jews and your life here is coming to an end" (Heb. 42; Eng. 56). The narrative, however, does not allude to the internal politics of Zionism that made such an option possible for them and not possible for others. The negotiations between the Zionist Organization and the German government allowed for individual Jews and families—such as Franz Rosenzweig (in the novel) and the Weis family (of my own trainer in the Betar youth movement)—to migrate to Palestine, given the availability in Palestine of means of support (as stipulated in the "transfer agreements"). The fundamental principle of these negotiations was, for the Zionists, to secure the selection of "suitable" candidates for transfer."[33] This provides some of the background against which Kaniuk paints his skewed portrait of extremism, distinguishing between the momentariness of Jewish extremism and the symptomatic extremism of the Arab.

In January 1941, the LEHI (Freedom Fighters for Israel [Stern group]) Zionist underground organization sent Naphtali Lubinczic to Vichy-controlled Beirut to meet two representatives of the German government. One was from Military Intelligence, the other from the Foreign Office. He handed them a memorandum proposing collaboration. They sent the memorandum to the German embassy in Ankara, where it was found after the war. The document was titled "Fundamental Features of the Proposal of the National Military Organization in Palestine (Irgun Zvai Leumi) Concerning the Solution of the Jewish Question in Europe and the Participation of the NMO in the War on the Side of Germany." Lubinczic told the Nazis that "if the Germans thought a Zionist state would be politically inexpedient, the LEHI would agree to the 'Madagascar plan', i.e. the deportation of European Jewry to the island of Madagascar, under German domination."[34] The German government showed no further interest in this proposal. Nevertheless, in July 1941, Nathan Yellin-Mor, second in command of the LEHI organization, sought to reach the Nazis again in neutral Turkey. He was arrested en route, in Syria, by the British in December of the same year.[35]

This provides a perspective on Kaniuk's depiction of a German Jew encountering Kafur, a Palestinian Arab nationalist, as a degenerate in 1917, and, in 1936, as a "little Fuehrer." From this point of view, his lighthearted ironies about Zionist political cynicism can be taken to represent what is possible by way of criticism and what is necessary by way of the balance required of criticism in the literature of liberal Zionism. They indicate at least the limits within which Kaniuk hopes to shift the sentiments of his readers toward a more liberal position toward the Arab. But they rely, within those limits, on the difference between a figure of unqualified and symptomatic extremism and an extremism implicit in certain situations as, at most, a behavioral problem, not one of character.

The last time we hear of Kafur, he is not even mentioned by name, though the attentive reader will recognize him by association. The time is spring 1948, the "event" the next major Zionist-Palestinian military confrontation. We are told that "only [Azouri's] dying uncle, lost in the remnants of his last hope, set forth at the age of sixty-seven to do battle on Mishmar-haEmek, and came back broken and died of a broken heart" (Heb. 62; Eng. 87).

In one sense, the novel is the story of "Uncle Kafur." It is also a history of the Palestinian national movement prior to the calamity of the 1948–49 war, told as a parable based on Yosef's dual identity and organized as a genealogy of

Arabness. The history of Azouri's family, as well as the others from whose fate Yosef seems so terribly detached, shows the decisive role of genealogy in Kaniuk's designation of the limits of Arab goodness. What we now know is that these limits refer us to several increasingly inflexible traits: unreasonableness, obsessiveness, extremism, self-indulgence, unfettered sensuality, and politics.

5

The 1948 War:
Irony and Self-Righteousness

A History Constructed

"After all," says Yosef, "Azouri was born into a history that saw the 1948 war as a British-Jewish bloodbath; while my mother Hava was wounded in a wearying attempt to save Jerusalem from the Arab Legion,[1] Azouri's brothers were talking about the theft of the land from its owners" (Heb. 45; Eng. 61).

In these few lines a whole history is constructed yet there are two questions that remain: (1) What is the referent, in the context of the narrative, of the phrase "British-Jewish bloodbath"? (2) What is intended by the juxtaposition of Yosef's Jewish mother risking her life "to save Jerusalem" and his Arab uncles "talking about the theft of the land from its owners"?

The debate about the fairness with which the British authorities governed Palestine between December 1947 and 15 May 1948 is by now beyond resolution. Some Zionist historians argue that the British favored the Arabs. Other historians argue that they favored the Jews. For Yosef, the debate is beside the point because, for him, the Palestinians are simply "not there."

Regardless of their position on this question, most historians, both Jews and Arabs, agree that the British government kept its political commitment in general to the Zionist colonizing enterprise in Palestine. On the other hand, though its military command at all levels never diverged from any of the principal directives set by the government, the British army was less sympathetic to the Zionists. The limited armed conflict between the British forces and what were then called the "dissident organizations" (the "right-wing" IZL and LEHI), or the Hagana during the years 1945–47, ended after the U.N. resolution of 29 November 1947 partitioning Palestine, when the British government announced its resolve to withdraw by no later than 14 May 1948.

Thus, Yosef's reference to a "British-Jewish bloodbath," revises the history of the war. Instead of one primarily between and affecting Arabs and Jews, it is characterized as a crisis jointly faced by the Jews and the British. Thus, an ambiguous mix of Arab and Jew, Yosef, defines Arab history without any implication of Arab experience. It is as if Yosef sees history itself as the mirror image of his own contradictory identity. In both the history and the identity, the Arab is inessential, provides no perspective, is there only to witness others less ambiguous than himself. The revision also mirrors the militarized relations of Arab and Jew that now define and constrict so much of Israeli society. The war was "a British-Jewish bloodbath" because the Arabs constituted a mere condition of rather than were parties to the only relation for which dialogue and negotiation were conceivable.

The second question is more complex. Hava was wounded while driving in an armed convoy in, as Yosef put it, a "wearying attempt" to break through a blockade of the main road to Jerusalem by Palestinian-Arab militia (Heb. 59–60; Eng. 82–84). These militia were headed by Abd al-Qadir Husayni, who had been appointed by his uncle, Hajj Amin al-Husayni, mufti of Jerusalem, to command the Arab military forces in Palestine.[2] The mufti was the Palestinians' greatest adversary against Abdullah, then King of Transjordan, who had rejected the establishment of an independent Palestinian state. Abdullah had coveted Palestine and had hoped to annex it, or at least those parts of it left after the establishment of the Jewish state.[3]

On the whole, the Zionist military strategy was offensive. It was designed to secure the establishment of the Jewish state in Palestine. This included controlling the main road to Jerusalem, the city itself, and its vicinity. Its purpose was, as far as possible, to gain a larger territory than that allotted to the Jewish state by the United Nations. Thus, "saving" Jerusalem meant taking it.[4]

Hava's "wearying attempt" contrasts with Yosef's uncles' complaint about the theft of the land from its owners. The first, the labor of saving, evokes the idea of a right to what one has earned. The second refers only to the violation of a juridical right over property, earned or not. The opposition of perspectives in Yosef's recollection, thirty-five years after the event, is, again, unequal. Hava's right is predicated on her suffering as a subject, therefore it is a right predicated on an expenditure. The Arabs' right is merely one in law, and therefore merely conventional. In this juxtaposition, only the Jew can be truly deserving. Because of the higher nature of Hava's claim, every Jew is represented by her labor. By contrast, a juridical claim identifies only a category of persons and subjects others to the limitations of the right that inheres in the category. A category is not a group, nor does it designate a subjectivity and therefore an enduring sense of right. Therefore, in this logical exhaustion of possible rights, there can be none left for the Palestinians but what they share abstractly, categorically, with all Arabs; and any instance of ownership will do, without regard to whatever relationship might have established it. Thus, no suffering or labor is necessarily associated with such a claim—only, if at all, accidentally. Therefore, the claim is amorally juridical. It induces no obligation of society as such, no sense of expenditure and depletion, no reference to what is deserved beyond what is merely granted. Therefore, it can in no sense be part of a legitimate politics, that is, one recognizably founded in righteousness.

This distinction between higher rights and conventional rights completes a circle that begins and ends with the inconceivability of a Palestinian experience equivalent to that of a Jew. What is erased in this remarkable passage, in which the labor of conquest takes priority over the property of victims, is not Palestinians, but the possibility of Palestinian subjectivity. Nor is the erasure political in the sense of a withdrawal, removal, or a taking away; it is rather an affirmation of Jewish subjectivity, because the latter now appears as purely positive, not oriented against an other, but oriented to and for a universalistic historical project, the salvation of a Jerusalem that stands for a *people*, rather than concerned merely with land, which is an object, there for anyone. By referring to Hava's "wearying attempt," Yosef fills the Jew with rights and history beyond temporal law, rights that can be opposed only by those who oppose humanity itself, in this case the Arab Legion and the Palestinian militia, which in the Zionist Hebrew vernacular are called *knufiot poriim* (bandit gangs).

On the other hand, the moral inferiority of property rights does not discredit Yosef's uncles. It merely leaves them with a calculable loss. In this way, the sense of a legitimate antagonism is sustained, but the legitimate direction of its moral resolution is implicit in how it is depicted at the outset. The uncles only meditate on specific rights derived from a specific state. Hava suffers for the sake of a people, and for a history the moral dimension of which is visible only through that people's experience. This is given added rhetorical force in Yosef's dramatic reference to 1948.

Yosef opens this part of his confession with the following:

In Acre where my mother and father were later to meet, a great kingdom once came to an end with a magnificent flourish. In 1948 a few Jewish shells put an end to the Turkish reign of hundreds of years, when the Israel Defense Forces conquered with a single three-inch mortar what Napoleon had failed to conquer. (Heb. 46; Eng. 61)[5]

It is significant that the English translation of this passage changes key expressions, possibly to aid the English reader in negotiating the complexities of the Palestinian-Israeli history. On the other hand, it alters the tone of the novel, diminishing the sense of irony present in the original: "In Acre where my mother and father were later to meet, a great kingdom *once* came to an end with a magnificent flourish." The added word "once" moves the action to a distant and symbolic plain; and, in relation to the "once," "where my mother and father were later to meet" casts the battle itself as fantastic, and the meeting epic, heroic, anticipated. The Hebrew passage alludes more directly to the medieval Crusaders' Acre of the twelfth century, and operates satirically to convey a sense of the puncturing of pretense, the pretentiousness of celebrating Salah-al-Din's victory over a so-called great kingdom. This demeaning of Arab history, the gloating, is lost in the English translation.

This is confirmed by the next sentence of the English version: "*In 1948 a few Jewish shells put an end.*" There is still the sense of great accomplishment, but not that of puncturing pretense. The insertion of the words "in 1948" specifies a moment, as if the statement is intended to inform rather than to characterize. It renders the sentence innocent, without the cutting edge of the original and without what might appear to the English reader as untoward gloating. Finally, the translation omits the word "Arab," which appears in the Hebrew in the hyphenated expression "Arab-Turkish." The primary effect is to neutralize for the English reader the original reference to the Arab as an object of scorn. For the Hebrew reader, the "Arab-Turkish reign" was, like Napoleon's, pretentious rather than truly mighty.

The translation was doubtless intended to reduce the tone of racialism and arrogance that might have been somewhat offensive to English readers, especially in light of the facts. Indeed, Acre was not conquered by the Israeli army with only a few shells from a single three-inch mortar. In a book dedicated by the IDF to the Carmeli Brigade, the description of the battle takes eleven pages. According to the U.N. resolution partitioning Palestine, Acre was to become part of the Arab-Palestine state.

As there were no Jews living in Acre in 1948, its 15,000 Arab citizens felt secure, at least during the first months of the conflict. However, following the fall of Arab Tiberius, Arab Haifa, and other Arab towns in the Lower Galilee district of the country, a siege was gradually laid around Acre. A flood of refugees came into the city, in numbers estimated at 35,000.[6] The siege was completed by the destruction of bridges on the roads leading north to Syria and Lebanon. Only then did the shelling by three-inch and six-inch mortars commence, and it was systematic and devastating.[7] During the siege a typhus epidemic broke out. Intelligence sources reported that the situation was desperate and that Acre would not be able to defend itself against a Zionist attack. The operation order to the attacking forces said, among other things:

> The city of Acre is under siege for the fourth day. A reinforcement of fifty fighters arrived yesterday in Acre. According to earlier information they had 100 fighters of which some have already run away. Their fire power includes 2 heavy machine guns, 4–5 medium machine guns, and about 70 rifles. Our forces: 3 NCO (mechanized) companies . . . + 2 regular companies . . . + 1 supporting arms platoon. Mission: to attack the city with the intention of killing its men, setting property on fire, and bringing the city to surrender.[8]

The general attack lasted twenty-four hours, 16–17 May 1948. Had the story been told by its Arab residents, no doubt many Havas would have been mentioned for their exemplary heroism. Above all, it would have been impossible to ridicule the defense of Acre by identifying the defending forces with pretensions and characterizing the Zionist attack as a puncturing of it. Yosef's account gives voice to a certain exaltation, a reflection on an achievement of historical stature by a people who had been reviled by others as they now revile those they conquer. The sentiment is understandable, but then so would have been a similar sentiment on the part of the Palestinians if the situation were reversed. What is important is that Yosef speaks here for his Jewish against his Arab self, just as he spoke against his rejection by the Israeli military on the ground that he was, after all, a Jew and therefore should be permitted to be moral, to *choose* whether or not to do his duty.

The Transcendence of the Private and the Incidental

Kaniuk's novel transcends the private and the incidental in its special use of psychology, its reference to the historical dimension of politics, and its invocation of culture. Its ambition is to present a saga of two conflicting nationalities. But it constantly reiterates the ethnocentrism of its original assumptions and the dependence of those assumptions on conquest, dispossession, and contradictory identity. It protects the Zionist myth from any criticism of its underlying invidious distinction by a poetics of dispersion, of chaos, of essential righteousness, and of utopia. The myth appears everywhere, casting its sense of the heroic and the historic on one event after another, regardless of type, whether fact or fiction, whether great or otherwise insignificant.

This is particularly evident in the novel's references to what it admits as Arab politics. Because these references bear on Yosef's relationship with his father, and therefore with the Arab portion of his own identity, it requires some discussion. In this account, Yosef's sense of his father is intertwined with ambivalence toward the "Party" as emblematic of politics.

> Azouri did not fight and was busy with Party affairs. He spoke of Jewish Arab
> brotherhood, but believed in no more than what he saw with his own eyes.
> Young women from the Jewish sector mingled with those tough men who
> formed the nucleus of the Party. There were dreams and there were meetings,
> and when the 1948 war broke out and Azouri was in Acre. . . . (Heb. 62; Eng.
> 86–87)

Yosef never refers to the "Party" by name, yet, from the allusions he makes to it, one can safely assume that what he has in mind is the Palestinian Communist party which, together with Jewish Communists, eventually established the Israeli Communist party (MAKI). My discussion of the "Party" relies on this assumption.

Given the ideological context in which "communism" was then perceived, to write of "the Party" without naming it was to invest the referent with the quality of something sinister, monolithic, and secretive. It was to incorporate politics into a field of dark forces in which people "mingle" without any greater purpose than can be imagined from the ganglike conjoining of "young women" and "tough men."[9] The image is, to be sure, softened by the reference to "dreams and meetings," but we are left with an impression of "Party affairs" and "busy-ness" as a reflection of idealism without hope and therefore tinged with a danger reinforced by reference to a "nucleus" of "young women" and "tough men."

By definition, any internationalist party committed to a democratic, binational political solution in Palestine, and determined to include Palestinian Arabs as equal members in its ranks, is anathema for Zionism. Of all the organizations under the Zionist umbrella, the Hashomer Hatzair kibbutz movement took the position furthest to the left, both in its social program and on the issue of coexistence with the Palestinian people. But, while espousing "a binational society" in Palestine and equal political rights for Arabs, at the same time it defined itself as a Zionist organization and adhered to all Zionist ideals. Thus Hashomer Hatzair was confronted with a contradiction: on one hand, "territoriality," that is, political inclusion *in the party* of all ethnic and national "groups" existing in the "territory," and on the other, not to be excluded from the Zionist, exclusively Jewish, utopia. This contradiction was never resolved.[10]

The central principle of Zionism was the *exclusion* of Arabs from Israel (and even more generally, though in a different way, the exclusion of all non-Jews). Therefore, it is not surprising that many Zionist politicians, academicians, writers, and artists hold extremely hostile attitudes toward Jewish members of the Communist party, especially women (whether married or not). In this respect, the Zionist reflection on Jews sharing politics with Arabs is analogous to the Orthodox proscription against intermarriage.

For Palestinian Arab members of the Communist party, however, the situation was and remains somewhat different. Although hated by the landed aristocracy and other bourgeois, religious-orthodox, and right-wing nationalist groups, the party played a significant political and cultural role for working people, including the peasants. Throughout most of the British rule in Palestine, the party was not allowed to function legally and therefore was forced underground. Party members were brutally persecuted; its leaders and cadres were frequently held in prison for years or exiled from the country.[11] Of its Jewish members, thousands were sent back to their "countries of origin." The Palestinian-Arab branch of the greater Communist party had objected to the war of 1948.[12] It was the only Arab political force that survived the war, and was the first to reorganize itself afterward (within MAKI) in opposition to Israeli control and the military government by which that control was implemented.[13]

However, the subtext of Yosef's reference to the Party is not politics, but merely a presence within his discourse. The subtext has to do with the relationship between Azouri and Yosef's dual identity. There are key passages that bear on the relationships among paternity, identity, and ambiguous or otherwise uncertain classification.[14] As with every part of the narrative, Yosef's confessions pursue the Arab part of his identity in an effort to displace it as a cause of anything but the error others have made about him based on his duality. However, Azouri is both father and Arab.

Thus, his depiction and its role in Yosef's "confession" is complex. Part of this complexity lies in Yosef's sense of Azouri as never quite what he seems to be. Thus, Yosef says of Azouri that he "spoke of Jewish-Arab friendship but believed in no more than what he saw with his own eyes." In a related context, he remembers that Azouri "was active in the Party out of a need to belong, to harness himself to something bigger than he was; but I know that Azouri was as much a Marxist as I was a Turkish monarchist" (Heb. 61; Eng. 85).

There is some power in Azouri's cynicism, but it is too isolating to be felt as truly authoritative. Yosef feels that Azouri lacks the political perspective he claims, and that he may lack political conviction as well. Although this confers on Azouri the minimal condition for being a good Arab—a lack of politics—it leaves him with less definition than he needs to be fully and unequivocally paternal. Yosef writes about Azouri's stay in France, where he taught at the Sorbonne for six months (1946): "They say he had a woman there who was married to another man. She used to come and see him. Did he love her? I never asked him and he never told me" (Heb. 61; Eng. 85).

This de facto inaccessibility is matched by Azouri's apparent indifference to those who may have loved him—especially women. "To the women he met in the Party he was hard and casual. They went in and out of his [bed]room[15] without complaints. Azouri was the blue-eyed boy of the town"; and, "A Jewish woman from Haifa who was in love with him used to come [to Acre] and stay with him but he did not go to bed with her. He told me that she had once been his brother's girlfriend" (Heb. 63; Eng. 88). Azouri had principles, but Yosef could find in him no definite center.

Politics: The Issue Is Paternity and Lineage

As for politics, Yosef writes of Azouri that "there were dreams and there were meetings." That paternity is the issue is clear in Yosef's account of the lineage of Azouri's questionable authenticity as a moral subject:

> His [Azouri's] father went to Kfar Yassif and joined the Qawuqji fighters for a while and he may have fired a few shots here and there, perhaps he took part in some battle, but for whatever reason this family was not eager to fight. Like many others they shouted, denounced the Jews, but they didn't shoot. (Heb. 62; Eng. 87)[16]

Azouri, despite his "dreams," did not even "curse; and he didn't join the the grumbling chorus. He refused to hold a gun in his hand" (Heb. 62; Eng. 87). Azouri's father's own refusal to fight may have been the result of a lack of enthusiasm, or it may have reflected some cowardice on his part. But Azouri's refusal is more complex, and Yosef cannot quite get the point of it:

At least his refusal seemed to be part of a constant and less expedient disposition than that Yosef attributes to his grandfather. Yosef knows this only through others, but through Azouri's reputation in general and not simply evaluations of his conduct by specific others: "Azouri's friends in town always looked at him with admiration; they saw him destined for greater things than war" (Heb. 62; Eng. 87).

We have already learned that very little is greater than war. Yet the reader expects to hear what it is about Azouri that motivates his friends' admiration of him. Azouri's status in the community as a man of forty-four years of age, an intellectual with five doctorates, a historian of the Zionist-Palestinian conflict, and a leader of "the Party" complicates Yosef's understanding of his refusal to fight. Together, Azour's reputation and inaccessibility create for Yosef a mysterious figure who inspires in him even more than respect. In the midst of war, "Azouri sat at home; told his father, when the war is over let me know who won. He wasn't even interested in the radio his father had bought" (Heb. 62; Eng. 87). Here, perhaps, is the special authority of one who can afford to be indifferent and to be so for reasons impossible for a son to understand.

What we are left with is a distinction between Azouri the father and Azouri the Arab. This is a duality that Yosef finds in his father analogous to the one he cannot avoid in himself. Yosef sees the positive aspect, the father, surface over and even against the negative aspect, the Arab, just as the community saw Azouri as more than Arab. This "positive" aspect constitutes an estrangement. Yosef recognizes the special power of his father, but only in order to forget it:

> A man who stood on the Acre beach for two nights and two days and never fired a shot, and Israeli soldiers pushed him into the water, and made him stand at the water's line, and wanted him to go back to some Arab past in the sea; he'll never forget it, he said, but he added, "You know what? I've already forgotten. What I have not forgotten is my mother. In 1948 she was fifty years old. A beautiful woman, but old." (Heb. 66; Eng. 99)

Yosef forgets what his father will "never forget," and remembers what his father's indifference to women otherwise makes forgettable. Yosef's dual identity requires two pasts—one that refers to the father who subsumes him, the other that recollects the mother who could have given him meaning and conviction. Paternity completes itself for Yosef as the mystery of the father's desire and the emergence of the son's.

On the other hand, Kaniuk adds an unexpected confusion, thereby reinstating doubt and ambivalence in Yosef's attempt to reconstitute a useful genealogy of his identity: Azouri's mother cannot have been fifty in 1948, because she would then have been only six years older than her son (see Heb. 28, 32, 39).

In 1948, Azouri was forty-four years old. His brother was four years older than he. How can their mother have been fifty years old? What is at issue in the narrative is not her age, but the resemblance this comparison of age difference creates with her son. What is important, then, is what Azouri makes of her, and what Yosef is then able to infer about Azouri in relation to himself. Azouri remembers his own mother's abandonment of his father. The purpose of this memory is to duplicate throughout Yosef's lineage the abandonment and the characteristic of forbearance. It is through the mystery of what lies behind forbearance that Yosef discovers the power that his father, any father, can have over his son. Azouri speaks through Yosef, the son authorizing the voice of the father and through that authorizing the father's own account of the forbearance of his father before him.

> My father went to Kfar Yassif. . . . His wife sat at home: a traditional Arab home, said Azouri. I was sort of an inexplicable clown. What was my father? He studied once in some school, a minor clerk in the British mandate. My mother was beautiful and she burned with hatred. . . . I went to Haifa. . . . When I returned, my mother was no longer there. Do you understand how a son feels? And I'm an Arab, Yosef, an Arab son of an Arab, who hears that his mother ran off to Tunisia with an officer from the Qawuqji army. . . . Pleasure came my mother's way again, from one who came from Iraq. I'm not sure where he came from, but I found an empty house. My mother didn't know how to write. My father came back and found that his wife had become a refugee in Tunisia, gone off with a mustachioed officer. . . . I cried for him, but he didn't cry. He was a strong man unlike his brother, Kafur, a realistic man, close to the land, not a big talker. He sat quietly. His pride was hurt and he didn't say a word. (Heb. 66; Eng. 93)

Azouri, who usually forbears, weeps for his father, perceiving strength rather than indifference in his refusal to speak. In this, he shows himself to be moved by his father as Yosef is by him.

Beauty and passion, a gendered Arab reality, the feelings of Arab sons, betrayal and pleasure, mystery and intimation, pain and forbearance—these are some antinomies in the genesis of Yosef's duality. But at the end, in the juxtaposition of passion and forbearance, Azouri's memory reconstitutes the priority of one identity—that of the father—over the other—that of the Arab. The juxtaposition reveals, Yosef says, "strength." Kaniuk needs to qualify that strength, because it is still the strength of an Arab. He needs to do this so that Yosef's reflection on the relationship between identity and lineage will remain consistent. But it must also, for the sake of Kaniuk's project, reinvest Arabness in the strong father:

Later he remarried. He brought his wife from one of the villages. [At that time he was working as an interpreter in the military government. In the meantime my brothers had scattered, the house was almost empty. I had apartments in Acre and in Haifa and I had to stand in a queue . . . to get a travel permit. My father was in charge. Sometimes he was ashamed to look me in the eyes.] I wasn't angry with him, his wife was nagging him, she began to despise him. (Heb. 66–67; Eng. 93–84) (brackets added)

The material in brackets in the above quote is illustrative of a type of disruption Kaniuk typically inserts in the text. It suspends momentum and pluralizes the narrative at key points. In this case, the device reconstitutes Azouri's father's Arab pride and shame, and gives Azouri the chance to forbear: "I wasn't angry with him." With pride and shame comes yet a new arabesque, the Arab woman who now stands for the Arab traits by which Arab paternity distinguishes itself as other than a manifestation of strength:

She wanted him to take a knife and go and avenge himself on the woman who had betrayed him. It maddened her that he wasn't angrier, that he didn't kill her or himself, that he helped me obtain travel permits. She became more and more trapped in the hatred boiling inside her. (Heb. 67; Eng. 94)

This passion, bordering on obsession and madness, is not just that of any woman, but of an Arab—indeed, arabesque—woman. "In bed she gave my father a cold body. She never smiled. She cooked and withdrew into herself. One day she killed herself in the room" (Heb. 67; Eng. 94).

Kathe and Hava had similar problems. They also could not relate sexually to their husbands. The only difference, we can assume, is that they did not "cook"; at least we are not told they did. They, like Azouri's father's second wife and Franz's sister, killed themselves, in each case but one out of frustration at having chosen the wrong man. Franz's sister committed suicide after Germany's defeat in WWI. Frustration based on strength belongs to men, and especially fathers. Anger based on weakness belongs to women, stereotypically Arab women. None of the men kills himself.

We were sitting in the kitchen. First she screamed, go and stick a knife. But my father never stuck knives in anyone, a wasted Arab, torn from what he had grown up on without arriving anywhere else. I too, Yosef. He and I, mutations from which you were saved. You inherited anger from my parents' parents: not from me, not from my father. (Heb. 67; Eng. 94)

Here, I think, the monologue takes a fateful turn. Azouri confesses to mutations from which a son must be saved. But these mutations are the results of betrayal by women. Nevertheless, the confessional tone contributes an element of "good faith" to the relationship between Azouri and Yosef. Azouri's father is "a wasted Arab," as Hamlet might be said to have been a wasted prince. This qualifies paternity in just the way Yosef needs, as confirming in his own authorial voice the obligation of Arabness to give way to the Jewish subjectivity on which any authority depends. Azouri too is a man who tried all his life to be his best and ended up vanquished. He says, "I too, Yosef," and he shows that waste is not necessary when he compares the suicide of his own father's second wife to that of Hava: "Like Hava, she was a brave fighter in a lost battle" (Heb. 67; Eng. 94). The losses of Arabs as well as Jews appear against the standard of Jewish heroism.

Yet, there remains a further ambiguity. Kaniuk's ironies always end with final authority vested in the Jewish conscience. But they leave that conscience at least somewhat uneasy: righteous, but uncomfortable with what the righteousness of such a self may do to others. Kaniuk's liberalism succeeds no more than any instance of Zionist liberalism; but Kaniuk at least makes room for an Arab reality, though it is one that requires forbearance, which is a strength the vitality of which lies in forgetfulness. Perhaps Kaniuk is saying that Zionism can thrive only at the expense of memory. If so, then the Zionist self, the sense of being an Israeli Jewish subject, can survive only on the ground of an invented past, a fantasy that disguises the Arab as dreams disguise unconscious guilt and fear. In this case, we are beginning to see Zionism as the resistance of a subjectivity to itself, a version of what Azouri refers to as "waste." This is clarified in Yosef's depictions of Arab resistance, especially by Palestinians.

6

"The Organizations"

Consolidating Zionist "Theory" of Arab Politics

The umbrella coalition of the Palestine Liberation Organization (PLO) represents a broad spectrum of cultural, civil, and military organizations, institutions, and political parties. In *A Good Arab*, as in public discourse generally, however, "the Organizations" operates as a figure of speech. For Yosef, it names and homogenizes the politics of Arab resistance, thereby reiterating and reinforcing an established "covering discourse" on all politics beyond the stipulated boundaries of Arab goodness. It constitutes an image of diffuseness and extremism, of dispositions beyond norms and negotiation, of terrorism. Its force lies in its always insinuating more than it says, qualifying any proposition of which it is part and invoking for the Hebrew reader a sense of urgency and efficacy beyond what the law provides. This term consolidates the Zionist "theory" of Arab politics, and provides *A Good Arab*, with a referent that marks the point at which Arab goodness is tempted to betray itself.

"The Organizations" are identical things, galvanized by irrepressibly uncivil dispositions, and arranged like guerrilla bands rather than a polity or a disciplined military force. Even so pronounced a moderateness as Azouri seems to display fails to allay Yosef's suspicions that he is not really so. On the other hand, "the Organizations" share those Arab traits that make all intentionally political Arabs somewhat ludicrous to the Zionist consciousness: Arab politics is dangerous, to be sure, but, like the old empire, there is more posture than substance.

Yosef's image of "the Organizations" is articulated in two ways that, at certain points, converge. In the first, "the Organizations" are described behavioristically, by lists of activities. Description is simple, direct, and laconic. Palestinians, the subjects of these activities, and operations, are on the order of functionaries. For them, identity is totally realized in behavior and, as such, must never be seen as manifesting conviction, because any indication of conviction would imply choice, therefore reason. But when "the Organizations" are represented by Yosef historically, identity is no longer set by activity but symbolically within an allegory. In that case, Yosef's narrative becomes intricate, ambiguous, filled with pathos; and therefore it partakes of the greater narrative of his "confessions."

> They killed children on a kibbutz. . . . Sometimes when I look deep into my own heart, trying to imagine this tragic conflict . . . , an unbridgeable gap. Thus the ground was left for the extremists and for a war . . . which will last very long, for generations. It does not lend itself to an interim solution; in this game someone has to win. But the victory is also a sign of defeat, for the victor will bear all the scars and he won't have peace, neither he nor his enemies. (Heb. 102; Eng. 145–46)

The upshot of this is that readers are brought without warning, and as a matter of insinuation, into the Zionist problematic.

These two articulations yield a sense of Arab politics as the *appearance* of Arab interest and the *reality* of Jewish entitlement. There are acts and there are deeds, rituals and purposes. For Yosef, Arab acts and Arab purposes have no necessary connection. Therefore, for the Jew, the acts, lacking all reference but themselves, require a reaction appropriate to the danger of extremism. For the Arab, posited by the Jew, the mere fact that he or she acts is comic, because without the immanence of purpose an act can have only accidental connection to the actor, hence the essential ludicrousness of any Arab conduct that is not merely "good."

Yosef frequently compares "the Organizations" with Jewish "extremists," but never with Jewish political parties and organizations, and only with individuals. These are usually presented unnamed or strictly in role, as, for example, Bunim, Yosef's supervisor in the Mossad.[1] Bunim has a habit of using biblical terms in his everyday speech. He is fond of poetry (Heb. 18; Eng. 20) and has something of a sense of humor (Heb. 58–59; Eng. 81). He was a Hagana naval captain in the Jewish underground refugee fleet en route from Europe to

Palestine, and was commander of the port of Haifa in 1936, when the Rosenzweig family arrived (Heb. 22; Eng. 26). As a captain, he served on the boat that brought Dina's (Yosef's lover) parents (Heb. 18; Eng. 20). Bunim has the almost mythical qualities of a Zionist hero. Against his reasoned "extremism," which is noble as well, the Palestinians are both monstrous and ridiculous: monstrous because of their indifference to humanity, exemplified by their opposition to Jewish hegemony, and ridiculous because of the pretentiousness of their every act, owing to its lack of purpose—purposefulness without purpose. The "ridiculous" in A Good Arab, is frequently evoked in ways that cast doubt on the legitimacy of ridiculing a particular individual.

But all politics has, for Kaniuk and Yosef, its own field of righteousness and doubt, focused by dreams and the past, and by a consuming goal that broaches neither exception nor compromise. This is especially true for "Arabs in general" and Jewish extremists.

> Azouri played it safe, but it seemed as if he was really free of his uncle's curse, the dream of the restoration of the Umayyads, overcoming the slanders of the past, even if he did have a somewhat romantic attitude toward the Organizations. They killed children on a kibbutz, but Azouri didn't sound too convincing when he condemned their actions. Perhaps in the depths of his heart he admired their single-mindedness, a single-mindedness which he lacked (Heb. 102; Eng. 145–46)

Azouri failed to condemn murder. Yosef can only speculate on this equivocality. But the reasons for his conclusion—that purposefulness may be enough and "single-mindedness" admirable—are intended to remind us of Azouri's goodness, the goodness of his conduct, and of his inability to be not good even though he might wish it. Yet Yosef sees strength in the possibility that Azouri admired the "extremists," which is to say that Yosef finds evidence of strength in what Azouri could not will himself to do. Thus, Yosef, too, is tempted, and his own goodness therefore lies in his weakness, like Azouri's. The good Arab wants to be his opposite, but cannot. In this way, Arab goodness contains what is bad in the Arab.

> Sometimes when I look deep into my own heart, trying to imagine this tragic conflict, which so many patriots on both sides had made their own and patented, I think that the gap between Arab moderates, and Azouri really is a moderate, and Jewish moderates is greater than that between extremists . . . and thus the ground was prepared for the extremists and for war. I know it in my guts; it will last very long, for generations. It does not lend itself to an interim solution; in this game someone has to win. But the victory is also a sign of defeat—for

the victor will bear scars and he will have no peace, neither he nor his enemies. (Heb. 102; Eng. 145–46)

After further meditations along these lines,[2] Yosef remembers that Bunim once told him:

> If I were an Arab, not an Arab like you but a proud Arab, I'd join the Fatah. I smiled my obsequious smile for him, my "Arab" smile, and went on describing what was happening in Arafat's camps, what I saw there, what was going to happen. And he was examining the papers in front of him in earnest and with scorn for me saying, there isn't an Arab you can't buy. Only name your price; and then he stared into space thinking, how many Jews can't you buy? Was uprightness ever a Jewish trait? And then he felt so very lonely in his desperate struggle to justify the injustices he was causing. But he is a whole person, though he had erased the humanity with which he was brought up in order to oppress Azouri, so that he would be sure that he was right even when he wasn't right, because on the other side he was facing those who were professionally righteous, each a kind of Bunim. The world is full of Bunims and I'm dying here, lonely, longing, thinking. (Heb. 103–4; Eng. 147–48)

Yosef sees Bunim as a Jew who can imagine being an Arab, who defines the Arab as an enemy who can be admired—in contrast with the stereotyped Arab that Yosef can produce at any given moment in his reflexively "obsequious smile." In this reflexivity Yosef enacts the role of abject other to the utter indifference of his interrogator in this pitiless version of master and slave. Bunim's indifference to and contempt for Yosef yields for the latter an appreciation of the former, and through that compassion on the part of Yosef for Bunim in a world of enemies. But the self Yosef discovers within himself, one who can think thoughts "of love and accusation against himself," is unhappy and inconsolable, a morally desirous self surrounded by the "professionally righteous" and unable to find its own center.

Here we see abjectness as a surface, a disguise for a more profound sense of absence or void. This relationship between disguise and the absence it conceals provides Bunim with the Arab he expects, preserves Yosef's sense of himself as not that expectable Arab, and completes for the reader the image of one who must conceal himself because of injustice, but who conceals only the inner void that lacks any capacity for politics. The Arab *subject* (who is also a Jew) will emerge, as he must if Kaniuk's project is to be even partially fulfilled. But it will still be the Arab who cannot turn the tables because he was never really seated in the first place. This is an Arab who finally must be grateful for all liberal attempts to recognize him and his kind, even Bunim's demeaning sentimental recognition of an idealized Arab nobility, even Kaniuk's self-protective recognition of Arabness in *A Good Arab*,.

"Minorities," Derogation, and Lack of Distinction

Much later, the novel returns to "the Organizations." The following passage identifies Yosef's objects, the "Organizations," the "minorities," with the object Yosef himself had been in Bunim's eyes.

> Today the whole thing seems to me like a joke. In panic I fled from the Organizations, but the chase through the streets of Copenhagen in a Volkswagen bus was indeed ludicrous. Two youngsters who the Voice of Israel would doubtless have described as "minorities" were hot on my tracks, but I slipped away. They didn't have a chance; they asked people the way. I was insulted by the ease with which I escaped. (Heb. 110; Eng. 157)[3]

Here is the appearance of incompetence, a subjectivity of form without content. No one is there to speak for a truth beyond this weak appearance. But Yosef speaks with an almost affectionate irony, absent in Bunim's characterization of him. It must be noted that *minorities* is a derogatory term used by Israeli authorities and the Israeli media to refer to Israeli Arab citizens, either as individuals or in groups. It elides the fact that the only non-Jewish minorities in Israel are Arabs, and equates them despite their differences (whether Muslim, Christian, or Druse). Normally the term is not used to refer to Palestinians living in the Occupied Territories or outside of Israel. Yosef uses it ironically to comment on the false objectivity of the Voice of Israel, and, in the context of "youngsters," to both humanize the category and, with "hot on my tracks," to reinforce a sense of ludicrousness, as if Arab terrorism is an obvious joke.

But for Kaniuk, who speaks behind Yosef's voice, as its limitation, "minorities" does additional work. It blurs the line between two categories, namely, Palestinians who are a minority in Israel and normally have nothing to do with "terrorists" and Palestinians who live in the Occupied Territories and are *the people* of their land, therefore "terrorists" by definition. It also implicates all that is, in Israel, associated with "the Organizations." As for the paragraph as a whole, it pairs "the Organizations" with youthful incompetence, depicting them as not much of a threat. Yosef's sense of insult completes the parody. But what game does Yosef think he is playing in this episode? We will see that it has something to do with danger.

Kaniuk distinguishes the truly dangerous from the apparently dangerous Arab, though, again, at the cost of a refusal to acknowledge the legitimacy of

Arab politics, of the possibility of self-initiated action. This is why it is necessary for Yosef to insinuate the analogy between "the Organizations" and the Nazis, as in the following otherwise essentially plot-driven passage:

> I arrived in Rome and from there flew to Zurich, where I met Nabil, who said to me, we heard of what you were doing. Come work for us. You could write something. I told him, I haven't done anything, and he said, look, you worked for the Mossad and it's an open secret. Now it's your turn to pay. . . . Nabil suggested that I go with him to Beirut and I agreed. . . . The *Luftwaffe plane* was already cruising over Cyprus when Nabil, who had had too much whiskey, told me a few things, from which I understood that Bunim had decided to keep me guessing to the end. (Heb. 138–39; Eng. 196–97) (emphasis added)[4]

Parenthetically, it is worth noting that this passage protects its narrator, Yosef, from being identified with terrorism and terrorists. The trip is part of his adventure, and the fact that it is his "turn to pay" introduces precisely the element of just exchange necessary to neutralize the possibility that Yosef is, after all, another Arab. The sense of just exchange is maintained in Yosef's way of discussing those Arabs left behind in Israel after his "escape." This is evident in the symmetry he finds in Arab-Jewish relations, as well as in the reasons he assigns for the acts of others such as the writer, Kassem:

> Kassem had a sense of drama which he knew how to exploit for all the wrong ends. His plays were Palestinian manifestos about miserable workers dominated by Zionist imperialism. The plays he wrote in his head were those of a wasted Arab Chekhov writing nonsense. The poems he used to publish in Hebrew translation were sad. They were woven with hypnotic lyrical strength but his plays were cheap entertainment for yawning commissars. (Heb. 138–39; ENg. 196–97)[5]

Who Can Produce Art?

Kassem's writing is wasted, expedient, sad, tiresome, anything but political. Kassem is redeemed by his "sense of drama" against the insignificance of his political art. He is thereby resituated in the regime of instrumentalism—writing for a goal. Thus, his work poses no danger except to himself. He only betrays himself as an artist; and "art" stands for a realism outside of history, therefore a realism in which the Arab can be *subjective*, but not a true *subject*.

Throughout the novel, Kaniuk's attempt to find the Arab worthy of compassion appears desperate. He must find ways of diminishing all instances of Arab agency but that which belongs to individuals alone, or, like art, is conventionally institutional. We see this in passages where the politics of Kassem and Darwish are described as symptomatic, and their symptoms are made to appear symmetrical with those of Jewish writers.

> The tragedy for Jews and Arabs in Palestine is that their sense of justice does not let them translate their nonideological screwing into real art, [Kassem] once said to me. All Arab and Jewish protest, all this literature and poetry and art, drop dead before entering their frames [of reference]. The wise Jews do not produce art in Israel. They're good for their Diaspora but not for here and now; and we learned from them! (Heb. 138–39)[6]

The discontinuity between politics and art and the invidious continuity of politics and "the Organizations" are visible in the text, as part of its discourse, as a basis for identifying that portion of Arab life that must be recognized democratically, as symmetrical with the Jewish experience. The question is, Who can produce art? Certainly not those who live the tragedy of being forced to be ideological. Kassem is both militantly Arab and Jew-like in his obsessive meditation on justice. But he favors politics over art. His character in the novel is saved from the consequence of politics for the Jew's sense of the Arab by his wry lament and his sense of art as both life and futile—"not for here and now."

The category of extremism serves as the negative against which the goodness of the Arab can have its proper range. But, as we have seen, even an extreme can be neutralized. It would have to be if the goodness of the Arab is to include the artist, and Kaniuk could hardly be expected to advocate compassion for the Arab if the Arab artist were excluded. Kaniuk's category of art is, then, broad enough to embrace Kassem *and* himself—both last authentic voices against a world of Arabs, Jews, and readers.

But this is still the Jewish artist determining the boundaries of compassion and granting exemptions from the invidious meaning of Arab politics in this Zionist economy of moral judgment. This is what allows us to follow Yosef, after he arrives in Beirut, in his otherwise oppressively moralizing discourse—for example, on the failure of heroes to live up to their promises, therefore on the irrelevance of politics especially for Arabs.

Yosef's Visit to Beirut

I arrived in Beirut exactly two years ago. Since then so many things have happened there. I went with Nabil to a small hotel that stank of whiskey and hashish. The rooms were full with women who served as mistresses of officers in the Organizations, who brought up the children who swarmed the corridors. These were the Organizations whose heroes Laila wants to believe are saints. . . . The

man who aimed his Kalachnikov at me shouted, What do you want here? I told
him to go to hell. Freedom fighters do not sit on top of perfume, dripping bas-
kets full of gold, buying concubines by weight. (Heb. 141; Eng. 201)[7]

Yosef's desire for heroism is sufficiently elevated to raise it beyond the
advocacy of "terrorism" or "extremism." What is left out is always the terrorism committed by the Israeli state. But this could be "terrorism" only if an
Arab point of view were to prevail. For compassion to be possible, and to be
predicated on recognition, none of the parties can be political, though all
might defend themselves as individuals. But surely only the Jews' defense is, as
we have seen, legitimate. The agency, the subjectivity, that remains after politics is nullified, and then made finally Jewish.

How does Yosef produce this result? Sufficient evidence is inserted into the
narrative to make possible a chronological reconstruction of the events such
that we can see just where Yosef draws the line. We may reliably assume that
the "time" of the statement quoted above is in 1982. Thus, when Yosef says
that "since then so many things have happened there," he is referring to Beirut
since 1980; 1982 is the year Israel invaded Lebanon. In his introduction, Yosef
says that he "had finished writing [this partially confessional autobiography] a
year ago" (Heb. 5)[8] and then had to rewrite the manuscript before he could
send it to the publisher. This would mean that the manuscript was complete
by 1983. If this were the case, Yosef would have had ample time to grasp the
devastating impact of Israel's invasion on the Palestinian community in Lebanon. Being an intelligent and informed person, and having worked for the
Mossad as an expert telepath (forecasting events), Yosef would have known
that Israel had invaded Lebanon once before, in 1978. He would have known
of Israel's political and military involvement in Lebanon for many years before
that, if not because of his profession, then by generally available information.
He would have known how vital the role of "the Organizations" was to the
life of the Palestinian community in Beirut, and for the Palestinian diaspora
all over the the Middle East—especially in 1980, when a protracted civil war
was ravaging the country. The absence of any commentary whatsoever on all
of this makes of Yosef's disavowal of politics, and his constant neutralization
of them as they crop up in his narrative, a trope that organizes the figurative
aspects of the text rather than the reflection of a position he could have
defended on rational grounds. From that point of view, his elision of that history operates to reinforce the possible goodness of the Arab, which constitutes
the inability of Zionist liberalism to tolerate any degree of Arab agency or

active subjectivity but that of a disguised absence, abjectness, and a self-effacing disattention.

Throughout A Good Arab, Palestinian brutality alternates with Arab culture and melancholy—structures of feeling that allow for the possibility of Arab virtue. Thus, Yosef tells of his visit with the family of his uncle (Azouri's older brother) in Beirut. His uncle, a Maronite Christian, "was waiting for the Israelis to come and rescue him" (Heb. 142; Eng. 201).[9] Both he and his wife were teaching at the American University. After dinner they took Yosef to their bedroom, ostensibly to see his cousin Annette. It is a shocking scene.

> The room was enormous. Above the bed there was a closed window and underneath the window a small crucifix. The other walls were bare but for a huge photograph hanging opposite the bed with its shiny yellow counterpane. My uncle switched on the neon light which almost blinded me, and I looked at the photograph. In five boxes which had been photographed next to each other, the dismembered parts of a young girl dressed in a fine khaki suit could clearly be seen. Her face was slashed, her eyes had been gouged out and lay in a separate box which held her face. My uncle said, meet your cousin, this is how we found her. They slaughtered her, tortured her before they killed her, but they gouged out her eyes after she was dead. My aunt said, I took these photographs. (Heb. 142; Eng. 202)

This is melancholy to be sure, but it exemplifies a calculation—"I took the photographs"—predicated on a rage permissible only if politics has been neutralized, as in "waiting for the Israelis," and only in the context of a cultured expression of melancholy and a denial of Arab identity. Then Yosef's aunt and uncle took him to another room and his other cousin played the Moonlight Sonata on the piano. Later, they had a midnight supper, during which Yosef's aunt said:

> We'll screw those Palestinians. We'll gouge their eyes out of each one of them individually. . . . I asked my uncle, and you? aren't you a Palestinian? He said, me? I left Acre forty years ago. I'm a Lebanese Christian. When I left there was no Palestine. The Jews, in their stupidity, created a people and a homeland for the Azouris. (Heb. 143; Eng. 203)

The Judaization of "Taking Shelter"

This representation of a just rage is reinforced against Yosef's depiction of Palestinian life in exile in the persons of two other Palestinians in Beirut, a doctor and a poet. There is nothing indicated of the vital Palestinian intellectual and cultural milieu that existed in Beirut. Instead, there are attitudes and airs, expressions of a pseudoculture of melancholy:

> Nabil came to the hotel and took me to headquarters. On the way we paid a visit to the Palestinian library. I met a physician from Acre with an aristocratic air who knew Azouri. We had coffee. He didn't say much, and he looked at me. His longings were weary and sad. He looked at me and tried to see the al-Jazzar mosque through me. He spoke melancholically about the bay and Haifa. (Heb. 144; Eng. 204)

The "Palestinian library," if it existed by that name, was probably part of the Institute for Palestine Studies in Beirut. The institute kept the Palestine Archives until it was plundered by the Israeli army when it captured Beirut in 1982. It had been a center of Palestinian learning and research. By 1980, it was part of an elaborate network of political, cultural, and social institutions, in fact, part of a national infrastructure the PLO had begun to establish for the Palestinian community in Lebanon and elsewhere after September 1970. Thus, meeting a physician in the "Palestinian library" who "knew Azouri" (Azouri must have been seventy-six years old in 1980), a physician who did not say much and looked at Yosef with weariness and sadness and "who spoke melancholically about the bay and Haifa," was for Yosef evidence of a general condition of passivity, depression, and torpor. This is reiterated in Yosef's brief but memorable encounter with the poet:

> I was taken to a poet whom we had all admired in Haifa. He sat sad and depressed, opposite me. At eleven o'clock in the morning he was already drinking straight from the whiskey bottle. . . . We spoke for hours. I had met him very briefly years ago in Haifa, when I was still in high school and attended, in the German colony, a meeting of Jewish and Arab writers at the Party club with Azouri. (Heb. 144; Eng. 204)

This sense of opposition between the admirable poet and the permanent exile, between a soul of profundity and its sad state of decline, speaks more for Yosef's own sense of isolation and division than about a general fact of Palestinian life. The poet "said nothing about his flight and about what had happened to him since he left" Palestine (Heb. 144; Eng. 204). Why is Yosef disappointed not to have the details of a "flight" that had taken place thirty-two years ago? Perhaps he had hoped that the poet's account of his own separation and isolation might have provided a kind of redemption for him as well. In the following passage, it is not clear that Yosef is able to distinguish himself from the poet, to distinguish his own internal self-loathing from that which he attributes to the other:

Perhaps he had compassion for me. Perhaps his hatred was too fierce for words. He was different from most people I met in Beirut. He knew I was an enemy, not because I had worked for the Mossad but because for him I was a Jew, and a Jew was a wound, was pain; and he perceived my own pain the way a person perceives his own shadow. Here though, he too was a Jew. Perhaps he was frightened by meeting me, which was kind of like looking in a mirror. (Heb. 144; Eng. 204)

What Yosef sees in this Palestinian Arab refugee is the Judaization of his own refugee condition, the Judaization of "taking shelter" (dons refugier). He finds this metaphor essential to resolve his own dilemma of self-division and antagonism. But this again serves the reader more than it could possibly serve the subjectivity of the Arab in Yosef. Through the Judaization of the concept of "refugee," that is, through the analogy of the image of the quintessentially Jewish refugee, it becomes possible for the liberal Israeli Jewish reader to have compassion for a Palestinian. But then, the Palestinian is only a surrogate, an accidental rather than an essential refugee, and such a compromised compassion can ultimately be no more than superficial, ultimately compassion only for oneself:[10] "A few minutes later we switched to Hebrew, as if the language had a reality beyond this room . . . which he knew how to hate in the words he was writing but for which he never ceased lusting" (Heb. 144; Eng. 204).

As for Kaniuk the universal refugee is the Jew, so for Zionism the universal language of the "refugee" experience is Hebrew, in which the Arab experience can be explicit only as a semblance of the experience of the Jew and as merely a referent in a speech that yields nothing whatsoever to that experience but what it has already chosen. Compassion is, then, for the Arab only if the Arab does not speak.[11] Parenthetically, the tendentiousness of this deviation of Hebrew to the status of universal language of the "refugee," preempting philosophy, is further indicated by the fact that the majority of Jews throughout the past two thousand years were neither refugees nor spoke Hebrew. The four main languages spoken by Jews during this long period were Aramaic, Arabic, Ladino, and Yiddish. The point of identifying Hebrew as the only language that speaks authentically of exile is not merely to provide a status (refugee) with a language capable of expressing its essence, it is to assert one voice in order to deny all others. "We exchanged enigmatic sentences," says Yosef. "Perhaps he was trying to warn me, if he could. He would disguise himself in my image and would pay the price once more, but he had burned more than one bridge and I understood his fear, his pain" (Heb. 144; Eng. 204). It is to recenter Israeli Jewish subjectivity according to the relation of Holocaust to

Diaspora, and to decenter radically any other subjectivity that might authorize a claim of moral right, a right to recognition.

Yosef and the poet share a Jewish aspect, but they cannot speak that aspect in any language but the one that condemns Yosef's other, Arab, aspect and denies the fact that the poet is only analogously a Jew. Indeed, even if the poet could have recounted the events of his "flight," it would not have been in the terms of migration enforced by the Israeli conquest. And Yosef's desire to hear those events recounted is a desire only for a ritual reiteration of what he must have known happened to the poet after his flight. These complexities, of language and voice, of biography and condition, of refugee and victim, of the Arab who is more than an Arab because a Jew in spirit, blur what would otherwise have to be recognized as a far more radical opposition than literary Hebrew can express.

Denial, Irony, and Memory without Context

For Kaniuk, compassion is possible only if opposition is neutralized, made separate from the incompatibility of its referents, because the possibility of Arab rights is the unyielding context of the novel's reception and the reason for its allegory of compassion. Yet, Kaniuk's writing against opposition leaves a certain surplus of feeling beyond meaning. The poet speaks of fighting "against those who took Haifa from his parents," but his enemies, "those," remain nameless. Thus, his momentary vocalization of his pain and anger points not at enemies, not at the fact of opposition, but at the loneliness and torment of a singular self. The poet remains a poet, and Yosef is left with a trace of nothing greater than an existential struggle that need not threaten anyone. This denial of voice, of the right to speak for others, provides one instance of Yosef's tendency to neutralize Arab politics in his references to "the Organizations." It is necessary for Kaniuk to establish this denial because "the Organizations" are otherwise what most threaten to reassert the voice of the Palestinians, blurring the line between the Arab and the good Arab, and thereby to negate the possibility of Jewish compassion for the Arab.

Yosef meets some of the heads of "the Organizations." One, a high-ranking commander, tries to milk him for information. Yosef finds the situation somewhat ridiculous. His interrogator is, compared with Bunim, "amateurish." Yosef reflects that Rammy could have made mincemeat of him "with one hand tied behind his back" (Heb. 145; Eng. 205). Yet Rammy and his friends were sophisticated enough to recognize "that they were playing parts in a cruel farce," something the commander could never understand. Rammy and his comrades would see, through an appreciation of Yosef's sense of them, an irony that the official Jew would likely miss. This ability to see irony shows that the Arab extremist is worthy of at least a modicum of compassion, even in the context of politics, for one can be compassionate to another if that other can laugh at him- or herself, especially if that other can also acknowledge his or her own capacity to reflect ironically, to laugh at him- or herself about what otherwise seems to be done with perfect seriousness. And what makes irony work is memory in the form of self-denial—the capacity to juxtapose things that are otherwise different so that each becomes ludicrous.

That night, Nabil took Yosef to a luxurious nightclub for a drink "where young concubines were doing the striptease, and the fighters rushed at them with desperate battle cries and bayonets on their guns." Nabil wanted Yosef to see, "probably," that "it was Azouri's dead uncle's[12] plot to bestow upon [Yosef] glorious abominations in their wild wretchedness" (Heb. 145; Eng. 205). Yosef does not immerse himself in the "abominations"; they are Nabil's contrivances, part of Yosef's "dead uncle's plot." But Yosef's innocence is not enough to redeem him as an Arab who is not an Arab. He has to experience the temptation of even greater license before his redemption can be complete.

In fact, nothing is or can be sufficient for his redemption. Yosef can only realize, over and over again, the experience of absence, of not being where he, one, is. Absence has its positive moments in Yosef's nostalgia, his fantasy of being *somewhere else*. This occurs even in the context of otherwise insignificant moments of intimate encounters. For example:

> Late at night I sat in a room that was rented for me. A woman that Nabil had sent to my room sat waiting in the armchair. She drank whiskey and for some reason decided to speak English with me. I didn't know who she was. She said, life sad here. My friend dead, was officer, dynamite finish. I belong Organizations, what you? . . . I was drunk and I lay next to her. She tried to undress me. Someone had paid her. I didn't want an actual woman. I wanted to hear the rattle in her throat, to smell the stink of an ideological whore. I didn't specifically want to penetrate her. This I saved for my fantasy. I told her to stop fumbling with me. I shut my eyes. I wanted to remember something that was hanging just at the edge of my memory. Suddenly it came to me, Dina. (Heb. 145; Eng. 204–6)

Yosef has already had his fuck. This virtually voiceless woman, paid for and drunk, is there only for Yosef to be somewhere else. If we could read the novel in its chronological order, we would remember that Yosef had conjured Dina up in his consciousness once before in a similarly charged situation, when Yosef and his friend Giora were fourteen years old. "They were dreaming

about girls. They looked at pictures of naked women." One day they went to a
party, with "boys and girls." One girl, Nina, was the kind he liked. "She had
big tits spilling out of her dress." She came to Yosef and asked if he wanted to
dance, and he said, "No, I want to fuck."

> Panting and heaving we struggled and then I entered her, and she let me go all
> the way in, and suddenly I realized that it wasn't going to work. But it was too
> late; I was already inside her. I shut my eyes. I put Dina in the pupils of my eyes,
> and she came and sat in them as if she had been there all the time without my
> knowing it. I thought that perhaps I was in love with Dina but I didn't want to
> think about her, and suddenly, when I was already in the seventh heaven of
> delight, I wanted to run away. She wasn't Dina. I convinced myself that she
> was Dina and I felt good. I whispered sweet words in her ear and all the time I
> directed my words to Dina. (Heb. 123–24; Eng. 176–78)

The difference is that Nina was not voiceless but powerful. She dreamed
with him, made demands on him, was the kind of girl he liked. Here Yosef
speaks to Dina through Nina. With the whore, he had only to think of Dina.
Perhaps his childhood innocence brought Nina and Dina together for a moment, and his adult encounter fulfills a separation of his authentic experience
with Dina from all other experiences of sex. If so, then this can be seen as a
development of his faculty of distantiation. It is as an adult that Yosef can
enjoy the pleasures of nostalgia, of the separation from life.

Yosef's intimate relationship with Dina had ended some ten years before
his adventure with Nabil. Thus, the fact that Dina's image fills Yosef's mind
any time he is with a "strange woman" gives a curious spaciousness to his adult
relations with women in general. Once Dina "enters" Yosef's stream of consciousness, we and he are taken back to a different time and to a fantasy to
which all women can be associated. We are then told an anecdote—for example, of Yosef's visit to an Israeli army camp where Dina was in training some
twelve years earlier. The anecdotes seem to float loose in Yosef's stream of
consciousness, a population of events without any concrete context but his
momentary unease with one woman and his momentary nostalgia for another.
Driven from one place in his imagination to another, so rapidly that he cannot
afford to admit what is real to consciousness, Yosef becomes at each moment a
victim of persecution, though he is his own persecutor.

Because his self-persecution is as nameless as historical persecution is absolute, the duality—reality and image—is magnified to the point of contradiction. Among Palestinians he is Jewish and among Jews he is an Arab. For one,
the other is real; for the other, it is the first that is real but unattainable.

Wherever he is, he is no place at all. For Yosef, to be is to not be. There is no escape. Yosef is at all times and in all places the epitome of the persecuted.

This is an irony that he discovers and rediscovers in himself, as he discovers and rediscovers it in others. But in himself the ironical juxtaposition of opposites is not ludicrous. He can escape neither of the terms, settle on no inclusive perspective. That is why he is driven by the real to nostalgia, and from that to the disorganized streams of association his imagination conjures up to enable him to function despite his uneasiness. As the epitome of the persecuted, he lives a life of denial and of hope, a life of desire and futility.

This opposition of the real and the imagined is the axis of this text, as it is of much of Israeli Hebrew literature wherever the "other" figures as central to the narrative and constitutes a moral "dilemma" for the Jew. The main feature of this "character," so far as it is *sympathique*, is that of permanently being *the* seeker of exile, or refuge. A "refugee as such" is, for this literature, one who lacks a homeland, and with it national identity, not merely one who has left home. Lacking such identity is tantamount to lacking selfhood, which is taken for the Arab to be a *personal* anomaly rather than a shared condition caused by conquest. Thus, Jews who refuse to accept *their* Jewish national identity once it is offered them by Zionism are anomalous in the same way. But the referent of this metaphor of the refugee is not merely identity. It is nation in the strong sense of self-government and place; and Yosef's duality, like all such instances of failed analogy, stands for and is emblematic of the desire for nation and a morality of that desire as if nation were a need and a legitimate good.

Kaniuk's Search for the "Last Jew"

What Kaniuk drives to the surface, I believe, is the anomaly of being both Jew and nationalist. That is, despite himself, Kaniuk exposes the Zionist idea as an anomaly for the Jew.[13] In contrast to the Zionist illusion that exile leads to its opposite, community, Kaniuk seems to say that exile has its own finality, paradoxically recognizable as the predicament of an "other." Thus, for him, the refugee is last, not first, after or in the midst of, but not before, community. In other words, the community of exile is not the same sort of thing as the fixed community of a place and an unbroken history. Given that there are no unbroken histories, the latter is, in any case, always a dream. Thus, Zionism's illusion is not exceptional, it is only anomalous, because the new or even renewed Jew of the Holocaust is nothing if not an emblem of broken history.

Zionism's illusion of "return" is, then, a denial of the very Jew for whom it promotes that vision of an unbroken history. The Jew seen as refugee is the last true Jew.[14] It is with this paradox that Kaniuk wants to confront his read-ers. But because it is an irony that can be appreciated only from the standpoint of a community of ironists, it leaves intact a vestige of the illusion of unbroken history. Only the Jewish reader can know this final irony; therefore, the reader must be yet above it, immune from it. But, as we have seen, to be above one's own contradiction is to be prior to self-criticism, including the self-criticism of Zionism that motivates Kaniuk. This is why the novel's self-critical demon-stration of paradox—the identification of the exile with a community, with an unbroken history—falls before its own radical insight.

Because this illusion of community can be maintained only negatively, against an other, the notion of "Jew" on which Zionism is predicated vanishes, becomes inessential. The *other* becomes, is, the essential term of Zionist con-sciousness. The Arab replaces the Jew as the source of Jewish definition and identity. The Jew is, finally, *not the non-Jew*. But, of course, the positive con-tent of this is, ultimately, the assertion of Jewishness as such; and such an assertion is, as a practical matter, an assertion against the Arab. This claim of identity, in the context of Zionism, is, in a way, too fundamental to last, a dec-laration of war: thus, as we have seen, the image of the warrior as a permanent agency on all sides.

Kaniuk's "last Jew," the exile, the final conscience, has one yet after it. That is the self-critical Jew whose consciousness Kaniuk can only allude to, as the reason for writing, but cannot make vital as the warrant for his novel's finally ambivalent critique of Zionism. If self-criticism, which is praxis, rather than exile were the object of *A Good Arab*, the novel would end with the Arab having achieved a subjectivity for which the Jew would now be merely an object, itself liable to judgment. This would certainly have allowed Kaniuk's critique to have transcended Zionism and, he believes, its only internal moral option to war, compassion. That this did not happen shows that the limit of Zionism's capacity for self-criticism is its inability to tolerate any moral judg-ment of "the Jew." Even a momentary subjection to the judgment of the other is unacceptable.

In Kaniuk's treatment of Arab politics, "the Organizations" stand for a denial of politics, a freeing of Arab goodness from what is inconsistent with it. However, freeing the Arab from politics, like capital's historic freeing of labor, produces merely an illusion of equality: on the one hand, the Jew whose poli-tics is part of his or her subjectivity; on the other, the Arab who, lacking poli-tics, has only the pure and unimposing subjectivity of the exile—without hope of community and therefore without a legitimate claim that utopian unity is possible.

Kaniuk leaves his reader with two concrete universals: active and passive subjectivities. These exhaust the moral universal of liberal Zionism, and demonstrate that for all its liberalism it remains caught in the paradoxes of Zionism's moral dependence on conquest. But this is not a morality that the Zionist subject can use to defend Zionism; and this may be what confuses Kaniuk. The Zionist is still a subjectivity vulnerable to critique, though not one that can be stated or written. If such a critique were to become explicit, then the Arab and not the Jew might be seen as victim and, therefore, according to the moral logic of Zionism, as the authentic subject of an opposition. That it never becomes explicit leaves Kaniuk with a problem: the Arab as moral subject is, for the Zionist, a formal possibility, and therefore a threat to Zionist righteousness. As a result, even liberal Zionist writers must contain that possibility by restricting the type of Arab who can manifest it. The good Arab can be the object, but not the subject, of morality. He or she can be valued but cannot value. To sustain this defensive maneuver, Zionism in all its cultural variations, including the novel, must constantly police the boundary between the good Arab and the Arab, no matter how much of its own irony it has to swallow.

Conclusion of Part I

This reading of *A Good Arab,* has allowed us to see more than we could have from a mere survey of Israeli Hebrew literary fiction. The relation of Jew to Arab constitutes, for Kaniuk, an allegory of authenticity. In this regard the novel meditates upon and confronts the moral dimension of a political fact. It aims to reinstate compassion within the authentic self of "post-Diasporic" Israeli Jewish society, though the post-Diaspora is precluded by its concept, its essential negativity, from maintaining any community by the community of conquest, hence, oppression. The identity of its protagonist, Yosef, is utopian in the way in which his duality is presented—as two parts, separable and, only in principle, equal. But ironies inevitably intrude that only the Israeli Jewish reader can experience with any sense of moral gratification. Yoram Kaniuk is aware of the destructiveness of the Zionist myth. And although, like other Israeli Jewish Hebrew writers, he strives to retain a Zionist resolution, the attitude and overwhelming presence of the Jewish consciousness conveyed by his novel denies any such possibility. Other Israeli Jewish Hebrew writers have striven in their own criticisms to "purify" even further the Zionist utopia, apparently on the ground that only beyond "evil and the Kelippah"[15] can it be found.

A *Good Arab*, also represents the total Zionist saga, personalized and embodied in the life experience of an extraordinary individual, ostensibly divided in two—an Arab and a Jew, a Palestinian liberal nationalist and a Jewish Israeli liberal Zionist. Thus, the narrative of A *Good Arab*, offers in compressed form not only an abundance of "actual" historical "events," the course of a whole century, but an interpretation of the significance of these events as they are presumably seen from the two oppositional poles of Jew and Arab.

Yet we see how this extremely self-critical Israeli Hebrew novel fails. Kaniuk has given the reader no way to avoid compassion within the text, but no way to live compassionately. He has at the same time welcomed his reader to a gratifying high ground outside of the text and apart from the experience of reading it—therefore to a position outside of experience. This inadvertent and unself-conscious intertextuality shows clearly that a moral Zionism cannot ultimately remain Zionist. Kaniuk offers his readers the opportunity for a self-righteousness *in regard to* the text that he demolishes thoroughly *within* the text.

This is the novel's "bad faith." Its context in the world, the militarization of the relation of Jew to Arab, comes finally to reassert its dominion over self-criticism by means of the very device Kaniuk adopts to avoid that very predicament. To establish a foundation for a liberal moral critique of Jewish-Arab affairs, he had to begin with a politics and poetics of identity from which escape is impossible. The politics of identity was necessary if he was to appeal to consciousness. But this is a self-limiting framework, fixed from the outset. It is the fundamental and self-defeating dilemma of an Israeli Jewish liberalism that wishes desperately to go beyond its own limitations but cannot even envision, much less conceptualize, its own dilemmas. Kaniuk's poetics of identity creates and reinforces unresolvable dualities at the center of Zionist moral thought. In my analysis of A *Good Arab*, this appears revealed within the complexity of a single text. I will argue that it stands for the operation of an entire genre of critical writing that takes the Zionist utopia as posing a moral problem to be solved within Zionism. In Part II, I examine works of three writers to this end: Shimon Ballas, Sammy Mikhael, and Albert Swissa. Israeli literary critics tend to regard these writers as belonging to an "ethnic group." Thus, their work is either ignored or marginalized, relegated to the category of minor works. However, I will try to show that these writers provide specific accounts of society that focus on the relations of intra-Jewish difference, as constituted by Zionism and its politics of inclusion, exclusion, and marginalization.

Part II

7

Oppositional and Insurgent
Israeli Hebrew Literature

Counterhegemonic Depictions of Self-Identity

Yehuda Burla and Yitzhaq Shami were born in Palestine, descendants of families who had lived in the country for generations. Their work, first published in the 1910s, was seen by critics to be, at best, "authentically Oriental" or "ethnic"—that is, culturally exotic, a critical disposition that runs consistently through Hebrew literature in Palestine, and later in Israel, from the 1920s to the present.[1]

Unlike Kaniuk, the Arab Jewish writers discussed below are in no sense "canonical." Their work can be seen as representing an essentially oppositional, virtually insurgent, tendency within Israeli Hebrew literature. Apart from the attempt to marginalize them as "Oriental," or as the expression of an essential ethnicity, the least sympathetic critics consider their novels as symptomatic, of identification with Palestinian Arabs or with the Arab Jewish "lower class," the "uncultivated *Mizrahim*" (Orientals), people presumably like themselves.[2]

The official Israeli use of the term *Sepharadi* or *Sepharadim* (Spanish Jews, singular and plural) is usually applied, at best, as qualifying a partial identity; at worst, it bears a disparaging connotation of the internal "other" (e.g., the "ethnic," *E'da* in Hebrew), in contrast with a putatively nonethnic *Ashkenazi*, which is taken to define authentic Jewish culture and identity as such. The term *Ashkenazi* or *Ashkenazim* is synonymous with *Israeli*, thus colonizing all other Jewish identities. The term *Arab Jew* does not officially exist in Israel, nor does *Israeli Palestinian*.

Ashkenazi culture has for a century systematically marginalized and suppressed Sepharadi (Spanish) culture and Arab Jewish self-representation. This was done chiefly by categorizing Sepharadi and Arab Jewish literary works particularly as "ethnic," and their authors as *sopherim bnei edot hamizrach* (Oriental ethnic writers), by omitting this literature from school curricula, and by failing to record it in current histories of Hebrew literature.[3]

Shimon Ballas, professor of Arabic Literature at Haifa University and a prominent Israeli writer, has confronted at least some of his critics. In an interview conducted by Yacov Besser in a fall 1992 issue of *Massa*, the weekly literary supplement of the Trade Unions Federation daily, *Davar*, Ballas responded to three articles by Gershon Shaked that had condescendingly and tendentiously characterized works by Ballas and Mikhael, and others, as a literature by *sopherim bnei edot hamizrach*.[4] These articles were excerpted from the fourth volume of Shaked's influential history of modern Hebrew literature.[5]

Ballas asserted that Shaked is the quintessential representative of the Israeli literary establishment, a powerful figure who has taken it upon himself to police the boundaries of Israeli literature and culture. For example, in Ballas's novel *A Locked Room*, the protagonist is an Israeli Palestinian and a member of the Communist party. In his criticism of the novel, Ballas pointed out, Shaked neglected to distinguish between the author and the novel's protagonist, as if there were no difference between the two, as if the thoughts, emotions, political views, and affiliations of the writer were revealed in the fictional life of the protagonist. Thus, Shaked argues, "Ballas' political standpoint is very pessimistic: he accepts the basic assumptions of the Arab, and does not see any solution of the problem but the destruction of Israel, a position to which neither the protagonist nor his creator are willing to admit." Ballas responded: "For this slander, he [Shaked] must apologize publicly. This is a malicious, personal libel. I demand that this paragraph be removed from the book that is about to be published, otherwise I'll take him to court."

Shimon Ballas has been an accomplished and well-recognized literary writer and editor in Iraq. In his interview, Ballas said that when he moved to Israel, in 1951, his political views were already established. He became actively involved in oppositional politics toward the Israeli state around issues having to do with social policy. His politics were neither "ethnic" nor in any sense arbitrary. Indeed, Ballas argued, Shaked's attribution of "ethnic sympathy" was not literary analysis but racism. Ballas's first Hebrew novel, *Hama'abara* (The transition camp), published in Israel in 1964, narrated the experience of an Iraqi community. This novel was the first in which Sepharadi and Arab-Jewish newcomers spoke with their own voice and from their own point of view. As authentically moral subjects, capable of rendering as well as accepting judgment, the characters were depicted as self-aware and conscious of their own history. It is in these terms that they are able to turn the tables on their oppressors, whether a functionary of the Jewish Agency,[6] a *paiil miflagah* (party activist), as they were once called, or an *ovedet sotsialit* (social worker)—all Ashkenazim, all associated at that time with the ruling party, MAPI, and many corrupt.[7]

The novel was well received, though less so in the temporary communities of immigrants. This is not surprising, given that the latter were more preoccupied with survival than with "high culture." What they read were stories of their own past glories, no doubt in consolation of their present oppression.[8] Despite its authentic success, the novel never became popular. It was excluded, to all intents and purposes, from public discussion and from the Israeli literary "canon."[9]

The critic and historian Gershon Shaked has completed the fourth volume of his history of modern Hebrew literature. His view of Ballas's work illustrates the point: for Shaked, the question is one of authenticity.

Shaked refers to Ballas as one of a "group," members "of the intellectual elite in Iraq."[10] In Israel, "here," says Shaked, they could only be "inferior" because they attempt to express their "personal humiliation through literary protest and revenge against the Ashkenazi who humiliated them." Through this psychology, Shaked is able to shift emphasis from the moral challenge posed by Ballas to the symptomatic quality of his work. Thus, Ballas's "support of civil rights for Israeli-Palestinians is based on a sentiment of humiliation." Ballas responded to Shaked's presumption, that

> I should not be regarded as having a principled political point of view but rather, as someone whose politics can only be regarded as a reaction to a humiliation which I, as it were, had suffered. . . . This is a distorted and racist representation. . . . In [Shaked's] view we were an elite only in the retarded world of Iraq, therefore we could only be inferior here. This is, indeed, condescending and it is distorted and racist.[11]

What Shaked cannot allow is for Ballas's texts to have the kind of authority he recognizes in other instances of literature; if he could allow that, he would be at least acknowledging the moral presence of the other, a presence Shaked is determined to deny. The danger such a presence poses to Shaked's

Zionism is illustrated in two of Ballas's most recent novels, *The Last Winter* (1984), and *The Other One* (1991).[12] These novels are virtually unique in that an Israeli Hebrew writer has produced narratives in which the state of Israel and its Jewish society are not presented as the final metahistorical agency. The characters see Israel as a proportional unit in a transnational geography, a rather parochial and somewhat suspicious presence, which is looked at with detachment, with some distance, and through a critical prism.

For example, Ahmad Haroun Sawsan, the protagonist in *The Other One*, sees Israel and Zionism from the perspective of an Arab nationalist. For him, Zionism and Israel are objects of apprehension and appear as two of many historical possibilities. The action in *The Last Winter* takes place in Paris. Its protagonist, Andre Sorel, has active political and cultural connections in many European countries and in the Middle East, North Africa, and Israel. Similarly, in *The Other One*, Sawsan reflects on incidents spanning more than half a century, involved in events in England, Germany, Iraq, Iran, Palestine, Israel, and the United States. His perspective is critical and anticolonial. Both Sorel and Sawsan are from the aristocratic intelligentsia. Both novels are narrated by old men in the form of political intellectual autobiographies. In *The Last Winter*, the protagonist dies before his story is finished. In *The Other One*, the protagonist requests that his story not be published before he dies.

The Last Winter is the story of the last months of Andre Sorel, a Jewish Communist born in Egypt and killed by unknown assassins in Paris in the winter of 1978. While in Egypt, Sorel spent years in prison, finally being expelled by the Abd al-Nasir regime. After some wandering, he settled in Paris, where he became a central figure in an international community of political exiles. Sorel was involved with Israeli and Palestinian peace activists, with leaders of the anticolonial struggle for national liberation in Algeria, with state officials of some emerging nations in Africa, and with leading figures of the Left in other countries.

Although the political activities of a small community of unaffiliated political exiles in Paris in the late 1970s may on the face of it seem insignificant, they come to stand for greater struggles and the possibility of compassion and solidarity that gives such struggles their human depth. The group includes Jews, Muslims, and Christians—Palestinians, Israelis, Egyptians, Americans, Argentines, Moroccans, French, and Germans. Their common concern is redemption through utopian means.

Paris of the late 1970s is portrayed in *The Last Winter* by a narrator who belongs to the city. This is quite different from Israeli novels in which the narrative proceeds from the point of view of a transient, one who is only momentarily not in Israel, one who will eventually return "home." Ballas's characters are, therefore, able to view events skeptically insofar as they have to do with Israel. They are never defensive of or apologetic for their "nation." Thus, one member of the group is Bashir, a Moroccan Arab. Bashir is a skeptical nationalist who lives in the midst of perpetual doubt. The group itself is radically secular. Interpersonal relationships among them supersede the formal boundaries of religion or national origin. Their polylingual and multicultural dialogues provide a politics of their political discussions. They live what they hope to understand. In this they try, not always successfully, to transcend their own nationalist tendencies and parochialism. Their awareness of limitations, and their willingness to engage them, signifies a sense not only of realism but of hope. Sorel's murder and a suicide committed by an Israeli do not refute their idealism, but rather humanize it. Sorel's death manifests the purpose of his life, the continuity of struggle.

Ballas's protagonist in *The Other One*, Haroun Sawsan, is a man approaching the age of eighty, an Arab Jewish Iraqi nationalist who, at the age of thirty-four, converted to Islam. On the occasion of his conversion, he added the name Ahmad as his first name. The story opens in 1980, a few months before the Iraq-Iran war began. Sawsan is the guest of honor at a party celebrating the publication of his most recent book, *The Jews in History*. The affair takes place at Iraq's presidential palace in Baghdad, and is hosted by the president (Saddam Hussein).

Sawsan's autobiography is written in his old age and recounts experiences of more than fifty years. Sawsan begins by saying: "While not lacking a measure of uniqueness, this is the story of a Jewish child from a small, drowsy town on the banks of the Euphrates who was confronted by a challenge—to break from the two bonds of tribalism and local traditionalism." He adds that, to meet these challenges, he had "to cut himself off from the Jewish experience, and then to approach unknown, more universal regions of consciousness, and eventually the broader span of human culture" (p. 25).

Nevertheless, the narrative explores aspects of Jewish identity that do not exist for Israeli Ashkenazi readers, or for Zionist historiography. These were, Sawsan argues, eradicated from Western European Jewish consciousness with the emergence of the European ideologies of Enlightenment, Modernism, and Nationalism, which, together with colonialism, dehumanized cultures, creeds, and peoples in all other parts of the world.

Sawsan is a radical critic not only of orientalist misrepresentations of Middle Eastern and Levant culture, but of the tendency of Arabs and Muslims to accept and internalize that orientalism. At the same time, he criticizes

Zionist separatist and parochial politics in Iraq, in the Arab world, and in general.

Thus, whereas the European Jewish characters of hegemonic Israeli Hebrew fiction usually find their self-identities expressed in reaction to the Zionist utopia—actually existing Zion—the identities of Arab Jewish characters in Ballas's novels are more ambivalent, tentative, and complex. They are instances, as Sartre might say, of praxis, totalization against totality, life against definition.

I was not surprised to find that Israeli literary critics concentrated on identifying the "real" types that informed Ballas's portrayal of characters. Such an emphasis is consistent with the cultural and ideological requirement that every work of fiction operate as an allegory. By that I mean that every figure must stand for a condition, an intention, an interest, a type that organizes events between the fallen Diaspora and the living utopia, or that represents a definite relation within the dialectic of Israeli Jewish identity and its other. More than narrative plausibility is involved—more than a sense that the events depicted could have happened as represented, more than "fictional truth." What is required above all is *historically* objective plausibility, namely, that specific events might have happened as described and that events of the given type certainly happened. In the canonical Israeli Hebrew text, historical referents are intended to inform as well as to instruct, and to inform about history as a whole, as is appropriate for a people that claims uniquely to make its own history and therefore to constitute the possibility of "history" as such.

A totalizing expectation of this kind demands that the writer be accountable to a standard of historical "truth." This is Shaked's reason for dismissing Ballas with the insinuation that his work is symptomatic of disloyalty to "the national interest."[13] Some critics, outside of the mainstream, recognized the two novels as a genuine contribution to Israeli literature and an unprecedented challenge to Zionist ideology. Still, their distribution was poor, and there was no support for them to be translated.

Andre Sorel gave his life in a cause—that of peace, social justice, and human dignity—he had fought for all his life, and Ahmad Haroun Sawsan *chose* to be "other." He insisted that Iraqi Jews should not collaborate in the destruction of their own ancient, and yet modern and flourishing, community. He died lonely and defeated, but, like Sorel, with no implication of futility. The difference they represent is preserved in their sacrifice, emblematic of the real historicity of Zionist hegemony.

For hegemonic Israeli literary criticism, however, it is inconceivable that an Israeli Jewish writer, or any Israeli Jew, for that matter, would choose the status of an internal exile, or would attempt to project alternative, multinational sources of identity for Jews. The Zionist imagination cannot accept the possibility of a Jew living in Israel *not by choice*. We will see this again in the response to Albert Swissa's novel *Aqud*.

After Politics Is Over: A Moment of Mutual Recognition

My intention is not to compare the depiction of Arabs by Ballas, Mikhael, and Swissa with depictions in hegemonic Israeli literature. I am, rather, interested in the ways in which these authors, all of whom were born in "Arab" countries, construct their depictions counterhegemonically. Although a comparison could no doubt shed further light on the nature of this difference, the way in which one depends on the other, I have chosen, instead, to situate Ballas, Mikhael, and Swissa in relation to their critics rather than to canonical Ashkenazi writers in order to highlight the difference their work makes at the point at which Israeli literature appears at its most self-conscious.

Sammy Mikhael was born in Baghdad, Iraq, in 1926. In his youth, he joined the Iraqi Communist party underground. In 1948, he was forced to leave for Iran, where he continued to be involved with dissident groups. One year later, he immigrated to Israel. Two of his novels, *Hasut* (Refuge) (1977) and *Hofen Shel A'rafel* (A handful of fog) (1979), reflect these experiences in the lives and fate of Mikhael's characters.[14]

Hasut depicts Jewish-Arab relations in Israel through the characters' confrontation with their internalized oppression. Their capacity to free themselves from their oppression within is predicated on their recognizing the external oppression to which they are relentlessly subjected. This, it transpires, is possible only through the entrance of the individual into solidarity with others. In that case, oppression is transformed into its opposite, namely, a source of empowerment for the subaltern. "Sound" judgment of political reality, therefore, becomes a means by which domination, its absolutist utopia, is exposed for what it is, that is, an illusion of mastery and of self-mastery. It is in this absurdity of domination that the oppressed of *Hasut* find their own subjectivity, the possibility of being freed from the internalized oppression that is otherwise the ultimate source of bondage and self-defeat. This is what actually happens in the novel. The reader is led, through the experience and growing self-awareness of the characters, to identify with the greater course of enlightenment and nonutopian liberation, which is the novel's own life. However, in regard to the "real" external oppression faced by the characters and those they represent, when we look closely at those who are "liberated" and those who remain prisoners of "illusion" and "inner oppression," we realize that we were led to expect more than the novel could actually deliver.

The novel's plot involves three intermarried Arab-Jewish families, over two generations of Communists. The Israeli Communist party is signified cryptically, by the term "the Organization."[15] The narrative transpires through the critical first three days and nights of the October 1973 war.

Against this background, then, the novel presents Jewish struggle, heroism, and sacrifice, as the dimensions of a space of excruciating endeavor in the midst of which Jewish consciousness discovers the source of its morality, national identity, while the Arabs remain "Arabs." Thus, the major individual antagonist to this struggle is embodied as an Israeli Palestinian poet and activist who thirsts for Jewish blood and is eager to reclaim "Arab honor" and the "plundered" Arab land of Palestine.

Valor in battle, devotion to the civilian population behind the front, righteousness of purpose, and dedication to the moral ideals of Israeli Jewry guide this novel's fabula. Its main protagonist, Marduch—a "Sumerian name"—had been a Communist revolutionary in an unnamed Arab country and, for many years, a political prisoner.[16] He is the "heroic" figure of the novel, engaged in a battle to defend Israel against the Egyptian army's advance through the Sinai desert. At the end, his fate is unknown; his identity remains, after reading has done its work, as the trace of great deeds. Marduch's wife, Shula, is confronted with a dilemma. She is instructed by "the Organization's" leadership to provide "refuge" for the unnamed Arab poet-comrade, in her home. After profound deliberation, she agrees. But Shula takes him in by way of endorsing her husband's principle that "providing refuge to a persecuted person is a supreme value." The absurdity of this instance of reason and its actual conditions is mirrored in the politics of the two main characters. The reason given for Marduch's joining the Communist party while he was still living *in an Arab country*, the country of his birth and the place where his family had lived for many generations, is that he is Jewish. The reason given for Israeli Arabs joining the Israeli Communist party is that they are Arabs. In each case, the condition of being an outsider determines what might otherwise be thought of as a matter of principle and the result of deliberation. Yet it is within this absurdity, this givenness, of a history to which all are subject that each character will eventually find him- or herself. Marduch's heroism is thereby humanized and made attainable. Over and over again, Mikhael writes of the paradoxes of oppression and of the impossibility of self-liberation without self-criticism and, through that, self-discovery.

Thus, Israeli Palestinians are perceived by Palestinians living in the Occupied Territories as "representatives of the Jewish State," and thus "of the oppressor." However, a Palestinian who visits family members in a refugee camp acts oppressively toward them. He flaunts his money to impress the children. He forces people to stoop in front of him, and to serve his whims; he attempts to molest a young niece and takes advantage of his widowed sister-in-law's despair. This internalization of oppression reappears in the consequences of the departure of the Israeli army from the area of the camp, on "Yom-Kippur's eve." The Palestinians then turn on each other, in a paroxysm of self-loathing that appears as a moment of freedom, or, from another point of view, a symptom of oppression by one's own kind.

Similarly, in Israel, Jewish women, members of "the Organization," are depicted as victims of their parents, an oppression by an older generation of dogmatists. Their mothers are portrayed as mean, doctrinaire, and nagging. Their fathers resemble scarecrows; they are supposed to be only frightening and impressive. The young women have married Arab men (members of "the Organization") because of their parents' expectations, and because of otherwise limiting social conditions their parents, out of their own failure, had created for them.

On the other hand, Arab men are married to Jewish women as a "bonus": "the Organization" offers them as an attraction to join, and, "as is well known," Arabs have great gusto for blond women with long hair and white skin.[17]

The first to discover "truth" and "light" in the midst of oppression and history is Marduch. As an active member of the Communist party "there," he was vulnerable to the police. Eventually, he was arrested and taken for investigation by "the sadistic, yet ignorant chief" of the secret service. Marduch was jailed, tortured, and held in chains for fourteen years. After this, he was expelled from the country. Israel was the only nation willing to take him in and to grant him "refuge." Marduch says that he was "dumped by surprise, against [his own] will" (p. 160).

In Israel he joined "the Organization," but could not find a place for himself among its Jewish members, because "they sat around cursing their own country." He "had no desire to be a wretch among wretches." Instead, he met with the Arab comrades and found that "they were in splinters, the remains of a strong body that had packed up and left." They "made [him] recoil, Those mean souled villagers who found the Organization to be a vehicle for their petty gains" (p. 163). This depiction of communists is immediately followed by the discovery of an exception:

But not Fuad. He's different. His head glides above the suffocating swamp like a swan's. The others have found some strange way to enjoy being suffocated. I respected Fuad because he really suffered from this strangulation. (p. 164)

Fuad, *this* Arab, sees with the same eyes as Marduch. Yet he is not Marduch, not a being such as Marduch. When Ido, Marduch's child, realizes that a war has broken out and his father has gone to the front, he screams "*Kus-emak ha'Aravim ha'tovim,*" meaning, "In the nakedness of their mother, the good Arabs" (p. 153).[18] In other words, when there is war, who is to blame? Naturally, "the Arabs," and Ido knows only *good* Arabs. Marduch went to the front "not out of fear of being punished for evasion," but rather, because once "he had seen that this was the right way, nothing could stop him" (p. 197). He, and not Fuad, *must* act, could will what would happen. This is the source of his heroism, beyond mere deeds. Fuad, by contrast, could only be heroic in knowledge, in suffering "from this strangulation." Marduch is enlightened, but at the cost of his momentary recognition of Fuad.

Shula, who narrates Marduch's life story in his absence, is next in discovering "truth" and "light." She describes the endurance of Marduch's moral rectitude, his struggle and past suffering, his intellectual and spiritual accomplishments, and their love. It is through Shula that the reader comes to know Marduch, and through her hears the story of their eleven years of marriage. Their child is retarded, and Shula wonders whether or not this was inherited from her family. The anxiety of this possibility is mitigated by her wondering whether or not there is a history of retardation in Marduch's family. Marduch himself says:

In a culture like the one in which I grew up, these things are difficult to detect, especially when they're not too severe. A person may be born and grow up and marry and have children and die, without anyone suspecting that he might not have all his wits about him. Not many children got the sophisticated kind of toys they have here—toys that may entertain them and make them happy, but also reveal their weaknesses. Not every adult had to learn how to use logarithmic tables, either. They didn't administer Rorschach tests and I.Q. tests. So perhaps there were cases like this in my family, and no one noticed it. (p. 139)

On the third day of the war, Shula pays a consoling visit to the family of her former lover, Rami, whom she rejected for Marduch. Rami had served as a colonel in the Israeli armored corps, and had, all along, occupied a vivid and loving presence in her life. When he is killed heroically in battle, Shula finds the inner strength for her self-liberation. She frees herself from the external forces, "the Organization," which held her in bondage for so long. She now realizes that the IDF (Israel's Defense Force) "is not like the French army, and not like the Red army." She says, "The Red Army was the people's army; the IDF is the people itself." Consequently, she declares, "I am leaving the Organization" (p. 381).

Marduch, however, was not lucky enough to be in a position to have made such a move before he left for the front. Shula has not heard from him since he left home, and she fears the worst. Yet she takes the liberty of announcing to her mother, on his behalf, that he too has left the Organization. She is aware that this is a lie, but she assumes that leaving would be the right thing to do at this critical juncture, and that Marduch would do the right thing. His is therefore a second-order liberation. None of the Arab protagonists, however, is liberated in any sense, neither in their inner psyches, nor from any external force that oppresses them.

The novel ends on a dramatic yet ridiculous note. At a late hour on the third night of the war, Shula awakens with a shock. In her dream, she saw Rami's dead body, and her mother insisted, "with hatred," that this was Marduch. While Shula is trying to sort out her confusion and overcome her fears, she realizes that she is not alone in her bedroom; she realizes that "a real figure stood between her and the open door." In her panic, she screams. It is Fatkhi (the poet). He did not intend to frighten her. In his love and concern for her he came to offer to take Shula and Ido to join a friend in Jenin, on the West Bank. His friend is a dentist, and he tells Shula that "both he and his wife are wonderful people." He adds:

> The Israeli armored corps has been completely destroyed at the canal. . . . Your army has finally been routed. At this moment there's no real Israeli force between the Egyptian armor and the heart of Israel."

Shula asks, "Where did you hear all this?" When Fatkhi answers, "From Radio Cairo," Shula responds, "Ah ha" (pp. 380–81).

A moment of implicit erotic tension flickers between them before Shula makes clear to Fatkhi that she is staying, and that she "would not abandon Marduch's house at such a time." She offers, on the other hand, to drive Fatkhi to Amalia and Emil, another intermarried couple in "the Organization."

> "You hate me," she said.
> "Does that matter now?"
> She said nothing. He rose, and his dry lips searched for hers in the darkness. She recoiled; he felt a chill as if a wall, cold as death had arisen between them.

At that moment they ceased being a man and a woman. He was just an Arab.
She was just a Jew. (p. 382)

The word "just," which appears twice in the closing sentences of the
Hebrew version, signifies inevitability, but it represents a moment of mutuality and, in that, a moment of self-recognition that neither imposes on the
other. This enlightenment lacks the pleasure of false, narcissistic enlightenment. It is "just" in the double sense of justice as well as "merely." It is real
under the circumstances, and therefore it is honest.

Clearly, this tale is told from Shula's perspective. It appears that her
achievement was only limited to substituting one orthodoxy for another. Yet,
her conversion makes it possible for Mikhael to humanize the Israeli Arab Jew,
Marduch, the Israeli internal other and, paradoxically, his Ashkenazi wife,
who did not have to go to war, but only had to renounce her Communist past.
Marduch's liberation, regardless of the validity of its politics, depends on
Shula; hers depends on merely an incident, after politics is over—a moment of
mutual recognition. This is where Mikhael leaves the subject of this dialectic
of oppression, and his reader—without romance or sentimentality.

All Men Are Equal, but Some Are More

Another of Mikhael's novels, *All Men Are Equal, but Some Are More*, is
engaged entirely with the aspect of reality as it is experienced by Arab Jews in
Israel.[19] The jacket of Mikhael's novel contains the following statement:

> In [this] bubbling novel Sammy Mikhael redeems the "Second Israel" from a
> conspiracy of silence and opens a window onto the painful reality of the silent
> majority. This novel tells the story of a mass immigration. Each of its protago-
> nists represents an archetype of all those thousands who arrived in Israel "from
> the East rather than the West."[20]

This only hints at what is disturbing about Mikhael's novel. Although it was
by no means the first literary expression of the Israeli Jewish subaltern class,[21]
it challenges one of the most revered myths of Zionist ideology, "the ingathering of exiles."

The novel covers a five-day experience in the life of David, its narrator,
beginning at 9:00 a.m., on 2 June 1967 and ending at 6:00 p.m. on 6 June
1967. David, a military reserve soldier, speaks while riding with a crew of five
in an armored carrier. The commander and radio operator are "Ashkenazi."
The carrier's driver and David are "Sepharadi." The fifth member of the crew

is a Yemenite, a distinct ethnic group of the so-called "Mizrahim." They are traveling from a location in central Israel to the southern border.

On June 5, at 3:00 p.m., six hours after crossing the Egyptian border into the Sinai desert, their carrier is struck by a shell and destroyed. The driver is killed and the other four are seriously wounded. David, who is in slightly better condition than his comrades, removes them from the burning carrier, which is about to explode. Despite the severity of his own wounds, he manages eventually to signal for help. Rescuers arrive the next morning, and he and his friends are saved.

During these five days David recollects the course of his life in a series of time frames. He remembers his family's experiences in Israel after they arrived from Baghdad in 1950. He then shifts to the present, where, during a military ceremony a few weeks after the war (1967), he is awarded a medal for heroism. These recollections juxtapose the immediate struggle of David and his comrades to survive with the sociologically mediated problems with which his family had to deal in overcoming the invidious conditions that followed their "settlement" in Israel. The two experiences are treated as analogous and as symbolizing the internal paradoxes of the image of Israel as a melting pot, as an assembling of diverse Jewish ethnicities into the newly established republican state. These paradoxes express a practical contradiction between the intense patriotism associated with the "settlement" of Israel and the absence of the sort of planning or infrastructure necessary to sustain the element of community presupposed by the unifying myth of the melting pot.

In this regard, one can compare *All Men Are Equal* with Bartov's *Each Had Six Wings*.[22] Both writers present the Israeli army as engaged in "settling" the new immigrants and in helping the younger generation among the newcomers to overcome alienation, isolation, and frustration. Bartov's novel represents the army through the figure of a remarkable woman soldier who serves as a schoolteacher for the newcomers and who, because of her military status, has more authority in the community than would normally be expected of a young teacher. In Mikhael's novel this same role is assigned first to David's older brother Shaul and later to David himself. Both novels gloss over the overbearing incompetence of the state bureaucracy and its priority of politics over human needs. Both novels fail to examine the implications of the conformism imposed by the Israeli army on Jewish youth. Both accept the ideological premise of this imposition, that the military serves society as a whole, and does so in a way that is both as humane as possible and responsive to community needs, especially those pertaining to the problems involved in assimilating

Jewish newcomers. As a result, both rely on an unexamined, and unexaminable, utopian vision of an existing society.

In *All Men Are Equal*, David remembers immigrants gathering at an unemployment agency and their mute frustration when the "good" jobs are assigned to the "Ashkenazim." The only overt signs of anger are shown by a gang of thugs led by one Abu Halawa.[23] But it is an anger that turns against itself. Abu Halawa's gang "works" for whoever is willing to pay the highest price. In addition, he operates as the chief pimp in the immigrants' camp. Bartov's novel says relatively little about that underside of "community." Thus, when a group of activists organize a demonstration in front of a municipal office, they are counseled by their benevolent soldier-teacher, who eventually intervenes successfully on their behalf.

Mikhael depicts a much more arduous and conflictual process than Bartov in regard to the "ingathering of exiles" and their "assimilation" to the civil "melting pot" of Israeli society. His novel is in this sense a more "realist" one than Bartov's. It refuses to minimize the tremendous human sacrifice involved in the project of unification. Both novelists bring their characters to a point within sight of Israel's "living utopia." Mikhael's characterization of the social dislocation, inequality, and suffering that underlie unification is, at the same time, a demystification. In fact, Mikhael portrays a rapid transformation of well-to-do Iraqi Jews into a community of failed and hopeless souls, in effect sacrificed to a future of benefit to their progeny. Its members began their journey by airplane stripped of their wealth yet dressed, optimistically, in their finest clothing. They have traded the prosperity of a nation for the promise of a society. They anticipate a joyful "return" to the ancient land of the Jews. What befalls them, however, is depicted, strikingly and ironically, as a reversal, and not a transformation of fortune. This experience is presented as unendurable. Yet Mikhael's narrator embraces it as a sacrifice necessary for the achievement of unity.

The fact that sacrifice is only remembered, is merely part of David's recollection, removes its sting and helps to separate it from the society for which it now appears as resource rather than as constitutive feature. Those who are its victims never tell their own tale. Their fate is one material element of David's self-consciousness, and the latter is a simulacrum of history reduced to an epic. David's memory, his reduction of real experience to a mere moment, subordinates suffering to a greater story of collective achievement. At the same time, it displaces suffering in general from society in general. It yields an idealism that can know itself as separate from suffering, and suffering as merely discipline. In the retrospect of David's life, which stands for the "life" of Israel itself, sacrifice may be accompanied by pain, but it is an abstract pain, a general pain without concrete victims, without debt. In the totalizing finality of this unity, nothing and no one is truly lost, and no obligation is incurred. David remembers the immigrants being taken from the airport by trucks to an old British military camp that had been turned into an "absorption center." It is called, without irony, "The Gate of Ascendancy." Scores of people, young and old, men and women, children and infants, are placed in barracks "to live" together through endless days and nights, without privacy, without proper facilities, without dignity. Where all bodily fluids mix, where sweating, farting, and lovemaking have nothing to cover their intimacy, and where all other human foibles are remorselessly exposed without hope of relief, the residents of the camp fall into despair. It is as if they had been forgotten by those in whom they had been led to invest so much hope. Finally, at the nadir of their suffering, and with the same degree of arbitrariness with which they had originally been assigned, they are abruptly taken on a cargo train to their "transition camp," a tent colony in Kheiriya, there to sit for years and rot.[24]

David recollects all of this immediately as a moment of a greater history. Nothing that happened to them seems to have had reason; nothing can or needs to be rationalized or explained. Only this greater history makes intelligible the first generation of newcomers' loss to misery and despair. David's father, a robust man in his fifties, had been a rich merchant in Baghdad, well known and respected in his community. Here, he is enfeebled, gradually losing his sight as well as his other faculties. Now he is wholly dependent upon his family, where only yesterday he was its source of strength. Shortly after arriving at Kheiriya, he dies futilely in a tent fire with his wife and their youngest daughter, theirs a sacrifice to a unity of which they could barely dream. In this sense, the being of community is demonstrated unequivocally by the otherwise irrational deaths of those for whom it could never be real.[25]

However, the novel overcomes one potentially subversive tendency, to become an allegory of the encounter of unreasoned faith with an arbitrary and incorrigible world, that is, of the absurdity of fortune and suffering. It emerges instead with another tendency intact, namely, the utopian denial of precisely the antiutopian history that had been disclosed. It does so by judiciously deploying a set of rhetorical devices that transform concrete experience into abstract context rather than into concrete history or even an object of irony. The following episode serves as an example:

> While having my tea I was teasing him: "Actually, what difference is a black lawyer like you going to make?"

> "Work." He didn't even bother to raise his eyes from the book.
> "Surely, even in lawyers' offices there're special jobs for blacks!"
> "Sit down and study!"
> "I'm talking seriously, Shaul."
> His hand caressed the book as if it was the curve of a woman's hips. "I didn't choose law accidentally," he said simply; *for the law* there are no ethnic differences; in court we're all *equal*. I believe it, and I'm sure that through law I'll be able to achieve equal rights, not only for myself but for all of us."
> "The old-timers in this country are able to bend the law—at their will."
> "Take that trash out of your head." (p. 111)

This is a dialogue between two brothers, David (the narrator) and his older brother, Shaul, who is studying law. Later, David protests what he considers Shaul's idealism, or naïveté. However, it turns out at the end that Shaul's personal success is the result of opportunism rather than adherence to principle. His and David's equality, as citizens of Israel, is predicated not on the law but on their bravery in war; not on history, but on power. The allusion to principle turns out to be merely a context of justification for expediency. Shaul's claim to be serious operates not to establish motivation but to establish position. What Shaul does is not predicated on what he believes, but on what he refuses to admit into discourse.

The restoration of utopia predicated on a military concept of unity finally, and paradoxically, confirms hope, though it is the hope of those who did not suffer. It occurs in a story of heroism so conventional that it erases precisely the predicament that it had initially, during the preheroic part of the novel, made trenchant and compelling to the reader. This restoration emerges as the narrator's autobiography, an account of a life intended to subsume and to some extent neutralize the horror that lay at its origin. Thus, it is by the device of individuation and then the elevation of the individual voice above experience, what autobiographical writing does so well, that the reader is drawn ironically back into the utopian vision as its very subject. In this way realism is transformed into its opposite. The reader ends by *appreciating* experience rather than *sharing* it. He or she is left with an ironist's view of suffering, but one that is devoid of self-irony. What emerges then is the coupling of a voice beyond suffering with a suffering beyond voice. It is to this emergence that we now turn.

The Army as a Figure of Utopia

David was twelve years old when his family arrived in Israel. He is thirty when he recollects these events. He had matriculated as an "external" student and had, at eighteen, despite his mother-in-law's objections, married an extraordinarily beautiful Ashkenazi woman from Poland. The couple divorced soon after having a child because, he says, of his mother-in-law's jealousy and protectiveness and her contempt for Sepharadim. This synthesis of ethnic difference through marriage, this moment of unity, fails. But the child, the surplus of a hopeless union, is neither "Iraqi" nor "Polish." He is *an Israeli* in the sense of being something new and complete, something that expresses the failed union, but as an impossibility rather than a contingency, that is, mere failure.[26] The child does not merely experience conflict; he *is* the embodiment of conflict. That is the center of his being and therefore the condition of whatever he does and whatever he can make of himself.[27]

During his seventeen years in Israel, David served in two wars, completed his studies, received his diploma as an accountant, and spent a number of years as a government clerk and as a foreman. He comes across as someone special, who has matured through difficulties that would have destroyed another less steadfast. To rise from the gutter, he had to make hard choices. Yet, in the end, it is only by his determination and, most of all, his courage in combat that he becomes a true citizen and a participant in a historic struggle. This "moral career," this course of self-discovery, is not itself an object of reflection but a condition. It appears as a series of incidents evolving plausibly and steadily through movement the telos of which the reader already takes for granted as its source of value. The narrative presents an allegory of overcoming that *appears* as history, and that operates to deny the virtual allegory of hope and futility that might otherwise have instituted a critically historical consciousness of that appearance.

But this substitution of one allegory (the myth of overcoming) for another (the falseness of opportunity) could not by itself have completed the task of effacing despair and what despair constitutes as an attitude and a way of being. It needs, as well, the telos of a utopian practice, an end to which everything can be subordinated, capable of displacing hope and therefore making irrelevant the sense of futility that must haunt every particular act in the light of so elevated an end. The result is a melancholy disguised by rituals of order and by celebrations of utopia, as if utopia had actually come to pass. The figure of this order and utopia is the army, which, in this novel, is more than an institution or a setting. The Israeli army is ultimately the protagonist in a far greater drama than David's, and it is this drama, this delusionary history, of which David's relatively meager story is ultimately no more than a fleeting signifier.

The army appears as society's capacity to mold individual character and its resource for forging a national unity. This confluence of substance and practice, value and production, makes the military the only adequate representation of society itself. In this context, civilian life, even magnified by suffering, is of little significance save as a backdrop against which the army demonstrates its own significance, or as a source of illustrations of weakness that need to be overcome for the sake of history. And the overcoming of these is, finally, all the civilian life that needs to be recognized. But then, it is, in effect, civil society against itself. The *ideal* of unity is thereby exposed as the *reality* of military life. The telos that informs society is reduced to a military truth, truth divorced from human need and the self-critical entanglements of intersubjectivity. This truth is as embodied in David as David is embodied in his function and the vision that informs it and typifies his conduct as what sociologists call performance of roles. David is, then, a personal abstraction. He becomes the exemplary figure in which utopia completes itself without being disturbed by memories of what had made it seem necessary and possible. David, the determined visionary, the vehicle of telos, now erases what is overwhelming in the lives of his parents. They become only his occasion, reduced to a mnemonic device itself part of the military economy of David's sense of self-determination, of being beyond contingency, his birth having been an uncaused cause. Their desire for peace has no possibility of recognition in the formidable military project of reconciliation. As a fact in David's biography, their longings and beliefs are no longer active in what can be conceived of as David's life beyond that biography. His new and abstract military existence erases the old fragile personalities who deserve reasons and respect, including the self he might otherwise have been. His biography, its telling by David as the story of the other he has become, deconstitutes the very idea of humanness that would allow his narrative to make sense outside of its particular, national, military context. Thus, the army not only constitutes a unique solution to an abiding radical problem posed by memory, it has the aura of something as magical as the living utopia itself. Indeed, in *All Men Are Equal*, it becomes that utopia and therefore comes to stand for all that needs to be envisioned.

Shaul, David's older brother, arrived in Israel one year ahead of his family. He says that he came "accidentally, just out of curiosity,"[28] and was "guided by people who risked their lives" in the Zionist underground (p. 25). After joining the Israeli army, Shaul was promoted to the rank of corporal. When the family disembarked upon arriving from Baghdad, his father was disappointed that Shaul, his oldest son, was not on the tarmac to greet them. Reuben, a family acquaintance, apologized for Shaul, saying that he was probably delayed by his military duties. This apparently trivial incident suggests, at the outset, the direction of the novel toward a "life" that will ultimately erase Life, toward a supercession of the civil by the military in the "living utopia" of Israel, toward a denial of history.

Shaul turns out to be the wise man, the experienced man of will and power who has *already* learned the ways of discipline and detachment. In one of his first conversations with Shaul, his father complains of having been sprayed with DDT as if he were an animal. Shaul replies: "My father, I know . . . listen. Around this small country we're encircled by enemies. None of them acknowledges our victory. If an epidemic were to break out among us, we'd all be lost" (p. 25). Thus, Shaul does not try to justify the need for immunization, but points out the need to avoid all criticism and all personal claims of right in the face of the military requirements of national security. In other words, Shaul advises, there is no past, only the future. What you were is nothing; what you are is all that is needed.

Shaul takes over his father's responsibility as head of the family, an obligation that increases as his father's condition deteriorates. A few months after his family's arrival, Shaul is promoted to the rank of sergeant. In spite of his condition and state of mind, the father is moved almost to tears by his son's promotion. But even this joy cannot diminish a greater bitterness. He appeals again to a history the utopia cannot abide:

> We thought, we'll come—like coming back *home*; Jews among Jews. One people. But it isn't so. Someone is dividing everyone into two peoples. You remember—in Iraq we had troubles, but we were not *inferior* to them! Here, thank God, Jews are not persecuted. But already before we came—our status was fixed for us as another class. A *second*-rate class.

After a moment of bewilderment, Shaul responds:

> And so, father, when I was persecuted *there*, I had none to complain to. I did not dare hit back. Here, I knock loudly on every door that's shut in my face. It ain't easy. My hands ache from the many doors on which I knock, and which no one opens. But at least I'm *allowed* to knock forcefully, and with noise. At the end, father, at the end someone will open. (pp. 25–26)

Shaul's response takes for granted a unity prior to struggle. Thus, while one may knock in Israel, no one should knock too hard lest he disturb the Jewish peace that allows each Jew, *in principle*, to be heard. This justification for denying politics and history is self-deceptive. Shaul, too, wishes to live under the conditions he knew in Iraq, but with the tables turned. This identification with the aggressor is the ultimate secret of his vision. He has taken the oppressor into himself.

What is most important is that at this early stage of the novel, Shaul's argument suggests a major Zionist theme. If only Jews convert to Zionism, if only they "return" to the "Land of Israel" early enough in their lives, they can save themselves from inevitable persecution and humiliation and find themselves as citizens of *their own* country. This cold-blooded, particularistic nostrum is Shaul's way, and finally the reader's, of simplifying history and denying experience. Shaul's response summarizes the novel's own solution to the Diaspora.

At the same time, Shaul is a figure of confidence and strength, in contrast to David's tentativeness and lack of clarity. The need for special effort on David's part is a constitutive feature of him. He is mired in the likelihood of failure and futility. For him to become definite, he must become different, make a difference. Thus, it is essential that David become a hero. Heroism will guarantee his transformation and erase his memory as the perspective of heroism erases history itself. But because a novel is not merely a resolution but the history of resolution—that is, an object of reading and not merely a moment or a thing—Mikhael's *book* nevertheless preserves what its *narrative* attempts to overcome. It contains an experience of pain and loss that the narrative tries to, but cannot, displace. And this is its de facto challenge to Zionism. Writing often leaves written the condition that the mind needs resolved. It is to Mikhael's credit that the novel ends without burying its *own* development as a text in sentiment and explicit self-denial. But the only reader who can have the benefit of its honesty is one willing to remember what has been read as well as to continue reading.

Shaul does not live in the ragged tent shared by his parents and siblings. Like the Zionist "pioneers," he has built his own hut, and like them he claims the principle of self-sufficiency as his own. In fact, it is his comrades, appearing one evening with lumber and a willingness to work, who assist him in its construction. Thus, his appeal to self-sufficiency is false. He is, in a different way, as dependent on others as his family is on him. This hypocrisy compromises the sense of noblesse oblige with which he provides for his father and heightens the ambiguity of such otherwise generous acts as providing extra food for his family. This appears when his father questions the legality of the gift of food, in effect questioning Shaul's authority and his honor. Shaul hesitates for a moment and again provides a glib answer to a serious question:

Look, here we all say *vuz-vuz*[29]—and it is a derogatory term, even with hatred. But I'm stuck in a military barrack with forty of them. Of the whole lot, ten were born here. . . . But the others aren't in a hurry. They are *vuz-vuz* too, but they roll into their beds in the big barrack, smoke, keep looking at the ceiling. . . . They have nowhere to go. Their families were slaughtered. Before you arrived in the country, I was like them. But I had, after all, the hope of meeting

with my family once more. *They*'re lying there, dreaming dead people's dreams. When they heard that *you came*—they got together to help, even the cook. I don't know if you'd understand, father . . . when they push something into my bag. Before I come here, they set aside slices of bread for their dead dreams. . . . No . . . this food was not stolen; it is *kosher*.
Father ceased eating and, pondering, moved his plate and lit a cigarette.
Are these the boys who brought the lumber for your hut?
Yes. (pp. 39–40)

Charity, even a son's toward a father, depends on the relative security of the donor. Food but no lumber; the moment of consumption but not the possibility of productive labor. These qualifications of the good deed are, like charity, intended to instruct. It is because of the surplus of material that Shaul can be both generous and moralistic. He can enjoy the pleasure of a life for which gifts can be measured, and therefore gratitude made rational. Unlike the reader, Shaul is *in* this novel. Thus, he is immune *from reading*, protected from his own memories, which the reader can hardly avoid. For the reader, and perhaps for the father whose life is what is *written*, though not what is *told*, Shaul is weakened by the self-deception, by forgetting.

His generosity is partly a sham, but it is reasonable in the light of the novel's own project—to achieve a measure of reconciliation without, denying that it is neither inevitable nor without dangerous countervailing temptations. Yet this tension between the textual motive of reconciling and the writing of difference that makes reconciliation a possible motive is what gives this novel its counterhegemonic bite. Through writing, Shaul becomes an episode in David's life, just as the textualizing narrative casts his father's life as an episode in a greater history. Reconciliation is always at the expense of those who need or want it.

Shaul refuses to get involved in communal affairs or to confront the thugs who continually harass the community, nor is he "ripe," as he says, for leadership: he learned in the army "never to act before you're ready" (p. 36). In any case, he says that he wants to complete his studies before doing anything else. However, after he completes them, he leaves the tent colony to establish a lucrative private practice as an attorney; like a proper utopian, he never looks back. Shaul represents the only attitude that can support the utopian vision, but the fact that Mikhael presents him with a measure of bad faith reminds his readers of faith, good and bad, and of hope, futile or not. Mikhael thereby retains the sense of a critique of Zionism—by showing what utopia cannot reconcile. But he preserves in Shaul's weakness the need to do away with criticism. This allows him to retain a grasp of the vision of unity despite having to acknowledge its predication on a history that contradicts it.

"Agenda," Politics, and Allegory

Shaul appears as strangely apart, even alien. His detachment, like the indifference of an aristocrat, objectifies others. It is one source of his power. But he also has a knack for gaining position, and this becomes a resource for David, whose own story increasingly becomes that of Shaul. Upon completion of his studies, Shaul eventually gains a national reputation as an attorney. He establishes himself in the upper echelons of power. When David uses his brother's name in applying for a job, it makes an impression. Wounded in the 1956 war, Shaul limps slightly on one leg, a Byronic flaw that adds to his charisma. He is not married, but has had a long relationship with a family acquaintance, Naima, who is married to someone else but with whom he has had two children. This relationship can be seen as another index of Shaul's character and its significance to David's moral development.

We learn about Naima and Shaul's intimacy when David senses some conspiratorial intent in their gestures toward each other. Shaul's hut is adjacent to the part of the family's tent that is occupied by David. One night David, hearing strange noises, cuts a hole in the material separating him from Shaul's room, and witnesses Naima and Shaul making love. David justifies this untoward violation of privacy by referring to vague fears he had for his brother's health. In fact, he allows himself to be deceived by Shaul.

We are led to believe that Reuben, Naima's husband, cannot father children, and that Naima is sexually unsatisfied in her marriage. Following several erotic scenes that David has witnessed through his peep hole, he hears Naima reveal that she is pregnant by Shaul. He understands this to be evidence of Shaul's virility, and of his generosity in satisfying another's, Naima's, need. But the episode has yet another significance. It teaches David a subtle aspect of the difference between strength and weakness, one that bears as well on the utopian image of Israel that informs the novel. Reuben is considered by Shaul to be "another of our weaklings." He had been elected to the Knesset, something Shaul considers "unbefitting" "Iraqis" or "Sepharadim." As he sees it, Reuben is one of those Sepharadim who makes his way into the political machine by being "smooth." Smoothness, expediency, and pretense are not the sorts of virtue that contribute to unity. They are attributes of a selfish temperament. They speak for agendas that are hidden and divisive. Shaul's own detached air also conceals such agendas, but for David this is a triumph of form over content, as, in fact, is David's own biography, which stands for Israel. But "agendas," hidden or not, can also stand for politics as well as strength; and it is this that must not be permitted to disturb Sammy Mikhael's allegory of emergence through becoming an instance.

In the 1950s, conditions in the transition camps were often poor and politically tumultuous.[30] Although demonstrations and protests ended, at times, in violent confrontations with the police, there were nevertheless reforms and occasional allocations by the government of resources to improve living conditions. But what is more important from the point of view of the immigrants themselves is that in these struggles they established new forms of political organization. For example, the Black Panthers emerged in the early 1970s from these struggles, claiming to represent the second generation of political activists in the immigrant community. However, officials and much of the press characterized all protest as "riot" and all immigrant politics as having been instigated by "thugs" or by anti-Zionist "elements" such as the Israeli Communist party. At times, officials hinted that such activities could only help "the Arabs."[31]

Mikhael avoids all of this in his depiction of the immigrant communities, conveying an impression of "good Sepharadi" for whom an Ashkenazi reader might have compassion for the injustice that had been done and respect for the stoicism with which they face the conditions of their lives. Mikhael's elision of politics is part of a yet greater, though ambivalent, purification of the utopian vision.

It so happened that David lost his job on the eve of the 1967 war, and then, as a reservist, was called into the army. His loss of moral stature in civil life is more than compensated for in his life as a soldier. His military experience radically departs from that of civil life, constituting not only a transformation of identity but the achievement of definite status against which civilian life is morally inferior. Entrance to utopia is, in itself, sufficient to fulfill it in one's lifetime. In a sense, David outgrows the civilian world, is in effect relieved of it: like a bar mitzvah, which brings the boy immediately into the world of authority and praxis, his entrance into the army constitutes both an end and a beginning, like the mere fact of Jewish Israel, itself a moment of originality and perfection.

The novel ends when the family, including David's ex-wife Margalit and their eight-year-old son Shai, attends the ceremony in which he receives his award for heroism. In the midst of the festivities, during which they are declared to be "a family of two heroes," the author's voice is heard attempting finally to clarify the connection between the novel as the author's idea and the written text that belongs only to the reader. David says, for Mikhael, with some bitterness,

> I received a document which establishes and testifies that I am an Israeli citizen. For the first time I behave as a citizen whose skin color does not constitute an impediment for him, as if it were a physical defect. For this, I had to go through a baptism of fire in war, and to hand over my beloved wife to another. . . .
>   Do I forgive?
>   Days will tell.[32]

Even though politics was erased, memory remains, at least under the surface of satisfaction. The sense of a predicament reemerges, a reflection on time and what it threatens to remove from self-consciousness. Thus, at the end, which is almost an unalloyed beginning, there is the possibility of a futility thought to have been dispelled by the incessant utopian appeal to unity. With this comes an implicit acknowledgment that utopia is still only a project, and the final means for its attainment remain hidden. Room is yet left for compassion and for criticism, but much remains hidden and uncertain.

Israel's wars are represented monumentally in Hebrew literature. Protagonists go to war, reflect on war, return from war, or are lost in battle, and these are not just conditions of their lives so much as what gives those lives meaning, and therefore, more generally, what constitutes meaningfulness in life itself. In any case, there is a greater memory constituted than mere survival or death. But, strangely enough, there are no true military conquests in these representations, and no others besides "us" whose fate is at issue, no practical interests or reasons involved. These are never merely wars "of position" or instances of "war" as such. The Jewish Israeli soldier is *away*, not *in* one place or another. He or she engages specific enemies in a battle of life and death in which the ultimate protagonist is utopia, something greater than the person or even than the state. While the Arab armies appear screaming, "*Etbakh! Etbakh! Etbakh!*"[33] Jewish Israeli soldiers are depicted inexorably moving forward, their deeds more important than words. Although they leave the battlefield with their enemies lying dead at their feet and with their heroes well defined, they never gloat. Jewish Israeli soldiers reflect only on their duty, rarely on the actual process of battle, and never on those they have destroyed.

> They sleep like reluctant fighters tired of war. Israel's soldiers do not return triumphant. They come home sighing with relief, there to count those who have fallen. They lick their wounds and try to suppress the terrifying sights from their consciousness. (p. 194)

Indeed, one finds a duality in all of Israeli literature analogous to that which forms the structure of Mikhael's novel, the opposition it constitutes between the author's idea and what the reader can apprehend. The former is utopian, and its futility is reflected in a constant tendentiousness in the author's prose. The latter, reading, is an experience, what Sartre calls "totalization," praxis beyond control. The idea leaves war as a moment of greater realization. Reading can hardly avoid its own memory of what is lost to the time of this realization.

Regardless of its compromises, and perhaps because of the way in which it manifests this unavoidable duality, *All Men Are Equal* challenges Zionism in ways not at all typical of Israeli Hebrew fiction. Its reluctance to acknowledge in the idea the past that is nevertheless inscribed in its text makes its own demand on the reader, but imperfectly so. It remains tied to the utopianism that Zionism increasingly identifies with its military project. The Israeli Hebrew reader is, because of the peculiarities of Israeli culture, a self-typifying reader. That is, Israelis read as tendentiously utopian as their writers write. As a result, one can see at least a possible, even likely, reception in the consensus-affirming attributes that are evident in such texts, those features that are on the surface and therefore taken for granted in the course of reading. Yet, the movement of reception, reading, cannot fully evade what the text demands be evaded. It is in this sense, that of an irreducible interaction of text and reading, that the novel provokes precisely the challenge that conservative Zionists fear. But in its cultural presence, as a book, a totality driven by a telos, the novel's effect is otherwise. It is the interaction of the two that makes it, simultaneously, critically ambiguous and uncritically certain.

Nevertheless, the subtlety of its valences tends to release the reader from the persistence of memory all too easily, especially in the context of so compelling a narrative and its allegory of spiritual striving. But this subtlety finally leaves unquestioned the military presence that embodies the Zionist utopian project. Mikhael's *writing* challenges Zionism in principle, but his *narrative* has left its most general principles intact. *All Men Are Equal* is counterhegemonic in principle, but that effect is limited, as it could only be, by the hegemonic culture into which it is invested. Though it leads the reader to the singular moral authority of the Jew, it nevertheless leaves that Jew, as reader, in the midst of contradictions, at the very edge of what Zionism tries to contain.

8

On the Morning of the *Aqedah*

The Author and His Novel

Albert Swissa was born in Casablanca, Morocco, in 1959. His family immigrated to Israel in 1962, and was settled in a newcomers' neighborhood in Jerusalem called Yir Ganim C'. His elementary and high school education was (Ashkenazi) Orthodox and Hasidic. He graduated from a *hesder yeshiva*.[1] But at age twenty-three Swissa abandoned his Orthodoxy and went to Paris, where he studied pantomime with Etienne Decaruox and eventually joined a traveling theater group. He has lived in Paris since 1985 and is currently studying movement and theater. *Aqud* is his first novel.[2]

Aqud comprises three parts, each of which can stand by itself. The first, titled "Aqud," is the shortest and can be read as a short story. The second, titled "Blessed Orphanhood," is a novella, and the third, "A False Effort of a Fading Memory," occupies the bulk of the book. The three together make one narrative set in a community of Jewish immigrants from North Africa. Initially placed in transition camps in Jerusalem, they were moved during the early 1970s from asbestos huts to a newly built neighborhood. By all accounts, this resembled a penitentiary, or area of containment. It was laid out in three distinct zones called Yir Ganim A', B', and C'.[3] The constraints of this setting constitute a first principle of unity in the novel. A second is found in the life of the three main protagonists, Yohai, Beber, and Ayiush.[4] They are children, not yet thirteen years old, and they provide the perspective and voice of the victims and heroes of *Aliyah*. Growing up in the newly built slum neighborhoods, they witness the sacrifice of their community to an ideal and, at the same time, are exemplary figures of its survival. The sacrifice and the struggle, the third principle of unity, are configured as a condition of bondage (*aqud*) and an obligation to wait. The protagonists define a zone of conflict, hence freedom, in the prison in which they find themselves, without preparation and for reasons they cannot understand. This struggle for emancipation can be challenged only ironically. The only available weapon for their struggle is a carefully contrived and disguised defiance—defiance of authority, and through that the development of a sense, often vague and inchoate, of both the oppressiveness of authority and how their knowledge of it constitutes their own power.[5]

Critics on Guard

Whereas Sammy Mikhael's *All Men Are Equal* was perceived, at least by some, as a daring attempt to "redeem the Second Israel from an acceptance of a conspiracy of silence," *Aqud* was said to be sensationalistic, culturally irrelevant, and without significant context. Apart from prejudice, this judgment depended for its justification primarily on the latter, the lack of explicit reference to context already taken as the essential frame for significant Israeli Hebrew literature. Without context, it was easy to find that the novel was pointless, about nothing but itself. I will try to show that *Aqud* is about resistance, and that it incorporates a context capable of supporting this reading, though it does not refer directly to it. Many of Swissa's critics, having failed to see context, failed to recognize that the characters were in fundamental opposition to its terms with or without consciousness of what their words and deed amounted to. From this, it was easy to see only self-indulgence in Swissa's characters, and in Swissa himself. Thus, they argue that his writing is pretentious, imitative, even coquettish, and that *Aqud*'s narrator is "artificial and hollow," the narration itself enveloped in an "Amazonian flowery rhetoric." But if this "style" is in fact itself a matter of substance, if it is appropriate as part of the author's subject, then such criticisms are misleading and beside the point. I will attempt to show that the speech of the narrator displays in its own rhetorical movement the struggle of the children to find meaning in their lives, when none is given from the outset, when they must find it in life itself. Thus, they are candid rather than merely obstreperous, and their refusal to conform to norms is their way of reflecting on both the arbitrariness of what are pronounced as standards and the fact that the norms, the law, hide a repression, that of power. They invent their own language of resistance, performatives, including gestures, that spoil the rituals by which memory is ordinarily neutralized and made to occlude access to what is honest and creative in life.

One distinguished critic, Ariel Hirschfeld, was offended by constant references in the novel to the scatalogical, as if victims should act only with the decorum and sensibility of the culture to which they are being sacrificed.[6] Hirschfeld finds such references, to shitting and peeing, particularly offensive when they come from members of the Moroccan Jewish community: "Of all the ethnic groups" in Israel, he says,

> the most ethnic is the Moroccan. This group intensified its own seclusion from other ethnic groups in the 1960s, turning itself into a spearhead of polarization. The thirst for literary expression which draws its energy from this character type, the discussion of which never lacks racial elements and energies, is immense.

Once having identified "style" with race, and after slighting the work of Erez Biton, a Moroccan Israeli poet, in order to illustrate his point, Hirschfeld goes on to say that the Moroccan ethnicity "has not yet established an artistic presence for the large and significant space it occupies in Israel. An artistic expression of this spirit, relative to the energies it emits in other spheres of . . . activity, has not yet appeared."[7] His point is that *Aqud* is not yet that "artistic expression." Instead, Hirschfeld claims, it "positions itself in the midst of a thirst for expression, as an index of the focal issue of this group—seclusion and repulsion," as if difference were not mediated and the perception of difference not itself an object for critical scrutiny, and as if any genuine expression would have to be external to the condition it expresses.

Hirschfeld accuses the Israeli government and the Jewish Agency of the World Zionist Organization of having been responsible for the "termites nests of exposed concrete; the malignant growths of the social perceptions at the heart of Ben-Gurionist methods of immigrant absorption," which are "suppressive architectural embodiments of statist magnitudes." However, Swissa, he says,

> is at the center of the issue, and he intends a great cry. He directs his vision at the immediate points of violence, not at the Jewish Agency or the Ashkenazim but at parenthood and sexual relations. He identifies properly the real style and disposition of the ethnic base to which he is giving form, never turning his eyes away from the harsh sight of humans on the brink of being animal.[8]

What begins as a universalistic critique of Swissa, that he ignores causes of misery, ends by endorsing a racialist characterization of the victims. Hirschfeld endorses the essentialism of discrimination for the good purpose of marking its oppression. But this undermines that purpose at the moment context includes politics as well as misery, because it excludes the former, leaving the issue of discrimination to be determined by the morality of the very will that discriminates. Policy, he says, is the source of the evil, an evil manifest primarily in the abjectness, total and defining suffering, of the victims. Thus, good can only come from a goodwill outside of the victims, in this case Zionism. Hirschfeld fails to acknowledge the thickly textured racialism intrinsic to Zionist exclusionism, and therefore sees *its* victims as victims of something else—ill will or bad decisions. But it is precisely Swissa's refusal to treat the victims as abject, as "on the brink of being animal," that gives his novel its power to disturb even the Zionist liberal and to expose the racialism that lies at the heart of Israeli Zionism, with its finalizing self-righteousness and its complacency about everything but itself.

Even Menachem Peri, *Aqud*'s editor, in his lengthy endorsement on the book's jacket, weakens in the face of so radical a tendency. On the surface, Peri's praise is unqualified, and, so far as this is concerned, Hirschfeld directs his wrath at Peri as ferociously as he does at the novel itself, accusing him of pretending critical detachment from what he wishes to sell.[9] Peri is the editor of the literary series that includes *Aqud*. His endorsement (signed "M.P.") is as long as a book review, and its intent is, understandably, to promote the book and the series. Other critics have attacked Peri in the same vein, accusing him of deception in promoting new writers who "do not yet 'deserve' it."[10] The real casualties of this debate—which is beside the point—have been the author and his novel. As in many such instances, the author became a cause célèbre and the significance of his novel was thereby removed from the discussion of literature and displaced to the more familiar and conventional discourse of propriety.[11] What is important as far as the novel itself is concerned, however, is not whether Peri was or was not trying to promote "his" author, but what he claims for the novel as context. Like Hirschfeld, Peri ignores what is most radical in *Aqud*, and for the same reason. He writes that "despite its materia,[12] *Aqud* is not a socioethnic novel," but a book about psychopathology: "Ayiush, in his refusal to accept the loss of his childhood, flees away from his 'bar mitzvah' to an amoral world, loses his mind, and probably commits suicide." Nor is it only Ayiush who is disturbed. Peri refers to

> the father, having had his own weakness exposed to his son, is also the son's object of love; the boys' difficulty in separating their personalities from their feminism; the father's feelings of guilt about having allowed his fatherhood to atrophy, by relinquishing paternal authority to his son; the romantic preserva-

tion of a lost childhood that turns into a concealed scroll torn to pieces by memory; an abject enjoyment of self-humiliation, among fathers too. A childhood from which one refuses to separate is also a world despairing in its cruelty. It is part of a spiral repetition. . . . The new reality where fathers cannot find their place is, in fact, a repetition of what happened to them "there . . . ";[13] and the fathers' finalizing emigration from one world to another is a metaphor for the "emigration" of adolescents.

The strategy of seeing derangement instead of perception, madness instead of honesty, is a familiar weapon in the defense of any status quo. Neither Swissa's editor, Peri, nor Hirschfeld has been able to acknowledge the deeply critical aspect of *Aqud*, the latter because of his overemphasis on ethnicity and therefore style, and the former because of what appears to be a desire to neutralize the novel's demands on the culture of oppression. What is lost to the critic is the reason of the author: lacking ethnic authenticity, his characters are simply of no account. What is lost to the editor is the reason of the characters: the context in which they create their lives is merely incidental.

If context is significant in this novel, and if the characters are truly cognizant and engaged, then Swissa must be seen as attempting to transcend the otherwise intransigent ideological limitations of Israeli moral discourse. If so, Peri and Hirschfeld must be seen as having neglected their critical responsibility in favor of containing *Aqud*'s counterhegemonic impulse.

It is, then, no wonder that for them the issue of value hangs almost exclusively on Swissa's language, whether taken as style or as symptom. Thus, Peri's endorsement of *Aqud* applauds the intensity of its prose:

> *Aqud* is shocking in its whirlpool of baroquelike language, in its powerful and often cruel depictions of reality, and in the flood of new materials never before seen in Hebrew literature. Swissa opens windows onto broad scenes, composing a great symphony. His language is wonderfully free, marvelously picturesque. At the same time, he shows a profound sensitivity to the multigenerational layers of the Hebrew language, which he displays fluently at his will.

Hirschfeld, on the other hand, finds in that same prose a profound failure:

> Albert Swissa presents the bitter, thorny, biting, and violent world of the Moroccan ethnic community through a contrived and empty narrator who wraps himself in Amazonian flowery rhetoric . . . , ugly waterfalls of "beautiful" words and Hazaz's[14] style of syntax. Swissa's narrator collects, uncritically and with bad taste, the panoply of styles of Hebrew fiction writers: S. Yizhar, Shamir, Oz, Kahana-Carmon, and A. B. Yehoshua. And he clutters his novel with them in an enormous effort to find favor.

But it is *voice* and not *words* that must be seen as defining *Aqud* as a novel of struggle. Throughout the entire book, the narrator speaks in the third person, never as a character. Thus the narrator is not a child, though he speaks sympathetically of and with the children. Sometimes these children express themselves directly from a perspective possible only from within the narrator's retrospection. This device in no way undermines, trivializes, or otherwise reduces the force of what the protagonists reveal about their universe. Indeed, it constitutes that force. The voice is that of the children, though the self-consciousness of voice itself is the narrator's.

Self-Emancipating Language

Perhaps the greatest surprise posed by *Aqud* to the Israeli Hebrew reader is its occasional secularization of a religious language ordinarily used for traditional purposes in order to declare a unity not possible for Swissa's characters. Yet Swissa does not desecrate religion. He is neither contemptuous nor, even for a moment, condescending. On the contrary, the integral reverence of Swissa's protagonists for religion is never in question. What is remarkable about his prose, so startlingly realistic to Peri and so dishonestly mannered to Hirschfeld, is that the children apply revered cultural references to their own gutter reality. What makes this an instance of self-emancipation rather than merely disrespect is that they are aware of the tension between the immediacy of their reality and the infinitely mediated meaningfulness of the religious referents. They intend that tension; they intend to grasp it as such and at all cost, because only by that grasp can they achieve their own voice, cunning and ironic and filled with the knowledge that the world of form is a sham.

Admittedly, the "abuse" of so traditional a language can only annoy proponents of "high culture." But for the children it is the expression of praxis, a going beyond what is expected; as such, its fluency is driven by humor. From this point of view one can only empathize with the children and rejoice in their ingenuity. Even for their parents, for whom religion is part of self-preservation, a form of personal and communal memory, any ordinary use of religious language tends to be somewhat reactionary. In the old country, their own attitudes had been fairly liberal and, at least to some extent, liberating. And there is a gendered aspect to this. Liberalism is personified in the narrative first and foremost by the women, the wives and mothers whose daily routines are seen to express a freedom only degrees removed from that of the children. The sensuousness of their movements and the intensity of their conversation are an ever-present background to the more overtly experimental

lives of their children. This is a freedom unthinkable in the traditional Ashkenazi home, or for that matter in any "dignified" Western home, a point made
by Yehudit Orian:

> One of the most boisterous chapters is that which depicts the extremely direct
> femininity of the Moroccan mother: her warm and broad bosom, the noisiness
> and bustle of a multiparous woman . . . whose motherhood is natural and real-
> ized without special exertions regarding her destiny. . . . Ayiush's mother
> together with her women friends comprise a kind of naughty mothers' harem
> laden with physical and erotic expression. The North African family is repre-
> sented as the ideal place to grow up without wounds.[15]

The liberalism of even the men of such families is illustrated in *Aqud* more
concretely by an episode in which a father looks at his twelve-year-old son,
whom he loves and of whom he is very proud. He is reminded of "the salon
parties in the company of handsome old men in Casablanca and Agadir, with
their well-tended silver, shiny moustaches, their glorious white hair, their
flourishing and perfumed coiffure; not the superfluous old men they are now"
(p. 51). In her commentary on *Aqud*, the critic Ariana Melamed describes the
metamorphosis of these men as a result of their move from Agadir to Yir
Ganim: "superfluous old men covered from head to foot with their black *jalabiyas*,[16] like . . . silent monks rotting in the synagogues located in bomb shel-
ters, and who are an embarrassment to the intermediate generation of parents
of these children."[17]

Swissa's own life provides a measure of support for the possibility of liberalism in the midst of religiosity. Commenting on his interview with Swissa,
Yigal Sarna writes that the author's father, a dentist, is strictly Orthodox and
has never read his son's book. Yet his mother reads "the lustful Henry Miller,"
and it was she who sent her son's first short story to a publisher. Swissa says
that a couple such as his parents, a strictly Orthodox man and a liberated
woman, is possible only in Morocco: "How greatly my father loves this woman
who is so different from him, and how tolerant he is despite being otherwise so
closed."[18]

The children of *Aqud* engage their situation not only through their secularization of traditional language, but by transforming its concepts. For example,
they occasionally summon mythological figures from the Bible and personify
them in order to share their tribulations. The result of this is a demystification
of tradition in favor of affirming life as it must, in any case, be lived.

Like Swissa, the children were raised in homes in which love was expressed
physically and with sensuous affection, especially by their mothers. But home

was overburdened by too many children in too little space, and by a degree of scarcity and disorder imposed from outside. The fathers' traditional authority had no base in the camps and later in the settlement zones. The children had no choice but to maintain their dignity with whatever resources they could find on their own. Educated in schools not of their parents' choosing, they gradually became aware that, for society, theirs were lives of degradation and violence. They understood that this was neither their fault nor the fault of their parents. The uncollected garbage and junk scattered around the streets of their fragile community show how little they count in the greater scheme of society, and their discourse conveys this knowledge.

The mayor of the city is always mentioned with irony. For example, in one episode he fails to show up for the scheduled inauguration of a street, which in any case did not occur. This indifference is sufficient to convince the children that their parents also do not count, anymore than their own lives have meaning, beyond the need to control, to their teachers, social workers, and other officials who represent the "system." The expressions are, then, products of an experience of dissociation from society, an experience that forces them to reflect on what others may take for granted. Thus, when Yohai and his father, Mr. Pazuelo, walked together[19] through the borough, they saw it as something "the dreaming heart needed actually to touch each time anew in order to realize in sorrow that this place was real and not merely built as a training field for bombing exercises" (p. 27).

One needs to listen to as well as read, almost enunciate with, the text, to see how the children's speech synchronizes with even their most profane acts, constituting an internal relation of thought and voice.

> [Yohai] had to shit, and he so much enjoyed shitting in empty lots. In empty lots no one could disturb him while he was shitting and telling himself stories, fondling, almost involuntarily, his member. The water in the puddle was terribly cold and it cooled his excitement to lower his pants. (p. 15)

Here shitting is poignantly subjective, a life-affirming act, a matter of praxis. It also evokes context and history in the midst of what is ordinarily permitted neither to be seen nor heard. Hirschfeld is shocked:

> The protagonists' emotional-sexual world in *Aqud* (it is hard to apply a word like love to this novel. The word "erotic" seems to have been borrowed too from another weird evolutionary stage) circles like a moth around an anus and from there it widens onto a whole ideational world—from the boys' and couples' buttock hills to the "Ass Mountain" and "Prick Mountain" of the mountains all around. His [Swissa's] anility oozes into everything. . . . The protago-

nist touches himself only when he squats to shit in the fields surrounding the neighborhood.[20]

However, imagine these lives depicted without reference to bodily functions. They would then appear ethereal and with only abstract intentionality divorced from the physical, material existence to which Swissa wishes to draw attention and, in doing so, to present as a material base of their reflection on oppression and freedom.[21]

I will discuss later and in greater detail the significance of such terms as "Ass Mountain" and "Prick Mountain" and the choices of names in *Aqud*. The situation of Yohai meditating while shitting is rendered poetically. We follow him on a harsh winter day, out of school because his father has granted him a day of grace before the execution of a punishment he is to receive for a gross transgression. He spends his morning hours of that fateful day alone in the open spaces. When we listen to how he perceives nature, the way he paints it with his eyes, the way he participates in it, we almost envy him. Paddling in the water with his little rubber boots, trying to make waves, he observes the sky:

> The white enveloping furnace steam flying swiftly in the wind, tarrying once in a while and creating gray-blue and deep blue swirls. Then the firmament split as a jet of shiny light sliced the world from one end to the other. (p. 14)

Yohai removes a sandwich from his pocket, about a third of a loaf of bread smeared with gravy. In his other hand he holds an unpeeled cucumber. He bites dreamily, once into the bread and then into the cucumber.

> A thin rain began falling. Not far away a mosque minaret jutted up, exposed to the sky. Birds in formation circled toward it, dividing into two groups and coming to rest on cypress tops near by. (p. 14)

This is the context in which Yohai shits, as it were, so eloquently. It gives shitting a significance beyond what it could have to the abstracting eye overly focused on the mere behavior. Consider in this same regard the intensity and love with which Yohai watches birds, and most of all the *nakhlieli*:[22]

> That's exactly, that's what I need. *Nakhlielim*, or a song about *nakhlielim*; And how much he likes flowers, and most of all *rakafot* [cyclamen], or a song about *rakafot*, or to collect them. When would he come back to collect *rakafot*? He will come back, he will;[23] what does it matter to collect, but the craziest thing is to be shitting next to *rakafot*. (p. 18)

The shift from "I" to "he" causes the narrator and the character to coalesce, and gives Yohai's desires the force of a reflection.

There is a temporal dimension to this reflection that has a beginning but no end. Yohai wishes for torrential rain to fall, to return home wet to his bones.

> His mother would slap his frozen cheeks, and then would sit him next to the kerosine heater, to warm up; and he would stare with wonder into the blue flame that would dry his socks and shoes.

When he finally does return home,

> his mother accepted him with a tormented and silent face. She put her baby daughter down, almost threw her on the bed, returned a puffed breast to her robe, and ran to him immediately. For him she was like a wild indifferent cat that already knew the boys in the neighborhood, and carried her kittens in the streets by her teeth. "Pity, pity, you've no heart," she said, while roughly removing his wet clothes, almost plucking his head from his shoulders. "He hadn't even breakfast for his sorrow. And working, he's working well [meaning "hard"] from dawn till night. May the Evil Eye have no power over him. Why he, he would've given his eyes for his father, blessed be his memory. Never mind, never mind, to-mo-rrow, *ya bnini*,[24] ev-ery-thing, eve-ry thing'll be all right." (p. 16)

Violence and Discovery

This unqualified love, this affirmation, despite everything, is of course nowhere else to be found. In school, Ayiush says, "we were taught a poem about *Lake Kinneret*. But we were also taught the *Shulhan Arukh*."[25] Teachers "would use red ink to grade us." Teachers also intruded without feeling into the children's "most cherished secrets." Thus, the children were confronted at all times with the need to lie and, at the same time, with the "tastelessness of lying." This was not for the obvious reasons, but because they, Ayiush says, hated having lies "forced" out of them, to have no choice but to lie because, cruelly, "a demand to speak truthfully was assumed in advance, and taken for granted." Eventually Ayiush becomes fond of lying, "the way they were once fond of telling the lies that were called legends." He too came to "tell legends and tales to all those who had gloomy faces," as a kind of escape (p. 150).

One of these "escapes" was the neighborhood movie theater. To afford it, Ayiush had to barter his bus ticket or his lunch. Then, he would walk to school through unfriendly territory, where he would have to confront hostile youth gangs or vicious dogs. One morning, as so often was the case, Ayiush was late to school. He entered his class and walked to his seat as if no one would notice. When his teacher, Mr. Lintzinski, got no response to his inquiry as to why Ayiush was late, Lintzinski grabbed the child's finger and started squeezing it in front of the class. In his agony, Ayiush took flight by becoming a character from a western movie starring Juliano Jema and Lee Van Cleef. Bearing his pain nobly, as such a character might, he mumbled something the teacher could not hear. Lintzinski intensified the pressure on Ayiush's finger and, as the pain worsened, Ayiush began to shout and make noises as if he were shooting, aiming with his free hand at the class and moving his body as if he were riding a horse. The pain finally became unbearable. Suddenly, Ayiush screamed, "You're a fuckin' blond and blue-eyed girl, yeh." Angered, the teacher maintained the pressure on Ayiush's finger. "I'm rraapping her . . . !" "What's that!?" screamed the teacher. Ayiush responded, "Rapping, rapping her, don't you understand . . . ?" Suddenly the teacher released the throbbing finger. "Then Ayiush leaned his pain-racked body against the teacher's desk and the class fell into a long gloomy silence" (pp. 152–56).

Ayiush's capacity to visualize an alternative world at a moment's notice allows him, in this instance as at other times, to assert a self where no self could otherwise be permitted. It exemplifies one way in which myths are transformed into what James Scott calls "weapons of the weak."[26] This reading is quite at odds with Batia Gur's extension of Hirschfeld's thesis. She concludes that "these children's reality is characterized by expressions of violent and animal-like cruelty," and that they preoccupy themselves with "humiliating, filthy, sexual games lacking tenderness." Yet, in contrast with Hirschfeld, Gur argues that Swissa represents the Ashkenazi world itself "as threatening," suggesting at least a modicum of rationality in the children's own apparent violence and cruelty.[27]

It is instructive at this point to consider the writer's own statements about the violence depicted in his own novel. In his interview with Swissa, Yigal Sarna raises questions about the "gang wars" and the emphasis in the novel on the violence of the children and their parents. Swissa replies that on the contrary, he

> decided not to write directly about violence. This was my decision. And I kept [the narrative] clean of violence for a purpose, since writing about it is like writing about love only as fucking. I think that both violence and love always stem from a much wider reality of emotions and climate. This book is my own emotional memory, my cultural and moral memory of that place and time. It is like having someone being cruel to another, and suddenly having compassion for one being cruel.

Sarna insists: "Did you purify the past? Do you build reality anew when you cleanse it of violence? Do you create—like a little god—another world?" Swissa responds:

The violence you are talking about appears as such from an external perspective, that of a Western person. When I lived there under those rules, it looked different to me. An animal in the jungle does not think it lives in a cruel world. From my experience I knew that that world was governed by a very strong emotional and moral system, something we, as Westerners, ignore right now as we talk. There is here, in this country [Israel], a denial of the innermost things which inhabit the Eastern emotional and intellectual world.[28]

This is why Ayiush's reaction to the teacher's violence is almost biblical in its passion. It reflects the heightened subjectivity of one who has been placed by violence beyond violence, who knows violence in its essence as merely a presence, as part of a moral universe that the teacher could scarcely grasp. Thus, his teacher could not be satisfied no matter what Ayiush did. He persisted in demanding that Ayiush explain his lateness, as if it had been the result of a decision, and as if being late reflects in itself *indifference* to norms and rules, the worst sort of transgression. "Ayiush took a heavy breath, the way children do because of their anger before they cry." Now, ready for revenge, he invented a fantastic story.

> Well, . . . so that's the way it was. On my way to school I saw a city gardener removing a strange lizard with yellow stains from a shrub fire. She was twisting in pain against the stick that he held against her belly. . . . So, when I approached the fire . . . , he told me [imitating an old and painfully excited gardener], that he had saved this poor lizard from the fire but that she insisted like a mad thing on going back into the fire. . . . Wait, wait, let me finish. He suddenly turned impatiently [to the teacher] as if they were friends. Then, "salamander," I shouted to him, this is a salamander! And it is written that she lives in fire. . . . It is. . . . it is . . . It's like taking a fish out of the water! I told him. He began to retreat. "You're torturing her." He was somewhat confused but he let the animal go free, and that. . . . And she turned on her feet, and sprang forth into the fire, sort of struggling in the coals 'till she actually got into the flames. . . . And there she sat in the coals, looking fearfully at me and then at the gardener. And we stood stunned over the fire . . . 'till we realized that we had been mad. We ran and brought more wood and shrubs so that she could live longer. That's it. This is it then. That's the reason that this is a very strange thing, and it doesn't happen to me every day. Th-i-s i-s w-h-y I w-a-s la-t-e! (p. 155)

Here Ayiush attempts to transcend his predicament by creating a universe beyond the need to make excuses, beyond the obligation to beg for forgiveness. What he cannot explain, why it was *necessary* to be late, he places beyond explanation, in the perspective of a tale in which lateness becomes irrelevant. In other words, here is Ayiush speaking in the deconstructive voice of the subaltern, beyond the knowledge of those who would rather put him in "his place" within what they cannot know. Within the subaltern world of the children, moral order is constituted by the pleasure they take in each other, and in the self-conscious pleasure they take in their own discourses. They respond to each others' pains, and soothe each others' wounds, for example, by spitting on dust and placing it like glue on those wounds, or by using spices and arrack, which they take "from their own homes, to stop the bleeding." Much of their tussling has to do with honor, but not the prideful honor of the truly self-alienated. Theirs is an honor that can, at least in principle, be shared. It reflects the violence of the world around them within the community of resistance that it valorizes.

For example, the leader of their band is David Ben Shushan, a lad of "spiritual elation who took his inspiration from the Bible." David designates from among the group military officers, judges, and consultants. Yohai, who always wears a headband around his shaven head and is known as a courageous fighter, is nominated to be second in command. One day, Muizo, another member, neglects his duty. The others unanimously vote, in a secret trial, that rather than being "excommunicated,"[29] Muizo should be punished and made to renew his oath of loyalty. David Ben Shushan says:

> Ya know, when Abraham our father made his servant Eliezer swear to him, ya know that he told him to hold his prick when he swore? Ben Shushan got excited and opened his eyes wide. "*Hakham* [sage, teacher] Ya'kub, my uncle, told me—all right, he didn't tell me but he sort of pointed at the *Rashi* commentary[30] where it is written—that he took it in his hand." He pointed his finger to heaven and posed for the sake of impression, "That's how Muizo will be punished and he is going to swear on my prick." (p. 12)

Yohai's father punishes him for participating in Muizo's punishment, sentencing him to exile in boarding school. The gang had forced Muizo to drink Yohai's urine. When the outraged parents and older brothers assembled to find out who was responsible, Muizo pointed at Yohai; and none of the others, neither the children nor those parents who knew the truth, had the courage to challenge David. Yohai realizes that he is to be the only one to take the blame, despite the fact that everyone knows he had not acted alone. His understanding that he is the victim of David's cowardice, and the cowardice of the others, including his own father, reflects his knowledge of how separate the world of the children is from that of the adults. He is willing to accept cowardice from the children because of their need for self-protection. However, the cowardice of the adults is, he can only conclude, merely part of their nature, their way of repudiating community in favor of power. Yet, despite his acceptance of unfair condemnation by his chums, his refusal to repudiate the community they share, he now knows that he is alone.

When he and his father arrive at Bnei-Brak, his place of exile, he finds it as strange as the sound of its name.[31] He enters the basement where the Orthodox boarding school is located, and suddenly knows that he faces far greater danger there than he had in Yir Ganim. Yohai finds the mutual flattery with which his father and the Moroccan *hakham*, who heads the institution, greet each other strange and frightening.

While they complete the admission formalities, they leave Yohai unattended for a moment or two. He immediately takes flight. The horrors he goes through in his escape, and his courage, are beyond what could be told simply. By the end of the day, exhausted and lost in what seems to be a larger city, Yohai is approached by an old man who speaks broken Hebrew with a Central European Ashkenazi accent. Yohai is suspicious but lacks the energy to resist the man's entreaties. The man treats him to a cake and a sweet selzer drink at a cheap coffee shop. Then, he takes Yohai onto his lap and plays with him as if he were a baby, caressing his face and saying, "You're still smooth, little boy. I likes brown boys. In Poland there is no brown boys." Suddenly Yohai vomits. Confused, the old man offers him another selzer, because "carbonated water helps to relieve gases from the stomach." He buys Yohai a lollipop and takes him by the hand to a cinema. Inside, it is dark and quiet, with only a few people in the audience. On the screen, a man and a woman scream at each other. When the man hits her she laughs, and even seems to enjoy it. Holding the lollipop in one hand, Yohai "felt in his other a soft thing, hairy and sticky; but he did not bother to check it out, since his eyes were closing into a deep slumber. He felt himself falling endlessly through a narrow passage lit by a bright light that had no source" (p. 27).

Yohai's escape takes him momentarily into a dark world of fantastic images, alluring sweets, and dull assurances, a world of few consolations and certainty none without debt. It is this that makes his caresses of the old man's penis as he drifts off to sleep something other than merely exploitation and abuse. A less ambiguous, less "deviant" rescuer would, under the circumstances and given all that has happened, have been pathetic, the episode off-color and sentimental. As such, it would have betrayed what the novel has already established as basic to Yohai's world and as conditions under which he could transcend it and in that transcendence find himself. For Swissa, for the struggle he attempts to elucidate, the dispositions of any single character, including the old man, are less important than what those dispositions become, what meaning they have, in the situation. The use of Yohai by the old man is part of a rescue, and therefore is for the boy a moment of consolation, though one laced, to be sure, with ambivalence.

This is not the only instance of so mixed a consolation in the text. There is another case, what critics labeled "the rape," in which one boy seduces another. In the third part of *Aqud*, Beber Sultan, after an earlier tender and mutually endearing sexual encounter with his stepsister, Yvonne, seduces Ayiush. Unlike Yvonne, Ayiush is unprepared and innocent, a gentle child bewildered by the feminine aspect within him. Beber undoubtedly takes advantage of Ayiush. But though this is not the beginning of a relationship, it is not merely a one-time event. Thus, Ayiush's feelings are necessarily ambivalent. In reference to this experience he speaks of Beber as a "criminal," yet he is offended by what he feels to be Beber's indifference, as if the two had truly shared an affection bordering on love. This ambivalence, like Yohai's about his rescuer, reflects the inevitable ambiguity of consolation in a world like the children's, fraught with multiple meanings and incapable of providing unequivocal satisfaction.

What arouses compassion for these children, rather than sympathy or pity, is their capacity to remain critically reflective, and their interest in right and wrong. By its emphasis on the children's reason, the rationality of their struggle, *Aqud* reverses the normal paternal order by imposing on the dominant moralism the existentially authentic social morality of self-discovery.

When Batia Gur says that, in *Aqud*, the "Ashkenazi world is represented as threatening, and, is derided," she fails to acknowledge that by placing that world at issue, Swissa reveals one that had been suppressed. Yet even then, the dominant world, the world of domination, is given its due. The children respect the fathers even as they separate from them, and Swissa respects the fathers' world even as he writes against its grain. Thus, as Yohai sits next to his father on the bus to Bnei-Brak:

> His father never ceased to surprise him. His movements were so guarded, so modest and personal, that every gesture came as a precious rarity. A thousand times he offered his son a peeled orange, and a thousand times he thrilled him. The boy licked his fingers and searched for something to say to him. Haa, yes, he'd ask him about a biblical matter: for example, what did Isaac think on the morning of the *Aqedah*? But he didn't; his father was immersed in travel prayers, and when he finished he took out a miniature Psalm Book and began to read. The boy determined that his father was *Tsadik*, more than *Tsadik*. (p. 19)[32]

Similarly, on the same day, at morning prayers, the boy looks at his father, thinking that "there is none in the world who can grace him with the look his father gives him every so often, a compassionate look, quiet and attentive, a look that says, beware and watch your soul, that's all you have in the world, and that's not much either" (p. 12).

This respect is returned in similarly small but significant ways. Even in the midst of guilt at having betrayed his son, Yohai's father reflects on his decision to punish the boy, saying, "I am not asking any favors of this world. All I'm trying to do is to prevent misfortune." Indeed, the children's world appears throughout the novel to include the parents. The lines drawn are not simply generational, though they are partly that. This is clear in the first part of the novel. At a certain moment, Yohai thinks of what his father had been like when he was his age, and he says: "He used to walk behind a donkey as an apprentice. And at the end of every six months he would return to his own father, kiss his hand, and hand him the money bag." Then Yohai adds that his father "had no fantasy in his youth, nor did he play in gangs" (p. 15).

This history, so sober and so different from Yohai's experience, comes back to him during his exile.

> [He] was surprised to see his father's ancient suitcase, which he had used when working as a dentist. For many years it contained his tools, which lay like unturned stones in the cupboard containing the Passover utensils. For his mother, giving the suitcase to Yohai was a sign of . . . [her] dream that [her husband] might return one day to his old profession. She stuffed an old sweater [Yohai] inherited from his father into the suitcase. He stretched out his arm and caressed the suitcase as if it were something marvelous. His mother noticed and said, "*eh oui, c'est la vie*, what used to be mundane will now become holy." And his father was moved and said, "*Ma'alin bakodesh*,"[33] and smiled to himself agreeably. Then he erased the smile from his face, but it still survived for a long time in his eyes. (p. 17)

Interpenetration of Generations

The second part of the novel, titled "Blessed Orphanhood," shows this same awareness of the interpenetration of the generations. The protagonist, Beber, is one of ten children. His mother, Yamna, complains of "the grinding weariness of having been delivered so many. Each delivery brought a 'prince' into the world, or a 'princess' . . . , a king who is not obliged to share the burdens of upkeep, since one father supports ten children while they are not capable of supporting one father" (p. 50). In Morocco, Mr. Sultan made his living selling old cars. Half car thief and half dealer, an urbanite merchant who knew the pleasures and companionship of great cities such as Casablanca and Agadir, he liked to travel to the rural hinterland of the Draa Valley, where his father's family had once lived.

Leticia, whom he had loved, "was the first in the Draa Valley who dared to emphasize the rounded parts of a Moroccan-Jewish woman" by wearing women's clothing "with high shoulders of the kind men wear in the great cities," and skirts which would "strangle her thighs so that she had to shorten her steps and bend her knees" while walking "on very high little red boat shoes that put holes in the dirt road" (p. 42). Leticia "disappeared from the world" ten days prior to the day she was to wed Sultan, eloping with his slave Salman, his "Moroccan Arab servant-partner in his smuggling business," "an ox of a man," the "enslaving slave" (p. 42). No one knew what finally happened to Leticia, but all suspected that Sultan murdered her out of jealousy. There was also a suspicion that Leticia was the mother of the little girl, Yvonne, whom Sultan had saved from an earthquake in Agadir. Yamna, his wife, was Leticia's younger sister.

It was Mr. Sultan who was reminded, while looking at his son (in the episode described above), of the handsome old men in Casablanca and Agadir— in particular of

> the metamorphosis these old men would effect around them from the moment they disembarked, slowly and authoritatively, from their carriages or their long limousines. They induced desires in young women's hearts, desires that were mixed with regret for being so young. They [the women] would urge their young husbands to hurry toward them with a customary flattering smile, to be first to shake and kiss their hands and to be blessed by their manliness. The presence of the old men would validate the wine . . . and the abundance of food and drink on the tables. Their maturity inspired respect from all members of the family, though their wrinkled brows hid, under the pretensions of well-acted fatherliness, an indifference and condescension toward the women. . . . Their eyes shining with alcohol, they would cruelly and impartially spread their philosophical opinions, profoundly contemptuous of the ungrateful world; then they would find it necessary to leave exaltedly and go to their private parties to share the company of Jewish prostitutes. (p. 51)

In all of this, there are sons in fathers and fathers in sons: the rough and iconoclastic Mr. Sultan, the son of his fond regard, and a memory that carries the weight of judgment. Here, in other words, are the life, affirmation, and ambivalence that we have so far seen only in the children.

The third part of Swissa's novel introduces us to the Monsanegor family.[34] Ayiush, the son, is the protagonist. His father, Mr. Monsanegor, had been a textile merchant, later became a book binder, and is now a stone cutter. Ayiush has recurring and disturbing memories of his Arab Muslim nanny and his mother's woman servant, Sulica. The family has a room in the apartment that serves as a kind of a living room "for the days to come." For the time being it is for storage, and is surrounded by a brick wall and fronted by an iron door. There, Mr. Monsanegor has stored all the furniture and expensive household goods that still have some beauty. The furniture, kept under white sheets, was for his older sisters' dowry.

In the parents' bedroom, there are closets and drawers all along the walls, stuffed with "black suits ready for night parties, fragrant perfumes and cosmetics, jewelry of silver and gold, and expensive textiles, preserved for the holiday that will occur when the Messiah comes" (p. 96). This is what remains of the wealth that had been brought from the old country. Much of it has already been pawned to cover "unexpected" expenses. A photograph that has been on the wall in Ayiush's room since he was a baby depicts the family at the time of their arrival in their new country. They are shown

> walking like astronauts in an old legend, legs raised high, careful not to step into the concrete crevices of the dusty dirt road. . . . They have white suitcases and elegant overcoats. . . . His brothers grin. They are sweating in their white woolen suits. His sisters wear sleeveless summer dresses, exposing their full-shaped arms. . . . If his mother were not holding [Ayiush] in her arms, it would have been almost impossible to distinguish her from her daughters, she had been so young and beautiful. [Ayiush's father is missing from the photo.] (p. 227)

These details indicate the social class, the style, and the sense of humor of the family. Above all, the picture is one of what sociologists call a "primary group," a small community of intimates that could exist as such only in the context of a yet greater community that they can take for granted. The depiction is in sharp contrast to Ayiush's later life as an immigrant, but it yields the sense of certain continuity of relations that runs from past to present, constituting a basis for some of the complexity of his reflections on his own youth.

Bondage and Defiance

All three parts of *Aqud* display a common motif: "the bondage" of persons, their coerced adherence to restrictions that leave little room for change and for the expression of self. Yet, they also present both change and the manifestations of self, and a sense of connection that even circumstances so dire cannot erase. The motif draws upon the biblical story of the binding of Isaac by Abraham. In the novel it is repeatedly articulated by a question: "What did Isaac think on the morning of the *Aqedah*?"[35] This, says Menachem Peri, is a

traditional question. As such it is "a 'well-used' theme of Hebrew literature."
But, he adds,

> here there are no fathers who bind their sons on the altar of national self-real-
> ization. Nor is *Aqud*, in spite of its materials, a social-ethnic novel. Its protago-
> nists are "displaced," between childhood and adulthood. The sacrificial altar is
> the "conspiracy" of the adult world, or the trauma of entering it.[36]

However, for the community of immigrants portrayed in *Aqud*, it is not possible for fathers to sacrifice their sons to "national self-realization," if only
because those fathers are not actively included in the project of "national self-
realization." The notion is in any case conceptually foreign to them, and in
terms of their own faith it is a heresy. For this community, sacrifice taken literally is possible only for God. Since Abraham's attempt to sacrifice Isaac,
human sacrifice is not permissible, even metaphorically. A person may choose
to die rather than to desecrate God's name, but this is a very different concept
from that of sacrifice. This difference is suggested in *Aqud* when children
choose to suffer terrible blows when they take God's name "in vain."

On the other hand, the entire community of Yir Ganim is *bound* for
sacrifice, but they cannot know *why* and *for whose sake*. While the children are
also in bondage, they are aware of it, and hold their parents liable for collabo-
rating, as it were, in the *conspiracy* of sacrifice, a judgment nevertheless qualified by compassion for the powerlessness of their parents. The children are,
ultimately, the objects of the project of sacrifice, but they still represent the
possibility of freedom for a community that has itself already been sacrificed.
What they offer is hope for the humanity of the parents when community has
already been lost. And so, the children oppose authority not because they are
nihilists but because they hate the nihilism of enforced passivity, the false
morality of obedience that enjoins passivity.

When, in the third part of the novel, Ayiush's father is summoned to the
school because of his son's behavior, the teacher tells him, condescendingly,
that students "in this school are admitted by grace rather than by right."
Ayiush interrupts: "Do not threaten!" (pp. 165–66). Ayiush had earlier tried
to provide his father with the information he needed to face the teacher with
confidence. But Ayiush finally gave up: "There were more powerful people . . .
who were interested more than anything in law and order, and his father was
their prisoner" (p. 165).

Similarly, in consequence of Yohai's long record of insubordination, in the
first part of the novel, he fears for himself when his father awakens him early in
the morning one cold, rainy winter day.[37] Yet his father touches him tenderly

on his shoulder. Despite the obligation he has to deal with Yohai's naughty behavior, Mr. Pazuelo is "saddened that a child must bear the burdens of grown-ups" (p. 9). Yohai recoils at his father's touch, but then, while still lying under the smelly blanket with his five brothers on either side warming his feet, he watches his father prepare for the day in prayer and by ritual cleansing. The narrator tells us that the "little boy had been taken with a sense of foreboding" that had possessed him "since last night . . . when his father and mother spoke to each other in French." Yohai meditates on his predicament: "What did Isaac think on the morning of the *Aqedah*? He was reminded of the time, last New Year's Day, when he stood next to his father at the rostrum, while his father led the prayers in the synagogue with his supporters on either side." While chanting a prayer, his father had wept in fear of God. Yohai remembers crawling under his father's prayer shawl and clutching his knee.

> The child was panic-stricken. He felt as if he were about to fall. He clung harder to his father's knee, fearing he might lose him. Daddy's about to be slaughtered. They'll slaughter me too. Mother'll cry. Daddy's a criminal. He's not well! Daddy's afraid. Daddy's himself the slaughterer. He's a certified slaughterer. He's slaughtering chickens. He's confessing to a severe crime, very severe, sodomy. For God's sake, give him relief! (p. 10)

The congregation is awed and silent; and in reverence for their leader in prayer, one of his supporters invites the congregation to sing the "*Aqedah*," a liturgical poem based on the story of Abraham and Isaac. Following this scene, Yohai's thoughts wander on:

> In school, they didn't know what Isaac had thought. Abraham was the whole story. But Isaac didn't know where they were going and he asked his father, Abraham, to tell him. And Abraham said that only God knew where a human goes when he is going. But finally, when he was bound, he must have known, because no one binds a human just like that. But the legends claimed that Isaac knew, and that in his righteousness he was happy to be God's sacrifice. (p. 10)

The binding of the child is also bondage for the father. But only the child can reflect on that paradox. Only one who is deliberately bound by others has that right and can reflect on it with clarity. The father's perspective, though he listens to God, is only that, a perspective.

Of course, Yohai's own reflections are not divorced from what is expected of him later in the same day. The presence of his peers at his "trial" justifies Yohai's punishment to him. He identifies with Isaac, and if Isaac survived he probably would too. This is expressed by the narrator as Yohai thinks, "When would he come back to collect *Rakafot*? He will come back, he will" (p. 18).

None of his teachers had ever dared to present such a justification of punishment as for the sake of the community, since the separation of Earth and Heaven must be absolute, analogous to the opposition of power and "subordination" in the secular world. Power justifies itself by reason and telos, subordination only by norm and obligation. *Aqud* is a poetic attempt to reconfigure and thereby overcome these oppositions, in particular the separation within the community and that between it and its world of power. Only doubt, fantasy, and cunning are available as resources for this metaphysical rebellion. In this sense, *Aqud* is a narrative of resistance, qualified though it must be by reference to circumstance and a sense of tragedy.

This is why Yohai elevates his father and himself to the fantastic level of Abraham and Isaac, why he feels free to speculate on his own fate, why he doubts all authority, why he allows himself to refuse and finally to flee. At the same time, he recognizes his father's predicament as analogous to his own. This is a distinctive feature of the novel, the powerlessness of fathers and sons in regard to each other and in the context of power directed from outside against both fathers and sons. But it is a feature that derives from the point of view of the child—the prospect of a critical position beyond the most obvious normative terms of reproach.

Yet, even the fathers occasionally reflect on this, and wonder why they had ever come to this country, this "place." And although Mr. Pazuelo is inhibited in his expression by his awe of the Holy Land (not merely the secular state of Israel), he nevertheless makes his frustration clear, if only against the Ashkenazim from whom he had once expected so much.

> For a moment Mr. Pazuelo was struck by joy at his own calamity. Deep in his heart he rejoiced at their failure. But he was not at ease with such feelings. "Sheer loafers," he said angrily to himself; "education, ha! And they even call that special education!" He detested them, their beards, their side-locks, and their fringed garments which for years had deceived him. (p. 13)

On the other hand, he still

> admired them; they were the Exiles of Exile. They had survived. They do not educate. . . . They are what they are, and what they have always been. He felt some relief in his heart. From now on he will be free of those gatherings that aroused in him such revulsion for and hatred of Israel. Heaven forbid. Never did the school headmaster or the class teacher speak to him privately. There were always two. They would abruptly disrupt the conversation and consult each other in their strange language [as if no one who counted was present]. (p. 13)

Contrary to those who see in Moroccan Jewish culture only "isolationist" tendencies and political ineptitude, it is interesting to consider the force of Mr. Pazuelo's critical meditation and especially that of his skepticism about the Zionist principle that Jews in Israel have "returned from exile." Mr. Pazuelo's perspective is a modernist one focused on secular dynamics, in contrast with what is fixed by God and unmanageable by humankind. This is exemplified when he says that the Ashkenazim are "the Exiles of Exile," because "they are what they are, and what they have always been." In other words, *they do not change*, but for their location. Relative to them, it is he and his community who are in motion, alive, engaged; and it is the world and not God that is the source of life. He does not, however, permit himself to dwell on the implication that the holy (of which he remains in awe) and its putative representatives (whom he doubts) are sources of death. He remembers the play of difference in his old country, where

> the Arabs didn't hate us . . . and at times would show respect for us. They simply wanted our money, nothing else. We had commerce with them. We resembled them in our customs, in our food, in our songs, in our dress, in our marital relationships; and as for God—we were closer to them than to the Christians [i.e., the French colonists]. They used to call us "Yahudin" and we would call them "Muzlemin." (p. 14)

In the midst of his anger and sense of futility, Mr. Pazuelo sees this shared life of diverse communities in a context of power and conquest, far removed from the traditional propaganda of Zionism and its justifications for its wars.

> But here came the godless brothers of the strange Yiddish-speaking Jews who made war and conquered their cities. Now they are anxious to get rid of the Arabs. They find it impossible to tolerate their customs and their culture. . . . It is no wonder that they left their own culture behind them and in its stead took on the culture of wickedness and sin. (p. 14)

It is in this light that Mr. Pazuelo reflects ironically on the delusions of his own community: "And we, he thought, a bewildered multitude, sickening innocents, pitiless, stupid, and unreasoningly blind, we accept the myth of 'the return from Exile'" (pp. 13–14), as if one could "actually" come out of exile and as if the identification of "exile" were without politics.

Ariel Hirschfeld suggests that the bondage motif in *Aqud* has a more restricted meaning, namely,

> the oppression of children by their fathers. In this novel there is the great *Aqedah*, with its principle manifest in the castration scene at the barber's. This scene transforms the violence depicted in the novel to Jewish metaphysical

magnitudes. If Ayiush is to have his bar mitzvah, he must go through a hair-cutting ceremony. This is only the external aspect. The content is the deep and burning insult he suffers at the hand of his father and the entire ethnic society, an insult that is ritualized. Ayiush's flight from this ceremony does not redeem him from his ethnicity. Without the obligatory religious ceremony he is abandoned like an animal, emptied of all context, a sign without signification.[38]

That is, Ayiush must be either inside or outside, and which one depends on his response to the culturally decisive fact of generational difference. If Hirschfeld is correct, these generational relations of a difference resolved through ritual constitute a latent unity that fails only when the individual refuses to be the signifier of the difference. Hirschfeld thinks that Swissa goes too far, makes too much of too little, elevates an individual's protest into an act of metaphysical significance.

But this ritual defines manhood for all Jews. It inscribes the Law, as it were, on the individual, every individual who can and should manifest the Law. It is not specific to the Moroccan community, but is part of all Orthodox Jewish observance, both Sepharadi and Ashkenazi. Ayiush's refusal to have his hair cut, and then the Bar mitzvah itself, is not merely the willful act, understandable though it may be, of an individual. It must be read in the context of the novel, which is a context of a struggle for the attainment of voice of a *community* of speakers. Hirschfeld chooses neither to acknowledge this as a possibility nor to recognize how it is actualized in the novel.

Ayiush's defiance, like Yohai's, must be seen in the context of two struggles, one of a community to survive materially and the other for it to survive as a way of life and as an affirmation of the experiences of its people. The children are both the emblem of and an instrument in those struggles. But they are also the agents of a yet more inclusive struggle of humanity that they represent in their subalterity. The latter is beyond the relative particularisms of generational conflict, ethnicity, and violence. To emphasize only these is to neutralize what is political about *Aqud*, and therefore to read the novel apart from its bearing on the Zionist claim that humanism derives exclusively from the standpoint of the anti-Diasporic Jew. Swissa attempts to demystify Israeli Jewish righteousness and to confront Zionism with its own contradictory attitude toward Jews themselves and its concomitant tendencies to identify an invidiously conceived otherness in the name of a false, imposed unity.

The Community of Children: Chronotype and Project

The community constituted by the children, beneath the surface of what appears to be the forms their sociation, is articulated in *Aqud* as a chronotype, a place/time, that is conceivable only in terms of the confluence of location and temporality. This confluence is not merely a trope of text. It is a condition of what the children do on their own account, as instances and exemplars of praxis. The achievement of the confluence is part of the children's work, against the reaction of a dominant society that would separate place and time, thereby reducing human agency to mere behavior and exchange. Without the confluence, place and time become separate dimensions, allowing exchanges to transpire and relations to be formed only according to a logic of calculation. In contrast, the children refuse all instances of exchange that require opposing what one does with where, among whom, it is done. Thus, they have no conception of surplus, or "free," time the use of which can be judged as proper or not. They do not perform "roles" or implement "positions." Thus, the violence is not, as Batia Gur seems to believe, behavior done when time is too free. It is part of a discipline and a praxis that is the very freedom of the children. The category of violence does not belong to them. It belongs to a situation defined, by the confluence of place and time, as a moment of a project, what must be done if one is to be honest and motivated by a desire for what Habermas conceives of as a liberatory community, what Sartre calls "totalization," and what Garfinkel might describe as a society of reproduction, of addressing conditions. The children's conduct is about relations, not about standards. For them, every act is, rather than part of a schedule, something infused with sociality.

This is expressed in the narrative in different ways. In one instance we are told that " . . . they came and asked [Ayiush] 'what are you doing?' And he answered, when I do, I'm asked, 'what are you doing?' And when I'm not doing, I'm asked 'what are you doing?'" (p. 262). What appears to the adults as Ayiush's "free time" is the only *real* time he has. It is the practical time of the children as such. For them, all time is the time of struggle, and all place is the place of self-realization in struggle. They have no special "other time" reserved for a "truer subjectivity," a time to pay the debts imposed on them by the adults, because such a subjectivity could only be removed from struggle, therefore without a meaning that could be lived. Consequently, they do not *have* any "spare" time for "more important" things to do, or "for leisure." It follows that when they leave the materiality of their neighborhood they are, as their parents warn, lost, but lost in a way that only the adults can fear, lost from sight.

When Yohai leaves Yir Ganim by bus with his father, we hear nothing about "place," or the succession of places, even when the bus goes through "Jerusalem." Yohai falls asleep, and his father awakens him only when they have to disembark. For him, they are *actually* nowhere. The *time* of the trip for Yohai is only a matter of then and now, and the series of *places* that appear externally to define the journey is in *reality*, for him, a field of simultaneous presences, a total situation of exile in which differences are merely locations outside of project, points of demarcation or passage that one can know but never experience. They are no more "places" in the lived sense than are names on a map.

When Ayiush searches for Gersha, who is "lost," there is no description of place separate from the movement of the search. In a sense, all places appear to Ayiush as defined by Gersha's absence; as substantially incomplete, as moments of his own desire for another.[39] When Mr. Sultan and his daughter travel to the "place" where the Independence Day carnival has been scheduled, it is not possible to guess that they are in Jerusalem, and that nothing occurs that resembles what is taken as "carnival." The two merely pass through streets that have no significance beyond the pure physicality of passage. This "outing" with his daughter, who is the apple of his eye, provides us with an unqualified opportunity to share Mr. Sultan's pleasure and, at the same time, his anger and frustration. His pleasure derives from the outing, from the mere presence of his daughter, fixed in his time and his sense of place. His anger reflects on its contradiction. For him, there is a *here* as much as a *now*. "Here" is a "place" beyond places, and he momentarily despises what it represents. It is a deterritorializing impulse that reflects the unreliability of all named territory for the immigrant. At the same time, he despises what he must do to the daughter—make her merely a presence—in order to enjoy her. Yet his anger is a feature of his own individualized praxis. It obliterates the boundaries that limit his own sense of instrumentality and identity. In this respect, Sultan is like the children as much as he is the denial of them.

When the critic Yehudit Orian says that she "could not reconstruct and arrange a vision of any concrete place . . . , any scene," she is reflecting not the novel's weakness but its strength. Of course, "Swissa's Yir Ganim could never be Amos Oz's Jerusalem or Yaakov Shabtai's Tel Aviv, or Gabriel García Márquez's Macondo."[40] After reading the novel for the first time, I also could not remember where the action occurred, that the characters lived in Jerusalem. If one did not know, firsthand, the city's streets, one might believe that the street "Costa Rica" was invented by the children. It took me a while to realize that this was in fact a real street, but only a "real place" for adults who can or must situate themselves independently of time and predicament in self-defeating irony, who can know the locations of things as other than settings of activity that takes absolute precedence over its name. In the novel, this street is not meant to be real in that adult, topographical sense. Its reality as a place/time is not available to those who live by boundaries and names, by economies of time *versus* place that are marked by "doing" *rather than* being. At one point we are told about the fruit groves that surround the "world," a universe that includes by name all the Jewish, Muslim, and Christian villages south of Jerusalem, but not *Jerusalem*.

At one point an object is seen on the horizon but it is not part of a skyline. It is merely a point of focus, "toward which birds are flying in formation." It is "a mosque minaret that pulls itself toward the sky" (p. 14), an object, not a thing, suffused with intentionality and movement. The only beautiful *place* to observe is the sky, which is not a location at all. This is where the children direct their eyes for many hours each day—toward their kites in the sky. They call one of them the "sun wheel"; and, in contrast, they name mountains around Jerusalem "Ass" and "Prick." This suppression of the negativity of adult place is not an artifact of Swissa's prose, not an excess of eloquence. It has its own significance, and it belongs exclusively to the children, to praxis.

Jerusalem, the Holy City, is thus radically secularized, deterritorialized. It is made absolutely mundane. In other words, it is stripped of mythology and recovered for life. This is why Swissa, rather then speaking as Amos Oz does of the "blazing blue," speaks instead of the "deceiving sun in the pale blue" sky *of Jerusalem*. In this transformation, garbage and trash, junk and open sewage, are not just the material properties of Yir Ganim. These are what make of Jerusalem a situation for these children and what make them instances of subjectivity beyond definition, power, surveillance. The only other writer I know of who has written such an unorthodox configuration of the place named "Jerusalem" is the late poet Alexander Pen, in his poem "Jerusalem, the Holy Whore."[41]

Naming and Signification

Names serve only as *virtual* signifiers for Swissa. In contrast, Sammy Mikhael's *All Men Are Equal* relies on the capacity of naming to evoke types. Apart from one character, Mr. Zidowitz, who is portrayed as an Ashkenazi opportunist, and another, Abu Halawa, who is portrayed as a thug, Mikhael's male protagonists have Hebrew names. The significance is clear in light of the fact that many if not most of the new immigrants from Iraq had Arabic names when they came to Israel.[42] The choice of Hebrew names is, in *All Men Are Equal*, an expression of a project, not merely a rhetorical strategy. But it is a project that separates instances of praxis as a matter of principle.

In *Aqud*, however, the names, with the exceptions of Rammy, David Ben Shushan, and Yohai, form a mosaic of linguistic types: Immo and Emme, Ayiush's two older brothers; Leticia, Yvonne, Beber, Tully, Georgete, Muizo, Koko, Mr. Sultan and his wife Yamna, Sitato the barber; *Hakham* Ya'kub abd-el-Hak, Ayiush's tutor for the bar mitzvah reading, and his wife, Ishtir; Mr. Pazuelo; Mr. Monsanegor; the family Shukrun; the family Shriki; Tonto Zaiish; Madam Arlette; Gersha; Mr. Lintzinski, Ayiush's teacher in the Ashkenazi Orthodox school; the twins A'z'iz'i and Makhloof; the night watchman in the mental asylum, Zeituni; Z'oz'o; Rabbi Eliyahu Buhbutt, of the Kabbalist synagogue. There is also a Dr. Goldstein, a dentist; and if there is a doctor in town, he is Ashkenazi. However, when Ayiush's school principal called him by his Hebrew name, Haiim, "Ayiush shot back at him, keeping his cool, 'Ayiush!'" And when Katie, Ayiush's younger sister, heard him speak of Rabbi Nahman of Breslow, she asked him, "What is Breslow?" Ayiush replied, "It should be some Ashkenazi name . . . and they laughed." Besides their colorfulness, these multilingual names are more typical and respectful of the cultures they represent than those in Sammy Mikhael's novel.

The use of names is part of the way in which these novels depict Arab culture. For example, in *All Men Are Equal*, Iraqi Jewish immigrants display a marked lack of sensitivity to the fact that their tent colony is built on the ruins of an Arab village named Kheiriya.[43] This is part of a depersonalization, a desubjecting, of Arabs. In light of this, the novel's protagonist is able *suddenly* to see the personhood in a single Arab. This token discovery occurs on a winter night, when David, depressed, is thinking about his divorce from his wife. He goes to the beach and enters the water "to cool" his anxiety. A wave u-pends him. Another man who happens to be in the vicinity comes to help him. In the ensuing conversation, which becomes personal, David realizes that the man is an Arab, "that an *Arab*, too, could become miserable because of a woman" (pp. 244–45). This momentary recognition of *an* Arab as *a* subject is predicated on the particulars of the moment—David's peril and the personal nature of their conversation. Subjectivity is not, for Arabs, a given.

In *Aqud*, however, the sentiment toward Arabs is quite different, and possibly compares only with that expressed by Ballas.[44] On one occasion, Mr. Sultan refers casually to "*Arab Jews*" and "*Arab Muslims*" in the Draa Valley of Morocco (p. 43). In the "concrete colonies of Yir Ganim," the narrator tells us, children profoundly identify themselves with Arabs as constitutive features of their "world." Yir Ganim is a slum, and the narrator looks at the contrasting "pleasantness of the nearby Arab villages," mentioning almost with envy the villages of Ein-Henyiah and Batir (p. 97), their fruit groves, vineyards, brooks,

and fountains. In another instance, on the eve of the Jewish Tabernacle holiday, "even the Arab peddlers who had already sold their merchandise hurried
to return to neighboring Biet Jalla and Bethlehem before dark. They swung
their sticks behind their donkeys, shouting while passing, '*Yid l'kher!*'[45]
Trembling and thrilling the heart much more than all the blessings here" (p.
206).

Aqud: An Antinomian Text

Yet, this sympathy is still not the crucial point of difference. In the first two
parts of this study I was concerned with a literature operating within the context of a strictly defined nationalist moral discourse. In *Aqud*, however, the
nationalist component of culture operates as an external imposition. Sympathy is qualified positively by identification. The Arabs and the Jews are what
Alfred Schutz calls "consociates," who "grow old together."[46] They are not
merely negations of each other. What makes *Aqud* unique is its endeavor to
free itself as a text not only from the nationalist restrictions on moral discourse, but from Jewish "identity" as an imposition on personal identity and
intersubjectivity. In this regard, I consider *Aqud* an antinomian text. And
although this may appear on the surface, to a secular, liberal reader, as an
inversion of political priorities, in fact, *Aqud* represents an attempt to be honest. In the Zionist context, it is not Sepharadic Orthodoxy that is pulling
Israeli nationalism toward an extreme, but secular nationalism that moves
Sepharadic Orthodoxy toward rightism.

Thus, whereas *A Good Arab*, presents an ambiguous identity within the
context of a secular nationalism in which dilemmas of political disloyalty
inevitably arise, the moral dilemma presented in *Aqud* is one that can moti-
vate a community. It has to do with the relationship between affirming life
through an acknowledgment of community and the affirming of God through
observance. A person's conscientious choice of, or even respect for, another
religion is experienced within the Jewish Orthodox community as shameful,
as much so as is the refusal of sacraments. Such a person is "other" and is liable
to excommunication (*herem*).

In *Aqud*, Ayiush is afflicted with this angst. He is beset by the memory of
his Muslim Arab nanny in Morocco, whom he suspects of being his mother.
This suspicion provides the psychological trigger for his eccentricities. But
rather than denying the possibility that he is part Arab Muslim, Ayiush comes
to believe that he was "deceitfully converted to Judaism" by his father. Ayiush
remembers the first three years of his life with his Arab Muslim nanny as idyl-

lic, as a "pure kingdom, which was probably lost too, and could never, God for-
bid, come back again." Thus, his life is "the false effort of a fading memory,"
which is the title of the novel's third section. This dialectic of identity has
been well recognized in the critical literature on *Aqud*, with the result that
critics have not been able to read Swissa for the radicalism of his reflection on
the relations of Arab and Jew, for his challenge to Zionist rationalism, and for
how moral his characters become in a world in which they are free only in the
context of bondage.

For Hirschfeld the narrator is "hollow." Peri dismisses the issue of morality
by focusing on "the romantic preservation of a lost childhood." Both ignore
Swissa's account of a dilemma that goes to the heart of Israeli moral discourse:
how to be, at one and the same time, Jewish (essence) and free (praxis), where
freedom has to do with being human rather than merely having an identity. In
Aqud, this issue is elucidated in the context of sin, punishment, repentance,
and grace.

Ayiush's punishment for misbehavior in school consisted of confinement
for an unspecified number of days in the family storage room. His father wanted to cure his son of the "disease" with which he was "infected." Nevertheless,
he realized this "was not just a body that [accidentally] acquired bad habits. . . .
There was something else at work in his son from within, inciting him against
his own father" (p. 167). Once the door shut behind him, Ayiush was left in
the dark, unable to see. The storage room was filled with so much worm poison
that his mother gave him mint leaves in the hope of protecting him from the
noxious fumes. In shock, he wondered how he had so easily consented to enter
that room. He could not comprehend the lack of reaction by his mother,
brothers, and sisters at seeing him so confined. He thought that they ought at
least to have waved goodbye, as they would have if he were going to study at a
distinguished *yeshiva*, or were going on an important mission, or if he was a
"gatherer" on the Sabbath, whose punishment was necessary as instruction for
the community.[47]

It is the last of these possibilities that preoccupies Ayiush, the fantastic idea
of a sinner whose punishment reconstitutes his sin as a social good. Not only
he but the punishing father may be such a sinner for the sake of the community's need for self-affirmation. The father must educate and punish. The suffering he inflicts serves a higher good, no matter the ambiguity of its intention.
Yet Ayiush reflects critically on another aspect of his pain, the personal
aspect. As "time went on without movement," doubts begin to disturb him.
Someone comes and sits beside him, someone who never bows, who refuses
orders, who demands to know why he is confined. Why was he so submissive?

Why does he obey his father? Is he really weak? Is his heart soft? Does he so badly need his father's shelter? Does he truly love this unreal home? "That night when all was silent, Ayiush prayed to his God from the depths of darkness and depression, like Jonah from the belly of the fish" (p. 172). This episode dramatizes the tension between Ayiush's sense of his individuality and the community in whose terms he ultimately knows and valorizes himself.

Often in the past, Ayiush found himself secretly wishing that "the wrath be ended; let father be ended, let everything be ended." When at night he would stand for hours on the bridge watching mute television through neighbors' windows, he was often struck by the urge to throw himself into the depths. "Surely someone would scream then, someone would at least find something to talk about." Then he would go down to the bomb shelter and masturbate.

This precipice was one on which all the children stood—where the self of freedom and despair confronted the public social identity riven with false hopes and moral compromise. This contradiction lent vitality to their lives. This essential ambivalence, so hostile to essentialism, testifies to the fact of oppression beyond any immediate experience of it. Ayiush thought of "the mother who had prostituted herself with such great love for the father who turned to her in his own lustfulness," the father who, as if by magic, suddenly returned when Ayiush was about to be thirteen. He thought about the house that had never really existed as he dreamed it, but was only imagined and lacked, in any case, any meaning he could grasp: "The more it is full, the more ephemeral it becomes. Damn this house!" (p. 104).

In an ancient book of penitential prayers that he had received as a present from his father, Ayiush discovered that his father felt guilty of unfathomable sins and misdeeds—murder, robbery, treason, adultery. Ayiush studied these in detail and saw in them the false pride of the secret sinner in confession, whose ambivalence made him incapable of repentance. He began to realize not only that he himself was destined to err and sin, but that he had inherited unbearable sinful propensities. His teachers told him that whoever does private acts, those he had done, that are not written in the *Shulkhan Arukh* commits sin. All these reflections are, for him, causes of shame, though not occasions for repentance. They create a sense of his own evil beyond hope of redemption,

> as that Muslim child that he could have been. That little piece of road on which he had already walked toward the *madina*,[48] his soft palm mingling with the Arab servant's tattooed hand, planted in him an ancient and unreasoning hatred of Israel, God forbid. Perhaps this is what his father means to suggest

when he points a finger and says that "the one who blackens others blackens himself." (p. 114)

Thus, we are confronted with a son and a father who are irredeemable sinners and, in obscure ways, partners in the same sin. Sinfulness, Ayiush says, both was taught to him and was given him from birth. Men have carried that burden of sin since Adam and Eve. But, for him, the ambivalence that constitutes his engagement with the situation makes being sinful the only way in which he can preserve his connection to the ruined community of his people. Children without hope, like "gatherers" on the Sabbath, are the moral fixtures of such a community's feeble self-consciousness, available as resources for its confused memory of what it had been and how it came to be what it is.

On Yom Kippur, Ayiush sensed that the people were treating him strangely: "With his childish inability or unwillingness to speak and tell others what he should," he was made to feel that "he is the only and last survivor of humanity. In despair and frustration, he takes a stone and throws it at the universe." We are told, on that day,

> the rumble of singing and prayer descended from all directions of the universe. Ayiush's heart held pitied the awkward and compulsively large steps he took as he walked along the small desolate paths. . . . [On this very holy day he was walking] toward, toward . . . , toward what he did not know . . . , [and yet he walked] with shame, full of regret, toward that which had not yet reached him but would reach him despite himself. (p. 190)

This is the narrator speaking of and for Ayiush as he walks home from the synagogue in the midst of prayer. When he arrives, he is overwhelmed by the solemnity, stillness, and silence of the beautifully decorated household, prepared for celebration and a great feast at the end of the fast of the holy day. Like Camus's stranger, he breaks the fast ahead of time, in violation of the law, curious to know what lies behind the notion that one must not eat more than "as little as an olive" on Yom Kippur. Ayiush

> had a vague and inchoate desire to stand on the other side of the barricade, on the side from which one can see the stones thrown by your own people aimed to kill you, by your acquaintances, relatives, and close friends, by the members of your family who are prohibited from mourning the dead sinner, the one who was stoned, the one for whom mourning obligations are not valid. (p. 191)

Here is an individual who, despite himself, attempts to measure God's rule by his own capacity to imagine its consequences. He wishes to know the rule as God knows it, to will it as if it could be his own, as if he might create the very law by which he [unlike God?] is bound. That this is a child's meditation is crucial, as only children are given the law without reason. Ayiush does not intend merely to be naughty, but only to demand that law be restored to the realm of freedom. We are told that Ayiush did not break the fast "in order to put himself apart from the community" but, on the contrary, to join it: "just like that gatherer, though two thousand years in his grave, is not forgotten, nor is his sin." Ayiush's struggle is thus not against his people but for them, for their freedom and for the identity that can know itself only if obedience to the law is chosen, willed rather than imposed arbitrarily. But then he can legitimately engage in this struggle to recover the lawfulness of the law only if others are also in need of such a reform.

As Ayiush leaves the kitchen, he hears the sound of running water. By the volume of it and its different pitches, he deduces that there are many people who have not gone to synagogue. Rather than being properly modest in their use of water on this day, they use enough to account for a great many sins. Ayiush discovers that the community is not what it has pretended to be. It, too, is engaged in challenging the arbitrariness of the law. His mood improves.

An androgynous midget whom Ayiush had conjured up in his imagination while confined to the storage room reappears. Ayiush walks with the midget from the kitchen to his parents' bedroom. There he takes off his clothes and enters the wardrobe. He digs frantically through the wardrobe, searching among hidden treasures and memorabilia. He finds an olive-wood box containing silver and gold jewelry, and a bunch of keys that he has never seen before. For a while, he reflects "on the doors they had left locked behind them" (p. 193). He realizes that his parents' past is a mystery to him, but that they have preserved traces of it. Sinfulness, memory, and alienation are brought together in this episode. Ayiush is Ayiush, but also someone else. Yet who that someone is has been kept secret; and he imagines that their denial of access to memory is the greater sin, and he is its victim. Like memory itself, this sin too must be shared by all, including Ayiush. Their refusal to share memory with him, the duplicitousness of that refusal, is the reflection of the community's need to recover its own commitment to the law through a reversal of its commitment to one another, and therefore through respect for those subversions by which the law can be chosen rather than merely received. But although this need can justify Ayiush's own conduct, his violation of his parents' privacy, he must face the likelihood that his heroic struggle will be rejected after all.

Ayiush searches through the wardrobe for something, though he has no idea of what it might be. Suddenly, he finds,

in a black shiny purse, a number of family photographs of men and women he
never saw before. Yet it seemed that there was something about them that he
had known in the past. He examined their faces, their unbuttoned collars, their
loosened neckties. . . . He was confused. They resembled each other. By their
posture, all the women were pregnant, although one couldn't know by whom.
. . . Here it is. Here is the longed-for photograph, another photograph. (p. 193)

Is it that memory cannot finally be kept hidden from one who searches? It
seems that Ayiush, after all, had a purpose in leaving the synagogue, and his
choice of that very day may also have been for a good reason. What other day
of the year could be safer for an investigation into memory and its suppression
than this day of atonement? He wanted to know who he was. A twelve-year-
old boy, who in a few days would be thirteen, was eager to find out not only
whether his life was worthwhile, but whether bar mitzvah is or even should be
part of that life. This is a daring thought for so young a child, yet it seems a
necessary one, given that he cannot be sure that he is Jewish and is, nevertheless, subject to Jewish law. Moreover, he believes that he should not be forced
to be Jewish. Whatever he is, it must be what he can will himself to be, what is
true to his life.

Ayiush had once thought that the term "tender in years" was engraved on
his forehead, as a sign of Cain, as if his lack of years declared him to be tender
and delicate, the years to come toughening him until he is weakened by old
age, and "he finally crumbles into the dust of the earth." That thought is
evoked by the photograph, that "strictly forbidden object" he presumed to
have been "left here temporarily." In it,

a gloriously robust child of tender years is seated like a little man on the lap of
an enormous woman. In his delicate, chubby hands he holds a water-and-sky-
like colored crystal fish. His blemish-free face is immersed in dream, free of
wounds, immaculate. His soft eyebrows jut forward like little frontlets above
full, almond-shaped eyes. He has a small and sensitive nose. His cheeks are
doughnuts, his lips red and soft like a cotton-worm. The woman's tattooed
hands are big and black, and she wears plenty of gold bracelets and rings. She
embraces him around his belly, protectively and with warmth, tilting his body
in a motion intended to turn his face toward the camera. Now Ayiush notices
that the child's eyes are slightly recoiling from the camera, or from what is
standing next to it. Although he is looking at the camera, his eyes are somewhat off center. His head is pulled upward and backward, toward the woman's
face. But the woman's face is missing from the photograph. It is not actually
missing. Someone had cut out the upper portion of the photograph. (p. 193)

In a fit, Ayiush destroys the maimed yet tantalizing photograph. He feels an
overpowering dizziness, as if he has been hypnotized. But he also feels great

happiness, "and a momentary exemption from . . . anxiety." Although incon-
clusive, the photograph nevertheless seems to have revealed the truth by its
inclusion of the figure Ayiush identifies as his nanny, a truth for which he was
willing to "squander his life." He ate, wondering whether or not he should
bless the food. But then he reminded himself that eating on Yom Kippur was a
transgression, so that blessing the food would be "a good deed" actually done
in sin. Nevertheless, in a presumptuous appropriation of the law, he did the
blessing. Then someone within him began to curse, and the midget said,
"Amen." Ayiush's desecration of the holy day, and his appropriation of its law
to his will, to the will of humanity, is part of a greater project than religion,
namely, to manifest the truth of community and of those who have need of
the community's truth. Thus comes into realization the post-Sabbatian, antinomian conception of *Mitzva ha'Baa ba'Aveira* (holiness of sin),[49] which is stated by the narrator in those exact words (p. 194).

Suddenly, Ayiush runs back to the synagogue and tries to enter it before
the prayers end. He is both terrified and excited. He enters wet and dirty, his
stained clothes revealing the fact that he has eaten. Everyone is preparing to
leave. They bless each other happily. His father is folding his prayer shawl. He
too is happy, though somewhat confused: "Less than thirteen years old, one
does not need to fast," they say. But Ayiush says, "We'll see next year." They
say, "He is alive! He is alive!" His mother massages his stiffened neck and says,
"He is alive! He is alive! And she laughs from the depth of her heart." Ayiush
thinks that "he is alive and nothing is dead in him; everything is as before" (p.
195).

He must, then, begin again and again, this Sisyphean figure who stands for
the possible value of continuing the quest for meaning, and who represents the
permanence and insatiability of history. "He is alive" means only that he is
still Ayiush, not the avatar of truth, not one who has come to a realization of
self, not one who has served others.

The Sisyphean Figure

Ayiush is shocked by his father's "blessing and curse," which he declares as the
time approaches for Ayiush to carry the burden of *mitzvot* (commandments):
"From now on your acts shall tilt the scales of your soul and that of the entire
world in favor of or against you. From now on, if your acts should lead you to
Gehenna I will not be there for you!"[50] Ayiush realizes then that he has no
alternative. He determines to leave home the next day, the day of his bar mitz-

vah, at an hour even before his father arises to awaken the family. "Tonight,"
his little sister will say, "he is taking revenge on his father for the loss of the
kingdom, for the treachery of his confinement in the storage room, for the loss
of the forelock which was his emblem, for his ugly birthright, and those wal-
nuts." Upon leaving, Ayiush sees his sister sleeping. Her innocence is evident
in her posture as she clutches her pillow with her small arms and legs. He
knows "that things could have been different, and it stung his heart."
However, he cannot stay, because there on the wall is "his bar mitzvah suit
hanging, calling to him and frightening him at the same time." And although
there is in the house a good warm smell of food and sweets, he feels that something has gone completely wrong; then, secretly, he leaves.

At dawn on the third day of his wandering, Ayiush realizes that he wants to
return to school. He suddenly longs to devote himself to study. He imagines
that he could become the school principal by the end of the next year; he is
prepared to suffer punishment. But while digging into the sores on his feet in
order "to clear them of the devils they had inside them," he is unable to complete these thoughts. A hot ball sticks in his throat. He sees the morning
spreading across the land and smells the sharp fragrance of the pine trees.
"Birds were leaping over one another and bending their heads toward each
other under low, cool strips of fog. And he let out a frighteningly joyful wailing, down toward Ein-Karem into the valley." The little man says, "Now that
you are wailing, you are free."

Ayiush is reminded of a huge buffet that sat in his room when he was a
baby. On it stood a glorious crystal vase, a present from his mother to his
father. In the family photograph hanging on the wall, they all looked like
tourists. Into his mind enters the voice of his father, saying, "That's how they
looked." Then his father disappears "somewhat wickedly," only to return,
reflected "in the vase with his head bent sideways on his shoulder." Ayiush
concludes that it could not have been his father "who took the photograph"
(p. 228). The little man of Ayiush's imagination tries to revive his memory of
his parents' divorce and his father's subsequent attempt to repent for having
committed adultery. Who is the greater "transgressor," Ayiush or his father?
And thus, what right does the father have to impose the law on Ayiush? And
what right does he have to determine Ayiush's identity?

But these are questions prior to memory and subsequent to the futility that
makes of Ayiush's life one of an "eternal recurrence." He stands for the contradiction between history and identity, destined both to remember and to
forget. His friends mourn him:

Now he is like a fish in a big lake, said Z'oz'o sadly. Nonsense, said an angry
Rammy, almost crying. He is like a crazed person, stuck . . . without purpose, as
if trying to build his nest in the sky, as if he had special treasures there. He is a
rejected object, simply higher than anyone else, simply more brilliant than the
sun. He is not a cloud to guide us in daytime, nor a fire to show us the way at
night. He is ephemeral. He is an *Epikouros*. (p. 261)[51]

One can sense the boys' confusion. They wish to express what cannot be
expressed about Ayiush and their sense of loss. They use the traditional
Hebrew word *Epikouros* to define what he means to them. Rather than "a sign
without signification," as Hirschfeld claims, *Aqud*'s narrator is a signifying
voice without recourse to adequate signs. It is the language and not the voice
that has failed. Rammy says that Ayiush was *"hefetz she'ein bo hefetz"* (a rejected object) (p. 261). As such, he is an object of desire, but of a desire that
rejects *itself*. Yohai says that Ayiush is like our "Tower of Babel, through
which God's spirit blows in order to disperse us throughout the world, and to
confuse speech. Soon we will be confused. Soon we will not understand each
other" (p. 269). But "we" understand ourselves now, and Ayiush is the spirit of
"our" life in anticipation of something other than mere life and perhaps
greater than the Law.

Among the bands of abandoned children, an unnoticed little boy cries. "He
stood agitated for a long while, at the entrance of the eternal street, Costa
Rica, waiting for the mayor to arrive" (p. 262). He begs the other children to
bind him to one of their carriages and push it down the slope, but none will.
Suddenly, he sees his father and mother approaching.

> Without confusion, and without haste, with composed and measured steps,
> Ayiush approached one of the abandoned or forgotten carriages, took it with a
> steady hand, and stretched the wire to stabilize its slight movement toward the
> slope. Then he placed one leg onto the carriage floor. He held the other leg
> ready at the side. He sent one more quick look over his shoulder and saw his
> father growing in size. His mother extended a hand forward. Now he felt truly
> that he did not need brakes. Now he'll push off and will finally understand it
> all. It wouldn't be long before he understood perfectly. His leg extended like an
> uncoiling spring and he started rolling down the slope. . . . His father and
> mother watched their eighth bar mitzvah bridegroom as he galloped in the
> wind toward the infinity of Costa Rica street. (p. 268)

Ayiush was gone, but his "little man"—the tiny female English doll his sister Katie gave him as a present, the one she used to call Madin Englander—
remained behind. On his last night, Ayiush ran in panic from a watchman, but
forgot his school bag. "In the dark interior of this old bag, reclining with his

back against the book *Our Motherland* (another irony), the little man was left
forsaken." Because the little man is now left alone and "has no one to talk to,"
he speaks to himself, chants a tender and sensitive elegy to Ayiush. I quote
only the last few lines:

> —All of this, though, is a decisive testimony from other places, very far away,
> where people are surely longing for us without our knowing, since they were
> left by all those who came here, to our place. Therefore they are the source of
> our longing for those places, and those remote people we were once, or that we
> could have been but did not know, or that we do not know anymore. (p. 270)

In Yigal Sarna's interview with Swissa, the author speaks in the light of his
memory of his own Muslim Arab nanny:

> And I am also an Arab child. In my imagination I can see myself living in a
> completely different world from that in which I live today. I am swept almost
> morbidly into the adventure of being an Arab child. And from my visit to
> Morocco, I absorbed something that overcame even the force of my Jewish
> existence. I refuse to deny these emotions, especially because of the hatred that
> prevails today between Arabs and Jews.[52]

Yet Yigal Sarna concludes this interview with the following, vaguely dismis-
sive, comment:

> All Swissa aspires for in his greatest dreams is to have a small place in Paris and
> a small place in Tel Aviv. This is Swissa's "balanced happiness." When he
> speaks of East and West, Swissa seems to me like an acrobat, cautiously walking
> the tightrope between a roof in Paris and a roof in Tel Aviv. Beneath his feet
> he sees the enormous residential buildings of Yir Ganim, and, close to him in
> the sky, a colorful kite.[53]

Thus we have the Israeli mainstream skepticism of a Jewish cosmopolitan,
who sees only an acrobat on a tightrope, balanced between Tel Aviv and
Paris, between the sky and the gutter, that is, one who sees only the possibility of taking sides—but not the inevitability of moral tension, therefore of
doubt in the midst of affirmation and of affirmation in the midst of doubt.

Conclusion

I have discussed some moral paradoxes inherent in Israeli Jewish culture, and analyzed them as expressing limitations of self-criticism and the capacity to recognize the "other" intrinsic to "the imagined community" of Zionist nationalism.[1] The paradoxes arise in two fundamental projections: of the relationship between Jewish identity and Jewish history, and of the validation of a sectarian morality by means of two tropes, the Holocaust and the secular global distribution of Jewish life called "the Diaspora."

The former organizes moral thought according to particular experiences. The latter establishes a utopian frame of reference for connecting life histories to an evolutionary movement of the Jewish people from dispersion to unity. Together, these projections constitute a "master narrative" linking texts, discourses, and moments of reflection in a dialectic of self and other. The assumption that Israeli Hebrew literature has a unique and transformative significance in Israeli culture is argued sociologically, historically, and theoretically. The case is a *prima facie* one, by no means conclusive. Nevertheless, the assumption is sufficiently justified to provide a framework for examining the ideological aspects of the texts I have selected for study.

The gist of the argument is that Israeli culture must be seen as more a matter of manifestation than latency. If this is true, then that culture must be understood as strategically organized around the problematics of explication, subject in all its public genres to a priority of allegorical forms of representa-

187

tion that combine symbols of totalization within a rhetoric of politics and morality. This is, in effect, the base of the Zionist superstructure. It is the field in which Zionist nationalism positions itself as a totalistic ideology, and the setting in which Israeli literature has its public presence as a source of cultural reflection on the intersection of identity, citizenship, and history. It is also the intersection in which writing and reading emerge as distinct practices. In that regard, literature and writers have a special significance in Israeli culture, influencing cognitive traditions, substantiating the continual affirmation/ assertion of Hebrew as a "national," or nation-giving, language, reiterating the perspective of Jewish unity implicit in the political conditions of Israel's presence as a country among countries.

My analysis runs counter to two assumptions in the sociology of culture normally taken for granted: (1) that *culture* refers to two incompatible realms —art and the practices of everyday life, and (2) that the latter, what ethnology would consider culture proper, operates in society as what Parsons called "a latent function," a latency of meanings, values, and norms that operates on both the manifest conduct of members and the manifest operations of societal institutions.

The first, though still prevalent in sociological research, has been thrown sufficiently into question by the "postmodernist" renewals of criticism that it is legitimate to begin with an alternative assumption consistent with recent currents of critical inquiry.[2] The second now appears inconsistent with most current ethnographic research, which has demonstrated that culture is essentially political, that it is generative rather than fixed, and that it embodies, as "practices," conjunctures founded in differences more than "traditions."[3]

I have drawn several conclusions from critical readings of texts, texts that were selected for their ethnological significance, in particular because of the publicity that attended their publication, their evident intention to cultivate a moral outlook on Arab-Jewish relations that could humanize the Jewish Israeli point of view, their attempt in this regard to provide for a self-critical recognition of Arab subjectivity, and the positions of their authors in Israeli life.

Among the most important conclusions of this study are the following. (1) The attempt to establish a critical base for rethinking, and reimaging, relations between Arabs and Jews reveals an a priori distinction between moral and juridical citizenship and an incorrigible identification of the former with authentic moral subjectivity and the latter with objects of judgment. This distinction operates at each point in the depiction of the Arabs and Jews, qualifying what can be thought of as Arab subjectivity in that context. (2) Reliance on this distinction expresses a certain "structure of feeling," in which the Jewish conscience articulates all terms of moral judgment from the perspective of an absolutely elevated subjectivity beyond history and validated as such by reference to the Holocaust. (3) The distinction, the identification, and the structure of feeling determine an irreducible dependence of Jewish identity (therefore moral subjectivity) on relations of exclusion and inclusion, hence on the need to reiterate constantly the constitutive negative identity of an other. (4) This other, constituted at all times as a matter of practice, is embodied in the figure of "the Arab" and humanized—so that morality is a type of knowledge as well as an attitude—by a distinction between "good Arabs" (individuals as juridical citizens or legal subjects) and "the Arab" (the category external to law and negative to morality). (5) The identity-driven articulation of that figure constitutes a barrier beyond which consciousness cannot penetrate, thereby eliminating at each last moment the possibility for Jewish *recognition* of Arab subjectivity necessary for the completion of any morally substantial autocritique of the role of Zionist nationalism in "Arab-Israeli relations." (6) The general problematic constituted by these tropes accounts for the ways in which Israeli literary criticism organizes itself in the function of a policing of culture. This is itself a genre, therefore a strategic formation. As such, it aims to diminish the force of the moral paradoxes of Israeli culture. What is threatening about those paradoxes derives from the same pressure for explication that makes Israeli culture intensively ideological to its "imagined community." The need to sustain a utopian politics, a need expressed in literary criticism as an altogether militarized politics of unity, tends to undermine whatever moral self-reflection might otherwise accompany the pressure of paradox.

There are certainly historical determinants of the transformation of cultural latency into a culture of manifestation, and of the regression of practice (the construction of society) in favor of theory (the construction of an absolute other, hence an absolute identity). But both need to be noted and studied if one is to understand the intractability of contemporary Israeli culture in regard to the other—the Arab—against which it increasingly defines itself, though with an increasingly evident loss of control. The texts I analyze illustrate this irreducible unease, this irrepressible ambivalence, about Jewish history and identity and all that is associated with them, even as they attempt to introduce a more generous self-critical moment into the dialectic of Israeli culture.

What we see is a culture whose resistance to criticism is uniquely tied to a need for self-explication that makes criticism itself a constant subvocal presence. Therefore, we see a culture always on the edge of self-criticism but never quite able to move beyond its own regressive tendencies. This contradiction of incessant utopian manifestation and unavoidably self-critical tendency marks Israeli culture as distinctively postmodernist. The key elements in the self-regulation of this formation—in which culture standing against itself must also stand against a definite subaltern other—are Zionism and racialist literary tendencies that configure "the Arab" as homogeneous, disposed, and beyond any reason that could be shared.

Zionism and the poetics of identity and otherness are decisive elements of the Israeli cultural "structure of feeling." But there are deeper, more generalized, operations that have to do with the relations of subjectivity to identity (mediated practically by territorialist projections), civic virtue to society (mediated ideologically by utopian idealism), and moral and political imperatives to history (mediated symbolically by religious sectarianism and the Holocaust). I have attempted to clarify the context of these operations in Jewish history, both its record and its delusions, and in regard to the historical politics of relations between Arabs and Jews. I have focused especially on the ways in which dissident literary fiction both challenges the moral and political themes of Zionism and, despite itself, ends by reiterating the episteme that organizes the reception of those themes.

Because of its role in contemporary Israeli culture, my investigation requires some consideration of Zionism's ideological aspect. In this regard, I have tried to show how Zionism constitutes a synthetic "structure of feeling," how it conforms to a model of ideology as a countergenerative, anticritical, repetitive type of discourse, how it serves to organize the apparently extraideological discourses of Israeli civil society, and in what ways it can be seen as a pervasive and currently irrepressible aspect of Israeli culture.

The language of Israeli Hebrew literature has to do work of a higher order than is normally required of fictional writing, reading, and discourse. Israeli literature is *first* of society and *then* organized canonically, ostensibly in relation to society. Israeli Hebrew writing can never be understood merely in terms of stylistics, as a matter of technique, or as modes of implementing authorial intention, because each of these constitutes an altogether impractical distance between texts and the community of which they are part and beyond which they cannot be read as having been possibly written (without the need for constant reinterpretive translation). Nor can it be seen as merely expressive, as a symptom that momentarily conceals specific motivations. Israeli Hebrew writing bears the burden of many discourses and the responsibilities of a certain historiography.

I have argued, however, that it does not follow from its implication in community that Israeli Hebrew literature is somehow more honest to itself, only that it cannot avoid its own dishonesty. This may well be so for any historical, mechanical, enforced unification of "a people" in which the collective forms of subjectivity and the socially practical orders of moral obligation seem to derive their validity beyond the space, time, and politics of experience. But there are relatively few cases of a cultural formation such as Israel's—and I consider this a virtue as well as a trial—which must constantly, as a whole, defend its own dishonesty. For most societies, dishonesty lies on the surface of the texts, the genres, the moral specifications of cultural formations that appear more systematically subordinate to other "institutions" than is the case in Israel. There, the moral burden remains especially heavy, and explicit self-consciousness remains perched on the edge of an abyss of the discovery that the self is indeed the other. These burdens give Israeli culture its special quality of ambivalence and its culturally critical operations their special determination to police the cultural practices.

Israeli Hebrew literature provides the quintessential object for a critique of Israeli political discourse precisely because of its highly spiritualized yet embodied referents, a historical people and a living utopia beyond which lies an unanalyzable but concrete, hence dangerous, otherness of being. Through the literary heightening of the symbolic and allegorical aspects of this myth, Israeli Jewish culture presents itself as a historical force that can be taken as an object of critique, therefore as an object of an altogether different subjectivity.[4]

In the second part of this study, I dealt with another aspect of Israeli culture. Ballas, Mikhael, and Swissa bear an ethnicity that represents for Zionism the other within. Thus, their authorial subjectivity constitutes a problem for which there are no obvious solutions. The fact that such a subjectivity cannot avoid being specially imputed in these cases demands a somewhat different contextualization from that appropriate to Kaniuk's A Good Arab,. Above all, in them the coupling of exclusion and inclusion cannot be taken for granted; and, as it becomes overt and unambiguous in their texts, there is at least a semblance of counterhegemony within the culture of those texts' reception. Ballas's novels The Last Winter and The Other One and Swissa's Aqud impose an obligation to reflect on oppression that cannot easily be assimilated to the metaphysically qualified dissidence of other critical writers. For one, the obligation is too general to remain within the omnivorous reach of Zionist interpretation; for another, the novels impute strength and subjectivity to their characters that stand firm against all instances of imposed or utopian unity. This is why so many critics of these novels have chosen to treat them from a strictly formalistic point of view rather than in terms of their content, the critical practices they disclose as part of everyday life.

The texts I have discussed in the second part of my study operate enough beyond the limits of Zionist nationalism to evoke a certain critical dread, but enough within those limits to allow it to be reduced to a failure of writing. Despite itself, Kaniuk's *A Good Arab,* reflects the hegemony of Zionism within Israeli Jewish culture; Mikhael presents a subaltern subject who internalizes hegemonic "strictures of feeling"; Ballas's and Swissa's protagonists reflect the possibility of a counterhegemony whose cultural base can only remain ambiguous, which is a condition that is itself counterhegemonistic. In a sense, both Ballas and Swissa have produced authentic extranational, one is tempted to say postnational, novels. To that extent, they speak within and of a history that subsumes rather than merely opposes that of the Jews, and it is that history that Israeli culture ultimately must recognize if it is to produce works that are genuinely self-critical in their moral reflection, if it is to permit the rediscovery of the self as other that is essential to recognizing the other and therefore to any nonsectarian morality.

Notes

Introduction

1. Edward W. Said, *Orientalism* (New York: Vintage, 1979).

2. Talcott Parsons, "A Revised Analytical Approach to the Theory of Social Stratification," in *Essays in Sociological Theory*, rev. ed. (New York: Free Press, 1954), 386–439.

3. Michael Riffaterre, *Fictional Truth* (Baltimore: Johns Hopkins University Press, 1990).

4. Jürgen Habermas, *Legitimation Crisis*, trans. Thomas McCarthy (Boston: Beacon, 1975).

5. Baruch Kimmerling, *Zionism and Economy* (Cambridge, Mass.: Schenkman, 1983). In his study, Kimmerling demonstrates the presence of an a priori Zionist ideological force in economy planning and shows that this pattern is continued from prestate Zionist economy to economy structuring in Israel today.

6. George R. Tamarin, "The Influence of Ethnic and Religious Prejudice on Moral Judgment," in *The Israeli Dilemma: Essays on a Warfare State* (Rotterdam: Rotterdam University Press, 1973), 183–89.

7. Hayden White, *Metahistory: The Historical Imagination in Nineteenth Century Europe* (Baltimore: Johns Hopkins University Press, 1973).

8. Quoted in Ehud Ben Ezer, "Where There Is No Vision the People Perish: Interview with David Ben Gurion," in *Unease in Zion* (Jerusalem: Jerusalem Academic Press & Quadrangle/New York Times Books, 1974), 75.

9. S. Yizhar, *"Hirbet Hizah," in *Arbaah Sippurim* (Tel Aviv: Hakibbutz Hameuchad, 1977), 86. Throughout, in notes, publications in Hebrew are indicated by asterisks. All translations from the Hebrew are mine.

10. Jacob Kellner, *The First Aliyot: Myths and Reality*, ed. and comp. Aharon Fein (Jerusalem: Hebrew University School of Social Work, 1982), 16. Page numbers for further citations of this work appear in text.

11. *Aliyah*, or "immigration," is a major idea of Zionism and the primary means for its realization. The term implies "personal participation in the rebuilding of the Jewish homeland and the

elevation of the individual to a higher plane of self-fulfillment as a member of the renascent nation." *Encyclopedia Judaica* (Jerusalem: Keter, 1972), 2:633. Indeed, the term is not value free. Literally it means "ascendence," "going up," "approach." In the same vein, the Zionist term for emigration from Israel is *yerida*, meaning "descending" or "going down." The Hebrew "value-free" term for immigration and emigration, is *hagira*.

12. Joseph Hayyim Brenner (1881–1921) was a Hebrew and Yiddish writer, literary editor, and publicist. He was born in the Ukraine, and in 1909 he emigrated to Palestine. There he contributed to two periodicals, published fiction, and continued his work as an editor. *Mikan u-Mikan* (From here and there), 1911, was Brenner's first novella published in Palestine that depicted life in the Zionist settlements. On 2 May 1921, Brenner was killed during a Palestinian insurrection against Zionist colonization and British government colonial policies in Palestine.

13. Joseph Hayyim Brenner, *Mikan*, in *Complete Works*, 2d ed., comp. Menachem Poznansky (Tel Aviv: Hakibbutz Hameuchad, 1955), 1:352. Page numbers for further quotes from this work appear in text. *Oved etsot*, in Hebrew, means "perplexed," "at a loss," "confused." In Kabbalh, *yesod* means "root" or "origin"; in ordinary use, it indicates a foundation, base, or ground.

14. Baruch Kurzweil, *"Between Brenner, Weininger and Kafka," in *Yosef Haim Brenner: A Selection of Critical Essays on His Literary Prose*, comp. Yitshak Bakon (Tel Aviv: Am Oved, 1972), 145.

15. This character's name is derived from the word *Diaspora*.

16. Yitshak Bakon, *"Introduction," in *Yosef Haim Brenner: A Selection of Critical Essays on His Literary Prose*, comp. Yitshak Bakon (Tel Aviv: Am Oved, 1972), 15. Page numbers for further citations of this work appear in text.

17. H. N. Bialik (1873–1936) was born in the Ukraine. Formally considered the greatest Hebrew poet of modern times, this essayist, story writer, translator, and editor exercised profound influence on modern Jewish culture. He participated in Zionist Congresses (1907, 1913, 1921, and 1931) and at the Congress for Hebrew Language and Culture (1913). He settled in Palestine in 1924.

18. Brenner's character Oved Etsot speaks of the "Congregation of Israel" as a whore who "cannot cease being a whore since this is her nature," and of Jerusalem as a "holy butcher shop, where holiness is sold by the pound. . . . this worn out old woman, who never knew shame . . . whose entire sense of value always dependent on what others thought of her." Brenner, *Mikan*, 1:345.

19. Brenner's abundant literary work was published at the time in poor form and with many distortions in various literary magazines, single books, and pamphlets. The first edition of Brenner's *Collected Works* was published between 1924 and 1930, and the second edition only twenty-five years later. See Joseph Hayyim Brenner, *Complete Works*, 2d ed., comp. Menachem Poznansky (Tel Aviv: Hakibbutz Hameuchad, 1955), 1:487.

20. Quoted by Nurit Govrin, *"The Brenner Affair": The Fight for Free Speech (1910–1913)* (Jerusalem: Yad Izhak Ben Zvi, 1985), 19.

21. The Hebrew word for apostasy is *shmad*, the same as for destruction, devastation, to lay waste, annihilate, wipe out.

22. Govrin, *"The Brenner Affair,"* 10. Ahad Haam (Asher Hirsch Ginsberg; 1856–1927) was a Hebrew essayist, thinker, and leader of the Hibbat Zion (Love of Zion) movement. (The Hibbat Zion movement was founded in Odessa in 1883. It preceded the World Zionist Organization founded by Herzl in 1897.) More than fifty people took part in this disputation by publishing their positions in print. Of them, forty signed either with their full names or with pseudonyms that were later identified. Among them (I mention only some of the names that recur in my text in different contexts) were Ahad Haam, Eliezer Ben Yehuda, J. H. Brenner, David Ben Gurion, M. J. Berdichevsky, and A. D. Gordon. Among participants who were involved indirectly (in private letters), we find the names of M. Usishkin, H. N. Bialik, and Z. V. Zabotinsky. The disputation

was conducted in Hebrew, Yiddish, and Russian, in some twenty periodicals and newspapers, in ten different places in the world. See Govrin, *"*The Brenner Affair*," 14.

23. Dan Miron, *"Landscape Scenes in Brenner's Palestine Stories," *Zmanim* (28 September 1955–9 November 1955), quoted by Bakon, *"Introduction," 31. For more on Brenner, see chapter 4.

24. Quotes in text are from Tom Segev, *1949: The First Israelis*, trans. Arlen Neal Weinstein (New York: Free Press, 1986). Page numbers for further citations of this work appear in text.

25. Israel argued that Palestinian Arabs were encouraged by their own political leadership to leave the country so as not to be in the way of the Arab armies in their surge forward against Israel. There is now ample available research that refutes this argument. For the most comprehensive study on the issue to date, see Nur Masallha, *Expulsion of the Palestinians: The Concept of "Transfer" in Zionist Political Thought 1882–1948* (Washington, D.C.: Institute of Palestine Studies, 1992); see also Walid Khalidi, "Plan Dalet: Master Plan for the Conquest of Palestine," *Journal of Palestine Studies* 18 (Autumn 1988): 4–37; Benny Morris, *The Birth of the Palestinian Refugee Problem 1947–1949* (Cambridge: Cambridge University Press, 1987); Michael Palumbo, *The Palestinian Catastrophe: The 1948 Expulsion of a People from Their Homeland* (London: Quartet, 1987).

26. Abbas Shiblak, *The Lure of Zion: The Case of the Iraqi Jews* (London: Al Saqui, 1986); Simha Flapan, *The Birth of Israel Myths and Realities* (New York: Pantheon, 1987); Wilbur Crane Eveland, *The Ropes of Sand: America's Failure in the Middle East* (New York: Norton, 1980); Uri Avneri, *My Friend, the Enemy* (Westport, Conn.: Lawrence Hill, 1986). See also *"Bombs against Jews," *Haolam Haze*, 20 April 1966, 12–13; this was reprinted as *"Iraqi Jewry and Their Immigration to Israel," *The Black Panther*, 9 November 1972, 5–6, 16.

27. Nathan Alterman, *"The First Million," in *The Seventh Column* (Tel Aviv: Davar, 1954), 49. Translation in Segev, *1949*, 96. Reprinted by permission.

28. Neil Smelser, *The Theory of Collective Behavior* (New York: Free Press, 1962), 79–130.

29. Dan Laor, *"The Mass Immigration as Content and Subject in Hebrew Literature," *Haaretz*, 20 April 1988, Literary section. Laor later published an expanded version of the same article, adding to the title the words "During the State's Early Years," *Hatsionut* 14 (1989): 161–75.

30. Ibid. (in *Haaretz*), 19.

31. Ammiel Alcalay, *After Arabs and Jews* (Minneapolis: University of Minnesota Press, 1993), 232. Alcalay adds, "Despite their canonical position within Israel, particularly when compared to Levantine writers, the works of many others are also difficult to place among a general readership. These include writers such as David Shahar, Uri Zvi Greenberg, Pinhas Sadeh, Benyamin Tammuz, Aharon Amir, Amalia Kahane-Carmon, Chaim Be'er, and Yoel Hoffman."

1. Israeli Hebrew Literature and Zionist Historiography

1. Simon Halkin, *Modern Hebrew Literature* (New York: Schocken, 1970), 115.

2. In contradistinction to this historiographic certainty, Philip K. Hitti opens his *History of the Arabs*, 10th ed. (London: Macmillan, 1970) with this statement: "As the probable cradle of the Semitic family the Arabian peninsula nursed those peoples who later migrated into the Fertile Crescent and subsequently became the Babylonians, the Assyrians, the Phoenicians and the Hebrews of History. As the plausible font of pure Semitism, the sandy soil of the peninsula is the place wherein the rudimentary elements of Judaism, and consequently of Christianity—together with the origin of those traits which later developed into the well delineated Semitic character—should be sought for" (p. 3).

3. Salo W. Baron, *A Social and Religious History of the Jews*, vols. 1–2 (New York: Columbia University Press, 1952).

4. Julius Guttman, *Jewish Philosophy* (Jerusalem: Mossad Bialik, 1963); Hitti, *History of the Arabs*.

5. Yehuda Slutsky, *"Haskalah" (Enlightenment), in *Encyclopedia Judaica* (Jerusalem: Keter, 1972).

6. Arthur Hertzberg, *The Zionist Idea* (New York: Atheneum, 1977); Shlomo Avineri, *The Making of Modern Zionism: The Intellectual History of the Jewish State* (New York: Basic Books, 1981).

7. David Horowitz, *My Yesterday: An Autobiography* (Jerusalem: Schocken, 1970), 18 and passim.

8. Fredric Jameson, *The Political Unconscious* (Ithaca, N.Y.: Cornell University Press, 1981); see also Jameson's "Third World Literature in the Era of Multinational Capitalism," *Social Text* 15 (Fall 1986): 65–88; Aijaz Ahmad, "Jameson's Rhetorics of Otherness and the 'National Allegory,'" *Social Text* 17 (Fall 1987): 3–25.

9. Pinchas Genussar, *"The Dialogue between the Labor Movement and the Renaissance Writers," *Iton* 77 (November-December 1988): 26–33; and *Iton* 77 (January-February 1989): 32–35. This essay is part of Genussar's Ph.D. thesis in literature.

10. *Shtetl* is a Yiddish word used to describe a kind of small Jewish town that used to exist in Eastern Europe.

11. Gershon Shaked, *Hebrew Narrative Fiction*, vol. 1, *In Exile* (Tel Aviv: Hakibbutz Hameuchad & Keter, 1977), 17–68.

12. Dan Horowitz and Moshe Lissak, *From a Community to a State: The Jews of Palestine as a Political Community during the British Mandate* (Tel Aviv: Am Oved University Library, 1977).

13. Genussar, *"The Dialogue."

14. Nurith Gertz, ed., *Literature and Ideology in Palestine in the 1930s, 3 vols. (Tel Aviv: Everyman's University, 1988).

15. I will refer to the "civil self" as *subject* in the dual sense of membership and agency or obligation.

16. It is argued that this sense of exclusion among Israeli Jews has doubtless been true since 1967. But, by the same argument, prior to the 1967 war, Israeli leftist intellectuals (scientists and others) regarded the term *tsionut* (Zionism) as a kind of joke, something used to extort money from rich American Jews. It is said that the country was becoming secularized, with long-overdue beginnings of concern over the deeply discriminatory character of Israeli government practices. By the same argument, shortly after the 1967 war, when the occupation settled in, those attitudes changed radically. The same people who were making fun of *tsionut* prior to the war were bitterly condemning those who dared to suggest that Palestinians had any rights, and would be infuriated at any criticism of Israel or Zionism. In many instances such criticism would be considered a dangerous disease that had to be fought. However, the second half of this argument does not explain the first half. I would suggest that in the early 1960s, Israeli leftists and liberals assumed that the Zionist mission was successfully accomplished; that its greatest achievement, the state of Israel, superseded Zionism; and that it should take over *all* the World Zionist Organization's earlier tasks. See, for example, Walter Laqueur, *A History of Zionism* (New York: Schocken, 1976), specifically his conclusion. This may explain why, for these liberals, *tsionut* became a joke. What most liberals and leftists had underestimated, however, was the as-yet-unsatisfied Zionist ideological ambition, its *endziel*. The 1967 war did not so much provide an opportunity for achieving these ambitions as it was their product. Once Menachem Begin took office as prime minister in 1977, he demonstrated, in flowery oratory and practical politics, his ardent advocacy, and the efficacy, of Zionism's grand designs. Indeed, there were liberal organizations and there was an Israeli Zionist Left. But the extent and relevance of their criticism is significant for the study of its limitations. Insofar as leftist Zionist parties are concerned, historical evidence would show that they, always, adjusted their political positions to the right. For a classic hostile response to a critique of Zionism from the

"Left" see "Eichmann in Jerusalem," an exchange of letters between Hannah Arendt and Gershom Scholem, *Encounter* (January 1964): 51–56. See also Norman G. Finkelstein, "Zionist Orientations: A Study of Ideology," *New Politics* 2 (Summer 1988); and his "From the Jewish Question to the Jewish State: An Essay on the Theory of Zionism" (Ph.D. diss., Princeton University, 1987). I owe my gratitude to Professor Noam Chomsky for presenting this argument, and for referring me to Professor Finkelstein's work. I am also thankful to Professor Finkelstein for offering me generous help with his studies on Zionism.

17. Erving Goffman, *Stigma: Notes on the Management of Spoiled Identity* (Englewood Cliffs, N.J.: Prentice Hall, 1963).

18. On 13 September 1985, Anton Shammas, an Israeli Palestinian author, poet, and journalist, published an article in *Kol Hair* titled *"A New Year for the Jews." He says, "In the absence of a constitution, [Israel's] Proclamation of Independence, although still considered in good repute as a liberal document . . . is, in my view, the AIDS of 'a Jewish State in the Land of Israel to be known as the State of Israel' [quoted from the Proclamation]. A mononational Jewish state contains its own seeds of calamity: the collapse of the state's immune system, i.e., its democracy. A monoracial, mononational state as established by the Law of Return is, in my view, the racist aspect of the Proclamation of Independence . . . on the surface of it, it promised 'complete social and political equality' for all; yet, it turns out . . . that the only democracy in the Middle East is dying. . . . what is to be done? Establish the State of Israel . . . (a united Israeli nation in which some are of a Palestinian Arab ethnic origin)" (p. 17). This article was rebutted fiercely both by the Right and the Left, and it provoked a harsh debate that still continues, mostly within literary circles. A. B. Yehoshua, Israel's preeminent Hebrew writer, who considers himself a member of the Israeli "Left," became Shammas's main interlocutor. In his first response, Yehoshua announced, "I am saying to Anton Shammas: if you want your full identity, if you want to live in a state that has a Palestinian character, with a genuine Palestinian culture, arise, take your belongings, and extract yourself one hundred yards eastward, into the Palestinian state that would dwell alongside Israel." Quoted in Yarom London, *"The Guilt of the Left" (interview with A. B. Yehoshua), *Politica* 4 (November-December 1985): 8–13.

It should be noted, however, that the Law of Return or the Proclamation of Independence is not consistent with the explicit decision of Israel's High Court (1961) that Israel is "the state of the Jewish people" in Israel and the Diaspora, not the state of its citizens; it is also not consistent with the complex system of land laws and administrative practices that virtually bar Arab citizens from about 92 percent of the land.

19. I am grateful to Professor Chomsky for drawing my attention to this High Court decision of 1989, and to that of 1961, as discussed in note 18, above.

20. Theodor Herzl, *Collected Writings*, trans. A. Barash, R. Benjamin, and A. Yaari, vol. 5, *The Jewish State* (Tel Aviv: Mitzpeh, 1939), 9–96. According to Hannah Arendt: "Herzl proposed a 'Jewish Company' that would build a state with 'Relief by Labor'—that is, by paying a 'good-for-nothing beggar' charity rates for forced full-time work—and by the 'truck system' consisting of labor gangs 'drafted from place to place like a body of troops' and paid in goods instead of wages. Herzl was also determined to suppress all 'opposition' in case of lack of gratitude on the part of people to whom the land would be given." In terms of nationalism, Herzl's thought was "inspired from German sources—as opposed to the French variety, which could never quite repudiate its original relationship to the political ideas of the French Revolution." Hannah Arendt, "The Jewish State: Fifty Years After," *Commentary* 1 (May 1946): 1, 6. For more on the German-related sources of Zionist nationalism, see Arendt's essay "Zionism Reconsidered," *Menorah Journal* 33 (August 1945): 162–96.

21. Michael E. Brown, "The Viability of Racism: South Africa and the United States," *Philosophical Forum* 18 (Winter-Spring 1986–87): 254–69.

22. See note 18, above. Yehoshua's comment reflects the "blood and race" conception of

nationalism and citizenship that traces back to the romantic period and reaches its most horrible expression with the Nazis, in contrast to the Enlightenment conception. It is worth recalling that liberal Zionist humanists in the mid-1930s, while despising Nazism for its anti-Semitism, felt an ideological kinship with the Nazis because of their emphasis on "blood and race" and abandonment of the "discredited" Enlightenment concepts of "brotherhood of man," and even argued that Zionists could appeal to the Nazis by making it clear that they shared the basic Nazi conception. See Joachim Prinz, *Wir Juden* (Berlin: Erich Reiss, 1934); also see Finkelstein, "Zionist Orientations" and "From the Jewish Question." I would like to express my gratitude to Professor Noam Chomsky for directing me to Joachim Prinz's work mentioned here.

23. Michael Riffaterre, *Fictional Truth* (Baltimore: Johns Hopkins University Press, 1990).

24. The same feature, though from a slightly different angle, recurs in my discussion regarding criticism of Shimon Ballas, Sammy Mikhael, and Albert Swissa in Part II of this volume.

25. Hayden White, *Metahistory: The Historical Imagination in Nineteenth Century Europe* (Baltimore: Johns Hopkins University Press, 1973), 7–29.

26. Tzvetan Todorov, *The Conquest of America: The Question of the Other*, trans. Richard Howard (New York: Harper Torchbooks, 1987).

27. For a sample of such portrayals of "the Arab" see S. Yizhar, *"The Prisoner," in *Arbaah Sipurim* (Tel Aviv: Hakibbutz Hameuchad, 1959; 13th ed., 1977) (trans. V. C. Rycus, in *Modern Hebrew Literature*, ed. Robert Alter [New York: Behrman House, 1975]); A. B. Yehoshua, *"Facing the Forests," in *Facing the Forests: Short Stories* (Tel Aviv: Hakibbutz Hameuchad, 1968) (trans. Miriam Arad, in *Modern Hebrew Literature*); A. B. Yehoshua, *The Lover* (Tel Aviv: Schocken, 1979) (trans. Philip Simpson [New York: A. Dutton, 1985]); A. B. Yehoshua, *Mr. Mani* (Tel Aviv: Hakibbutz Hameuchad, 1990) (trans. Hillel Halkin [New York: Doubleday, 1992]); Amos Oz, *"Nomads and Viper," in *Where the Jackals Howl* (Tel Aviv: Am Oved, 1982) (trans. Nicholas de Lang and Philip Simpson, in *Where the Jackals Howl and Other Stories* [New York: Harcourt Brace Jovanovich, 1981]); Amos Oz, *My Michael* (Tel Aviv: Am Oved, 1968; reprint, 1983) (trans. Nicholas de Lang in collaboration with the author [New York: Bantam, 1976]); David Grossman, *The Smile of the Lamb* (Tel Aviv: Hakibbutz Hameuchad, 1983) (trans. Betsy Rosenberg [New York: Farrar, Straus & Giroux, 1991]); David Grossman *Yellow Wind* (Tel Aviv: Am Oved, 1987) (trans. Haim Watzman [New York: Farrar, Straus & Giroux, 1988]); Sammy Mikhael, *Hasut* (Tel Aviv: Am Oved, 1977) (trans. Edward Grossman, *Refuge*, [Philadelphia: Jewish Publication Society of America, 1988]); Sammy Mikhael, *Trumpet in the Wadi* (Tel Aviv: Am Oved, 1987); Shimon Ballas, *A Locked Room* (Tel Aviv: Zmora, Beitan, Modan, 1980); Shulamit Lapid, *As a Broken Vessel* (Jerusalem: Keter, 1984); Ruth Almog, *Death in the Rain* (Jerusalem: Keter, 1982). See also my discussion of the works of Sammy Mikhael and Shimon Ballas in chapter 7.

28. This is the logic one would apply to any case of the moralistic denial of an other's essential humanity and the sudden recognition of that humanity in a moment of justifiable hypercriticism.

2. The Problematic of a "Good Arab"

1. Yosef Sherara, *A Good Arab, (Tel Aviv: Kineret, 1984). The English translation, which carries Yoram Kaniuk's name as author, is titled *Confessions of a Good Arab*, trans. Dalia Bilu (London: Peter Halban, 1987). Because of significant discrepancies between the Hebrew and English versions, and as part of my argument, I have attempted my own translation wherever I found it necessary. Translations in this book of all other Hebrew materials are mine.

2. This quote falls on page 5 in the Hebrew edition and on page 2 in the English. This will be the format of all citations to the Hebrew and English texts of *A Good Arab,*.

3. The author does not provide dates and is meticulously chaotic regarding his characters'

ages, biographies, and histories. Therefore, all birth dates and the times of other "historical" events I have extrapolated from the text.

4. An ex-paratrooper turned "liberal," Rammy is regarded by Yosef as an "outsider" within his own group. Based on Yosef's Jewish-Arab historical and identity "symmetry," Yosef sees Rammy as having "the same fate" as he. There is no indication in the text, however, that Rammy shares this perception with Yosef.

5. Marie-Helene Huet, *Monstrous Imagination* (Cambridge, Mass.: Harvard University Press, 1993).

6. It should be noted here that Menachem Begin (at the time prime minister of Israel) denounced this claim as hypocritical, saying that the 1967 war was also a "war of choice," a position that had been expressed ten years earlier by a whole raft of generals, beginning with General Mati Peled, and later by General Ezer Weizmann (now president of the state), and others.

7. See, for example, Amos Oz, *Poh va-sham be-Eretz-Yisrae'el bi-stav 1982* (Tel Aviv: Sifriyat Ofakim Am Oved, 1983) (translation, *In the Land of Israel* [New York: Harcourt Brace Jovanovich, 1983] and *The Slopes of Lebanon: Essays and Articles* [Tel Aviv: Am Oved, 1987; Vintage International, 1993]). In fiction, see Amos Kenan, *The Road to Ein Harod* (Tel Aviv: Am Oved, 1984); Benjamin Tammuz, *Jeremiah's Sin* (Jerusalem: Keter, 1984).

The argument of "Palestinian intransigence" or "right-wing extremism" was a pretense liberal Labor Zionists, including Peace Now personalities, used to present in defense of the Labor coalition governments who refused to move toward a political settlement. In fact, the most avid opponents of a political settlement, arguably, were Yizhak Tabenkin (a leader of Ahdut haAvodah) and RAFI (Ahdut haAvodah and RAFI are two partner parties of Labor governments). On the "panic" caused among Israel's political leadership in the wake of a full-scale peace settlement made by Anwar el-Sadat in 1971, see Amos Elon, *"'I Am Disappointed, We Stopped at the Middle of the Road—Israel Is to Blame'": An Interview with President Sadat of Egypt,"* Haaretz, 16 March 1980, 13–20. For an informative insider's account, with extensive quotes from cabinet records and other discussions from 1967–77, see Yossi Beilin, *Mehiro Shel Ihud* (The price of unity): *The Labor Party until the Yom Kippur War* (Tel Aviv: Revivim, 1980), especially chap. 4. I am grateful to Professor Noam Chomsky for these references. See also three works by Norman G. Finkelstein: "Zionist Orientations: A Study of Ideology," *New Politics* 2 (Summer 1988); "From the Jewish Question to the Jewish State: An Essay on the Theory of Zionism" (Ph.D. diss., Princeton University, 1987); "Myths of Conquest: Critical Reflections on Zionist Ideology" (unpublished manuscript, 1993).

8. Yoram Kaniuk, "I am Yosef Sherara," *Maariv Sofshavua*, 6 August 1984, weekly supplement magazine, 27.

9. Heda Boshes, "Incest as a Problem," review of *A Good Arab*, by Yoram Kaniuk, in *Haaretz*, 25 May 1984, 12.

10. Michal Sela, "I Am an Israeli Too," review of *A Good Arab*, by Yoram Kaniuk, *Yediot Aharonot*, 1 June 1984.

11. Amnon Navot, "Shedding Light on the Consciousness of the Other," review of *A Good Arab*, by Yoram Kaniuk, *Maariv*, 29 June 1984, 43. As Navot says in his essay, he was among those critics who, a short while before Kaniuk's public announcement, identified the writer by the novel's style and language. This process, then, began to bear on Kaniuk, finally forcing him to admit his deception publicly. See also Sela, "I Am an Israeli Too."

12. Navot mentions Rammy's *need*, as it were, to be serving in a paratroopers' unit as an example of such "an a priori" assumption by Kaniuk; he also mentions Dina's being a cadet in women officers' training.

I assume that Navot is using the term "external layer" in contrast with his designation of "materia," which he perceives as substantive *content*, meaning those materials that are not *sensational*.

13. Edward Said, "Narrative, Geography and Interpretation." *New Left Review* 180 (March 1990): 81–97. For the concept of the colonial-settler state as it pertains to Israel, see Maxime Rodinson, *Israel: A Colonial-Settler State?* (New York: Monad, 1973); also see Ibrahim Abu-Lughod and Baha Abu-Laban, eds., *Settler Regimes in Africa and the Arab World: The Illusion of Endurance* (Wimette, Ill.: Medina University Press International, 1974).

14. Boshes, "Incest as a Problem"; Sela, "I Am an Israeli Too"; Anton Shammas, "What About the Comma?" review of *A Good Arab,* by Yoram Kaniuk, *Kol Hair,* 5 May 1984; P. Alef, "On the Road to Despair," review of *A Good Arab,* by Yoram Kaniuk, *Zo-Haderkh,* 22 August 1984; Lea Dovev, "A Good Arab, Unreasonable," review of *A Good Arab,* by Yoram Kaniuk, *Kol Haifa,* 24 August 1984.

15. As in the Hebrew edition on p. 87; this text is missing from the English version.

16. This text is missing from the English edition.

17. Kaniuk, "I am Yosef Sherara." Arabic names in *A Good Arab,* are misspelled in Hebrew or are not possible as names: Yosef is a Hebrew name. As an Arab name it should be spelled Yousuf, Yusuf, or Youssef. Yosef's father's first name, Azouri, is not a first name in Arabic; his last name, Sherara, from the Arabic root *sha'ar* (a spark), should be spelled Sharara; a more proper form would be Sha'ara. For criticism of this aspect of the novel, see Shammas, "What About the Comma?"; Sela, "I Am an Israeli Too"; Alef, "On the Road to Despair."

18. Kaniuk, "I Am Yosef Sherara."

19. See the novel's introduction (p. 1), first paragraph, in both the Hebrew and the English versions.

20. Erving Goffman, *Stigma: Notes on the Management of Spoiled Identity* (Englewood Cliffs, N.J.: Prentice Hall, 1963).

3. Dual Identity: "To Be My Own Enemy"

1. These lines are missing from the English translation.

2. A debate erupted in the aftermath of Anton Shammas's publication of his novel *Arabesques* in 1986. Anton Shammas is a Palestinian Arab citizen of Israel. His novel is a first-person autobiographical narrative of a Palestinian Arab written originally in Hebrew. Shammas argues that he is a Palestinian Arab, member of the Israeli nation, writing in its national language—Hebrew. This follows his position that Israel should be "a democratic state of its citizens, rather than a Jewish state of the Jewish people." Anton Shammas, *Arabesqaot (Tel Aviv: Am Oved, 1986) (trans. Vivian Eden, *Arabesques* [New York: Harper & Row, 1988]). For the debate, see Sammy Mikhael, *"Arabesqaot haTsionutionut" (The arabesques of Zionism), comments on the debate between A. B. Yehoshua and Anton Shammas, *Moznaim* 60 (July-August 1986): 10–17. Anton Shammas, *"Milhamti beTahanot Anshei haRuakh" (My war against the intellectuals' windmills), *Moznaim* 70 (September 1986): 26–27. Yael Lotan, *"Lismoakh veLo leHitaabel" (Be happy rather than mourn), *Moznaim* 70 (September 1986): 28–30.

3. Although the actual meaning is "the house of the father of Yosef" (a grammatical form found frequently in the Bible), here, as I suggest, it implies a double meaning, namely, "my father's house" (Yosef's).

4. Kaniuk (here obviously as *the writer*) defines the "tragedy" as "Jewish-Palestinian" rather than as Israeli-Palestinian or Zionist-Palestinian, thus utilizing a Zionist trope whereby the entire Jewish people becomes a (monolithic) partner to the conflict and the Palestinian people an enemy of the Jewish people as such.

5. Yoram Kaniuk, "I Am Yosef Sherara," *Maariv Sofshavua,* 6 August 1984, weekly supplement magazine, 27.

6. It is impossible for me to provide a systematic review of the discrepancies in syntax, grammar, and punctuation between the Hebrew version and the formal English translation of this

book. However, the following instance from the English edition serves to illustrate the point: "What remains is therefore my own irrational theory, I was there, in potential. I had to be born in order to spoil the stereotypes that made things so simple for Bunim and Nissan, and also to understand them with the part of me that comes under the stereotype of "holocaust survivor." Not that Franz was actually a holocaust survivor, he got out before it happened, but his humiliation when they expelled him from the hospital, the Judaism they forced on him in the shape of the yellow star, were enough to make him into a refugee."

Among other things, it should be noted here that "yellow patch" *in Hebrew, in Israel*, signifies humiliation. As such, it works as a trope for the Zionist notion that European Jews in their powerlessness, meekly, had to wear a national symbol as a sign of their own humiliation. If later on (non-Zionist) Jewish historians termed it a "yellow star," they, I believe, wanted to signify a defiance of this intended humiliation, but that is not in Kaniuk's text.

7. Israel's Knesset Protocols, Absentee Property Law, 1950. This law assigned the status of abandoned property to all movable and immovable property of Palestinian Arabs who had fled to the neighboring countries during the war and later extended its jurisdiction to include the property of Palestinians who were declared "present absentees" although they did not leave the country. These were people who were not "physically" present at home on 15 May 1948, the day the state of Israel was proclaimed. Land, houses, property, and all means of livelihood were put into a custodianship of the Custodian of Absentee Property, and were later confiscated by the state. This property was then leased, granted, or sold for a symbolic price to Jewish newcomers, farmers, town dwellers, and kibbutzim. On this subject, see Sabri Jiryis, *The Arabs in Israel* (New York: Monthly Review Press, 1976), 75–134; Ian Lustick, *Arabs in the Jewish State: Israel's Control of a National Minority* (Austin: University of Texas Press, 1980), 31, 59, 61.

8. On 9 April 1948, a unit of the Irgun and Lehi paramilitary organizations attacked and captured the Palestinian village of Deir Yassin at the southern outskirts of Jerusalem, and slaughtered some 250 men women and children, whose mutilated bodies were stuffed into wells. The first Israeli account was published by Uri Milstein in the daily *Haaretz*, 30 August 1968. See also Larry Collins and Dominique Lapierre, *O' Jerusalem* (New York: Simon & Schuster, 1972), 272–82; M. Begin, *The Revolt* (New York: Dell, 1977), 224–27; Jiryis, *The Arabs in Israel*, 137–40.

9. Palmach is the Hebrew abbreviation for Storm Troops, the name of Jewish paramilitary units established in 1941 in Palestine, nominally to assist the British army in the defense against the approaching German assault, which never materialized. In 1944, these units went underground and formed a commando force against the British and the Palestinian Arabs. These units distinguished themselves in the 1948–49 war and became legendary. HaShomer, or the Watchman (1909–20), was the first Jewish paramilitary organization in Palestine; it served to protect life and property in the Jewish colonies, and was supported by the Zionist World Organization. The majority of its members, although not of the same political party, were ardent nationalists and in many instances exerted violence.

10. This is a pun on "drying of the swamps," which is to this day a distinguished Zionist metonym. (This text is missing from the English translation.)

11. This is a slightly changed name (*Michael* Halpern). Halpern is described by Walter Laqueur as "one of the early *shomrim*, [who] used to talk occasionally about the conquest of the country by legions of Jewish soldiers. But these were flights of fancy indulged by a few individuals, and no one took them seriously at the time." (Walter Laqueur, *A History of Zionism* (New York: Schocken, 1976), 228.

12. This is an acronym for an incipient Zionist movement (early 1880s) that initiated the first groups of Zionist immigrants to Palestine.

13. This, of course, is Kaniuk's ironic reflection on Zionist indoctrination of little children in elementary school.

14. Hebrew: "On the fifteenth [of the month] all Arabs will be dead." Azouri's response is in Arabic.

15. The "black lists" are the lists of mixed marriages and children thereof, or "suspected" non-Halachic conversions to Judaism.

16. Halacha is Jewish traditional law.

17. This means that here Yosef is assigning *his mother*, the daughter of a Jewish emigrant from Germany who left in 1936, the status of a "descendant of Holocaust survivor," thus granting himself the status of a second-generation descendant of a Holocaust survivor; and so every Jewish newborn of European descent after World War II could be regarded as "descendants of Holocaust survivors," which, from a Zionist point of view, is as important for its moral significance as is for traditional Jews being descendents of those who attended the Giving of the Torah at Mount Sinai.

18. By "in the original," does Yosef mean he read the "protocols" from the court's files? I suggest this is another instance of contrariness between the display of signs and their use (see chapter 2).

19. This is "incorrect"; Yosef was born in Paris, France.

20. In the context of this narrative, the allusion is to the Israeli Communist party.

21. Unless this is a reference to Azouri's historical research on the Israeli-Palestinian conflict, the reader would not know what this charge is.

22. By this he means a *Jewish* high school.

23. These are all demeaning colloquial terms used for Arabs in Israel.

24. Neli Milo, "Almost a Poem," review of *A Good Arab*, by Yoram Kaniuk, *Iton 77* 77 (September 1984): 51.

25. Amnon Navot, "Shedding Light on the Consciousness of the Other," review of *A Good Arab*, by Yoram Kaniuk, *Maariv*, 29 June 1984, 43.

26. Surely, Yosef did not kill his father. His comment regarding his mother's uniform is only an analogy. This swollen "oratory" could be another orientalist feature Kaniuk ascribes to an "Arab."

27. This "generosity" in the number of Azouri's doctorates is in itself an orientalist expression.

4. The Palestinian "Extremist"

1. In late-eighteenth-century England one finds the same moral conceptual base for "savage," "woman," "child," "primitive," "the people," "the mob," "the poor." Each invokes the irrational other to what Adam Smith called "commercial society," and to the calming rationalism of the Augustans. See Michael E. Brown, "Unaccountable History: Some Limits of Experience" (paper submitted for publication, 1993).

2. I consider Israeli-Palestinian citizens only. Palestinians of the Occupied Territories would present a slightly different issue, which I do not discuss here.

3. For another example of this "type," see the boy protagonist, Naim (the "good Arab"), in comparison with his uncle Hamid, "the Arab," in A. B. Yehoshua's novel *The Lover* (Tel Aviv: Schocken, 1979).

4. Adir Cohen, *An Ugly Face in the Mirror: National Stereotypes in Hebrew Children's Literature* (Tel Aviv: Reshafim, 1985); Fauzi El-Asmar, *Through the Hebrew Looking-Glass: Arab Stereotypes in Children's Literature* (Brattleboro, Vt.: Amana, 1986). See also my review of these two books, "Stereotypes in Literature," *Journal of Palestine Studies* 17 (Autumn 1987): 159–63.

5. The name is not spelled correctly here; it should be abu-al-Misk Kafur Sharara; also, the name (in Hebrew) of Salah-al-Din is misspelled in the quote that follows.

6. Edward W. Said, *Orientalism* (New York: Vintage, 1979). See specifically Said's discussion of Dante, d'Herbelot, Flauber, Lamartine, and Lane.

7. Nissim Calderon, *A Previous Chapter: On Nathan Sach in the Early Sixties (Tel Aviv: Hakibbutz Hameuchad Siman Kriah, 1985), 75–76 and passim.

8. He refers to "The Seventh Column," a political weekly feature by the poet Nathan Alterman that appeared in *Davar, the daily newspaper of Israel's Trade Unions Federation (Histadrut), and at the time the de facto mouthpiece of the ruling party, MAPI. Alterman's admiration of Ben Gurion and Moshe Dayan and their policies and politics, and their praise in his poetry, had become explicit already in the early 1950s. A number of Israeli literary critics have dealt with this issue. See Dan Miron, *If There Is No Jerusalem: Essays on Hebrew Writing in Cultural-Political Context (Tel Aviv: Hakibbutz Hameuchad, 1987), 56–67.

9. The foreign minister of the United Arab Republic (UAR), Kamal-ud-Din Hussian, on one occasion published a statement that was read to pupils at all educational institutions of the UAR. It concluded with the assurance that the "day of Hittin" was near (referring to the battle of Hittin, near Tiberias, where Salah-al-Din had defeated the Crusader army on July 4, 1187). From Al-Ahram, 15 May 1958, quoted by Aharon Cohen, Israel and the Arab World (Boston: Beacon, 1976), 324–25.

10. Uri Avneri, Israel without Zionists: A Plea for Peace in the Middle East (New York: Macmillan, 1968); reprinted as Israel without Zionism: A Plea for Peace in the Middle East (paperback ed., 1971), 79–89; Benjamin Beit-Hallahmi, The Israeli Connection: Who Israel Arms and Why (New York: Pantheon, 1987), 4, 22, 182, 248; Sylvia Schein, *"Joshua Prawer: In Memoriam" (lecture given at Haifa University, Israel). In her lecture, Schein says that "as a historian, Joshua Prawer holds an outstanding place among historians of the Crusades and the Latin Kingdom of Jerusalem. . . . The impact of his lectures at the Hebrew University . . . from the 1950s onward is best reflected by the fact that in contemporary Hebrew literature, history students are frequently depicted as working on some aspect of the Crusades." Schein's lecture was published in English by the Department of Near Eastern Languages and Civilization of the University of Washington, MESA Bulletin 25 (1991). I am grateful to Dr. B. Beit-Hallahmi for bringing this lecture to my attention.

11. In late summer of 1990, when the Iraq-Kuwait crisis loomed large, Salah-al-Din's image was invoked in Israel once more, this time, in analogy with the president of Iraq, Saddam Hussein. On this, see Yossi Sarid, *"Let Them Look for Me," Haaretz, 17 August 1990; Yaron London, *"So Long, Husseini, Nusseibbeh, and You Other 'Authentic Leaders,'" Yediot Ahronoth, 14 August 1990; Chaim Shur, "Gulf Crisis: PLO on the Wrong Track," New Outlook (August 1990): 5; Daniel Ben Simon, in "Notes from the Israeli Peace Movement" (special section), Tikkun (November-December 1990): 70–78. Yerach Gover, "Gulf Crisis, Palestinians and the Israeli Peace Camp," Social Text 27 (1990): 167–71. In literature, see Dalia Ravikowitz, *"Karnei Hittin," in The Third Book: Poems, 4th ed. (Tel Aviv: Levin-Epstein–Modan, n.d.), 29; A. B. Yehoshua, *Facing the Forests: Short Stories (Tel Aviv: Hakibbutz Hameuchad, 1968); Amos Oz, *Ad Mavet Sipurim (Tel Aviv: Sifriyat Poalim, 1971) (trans. Nicholas de Lange, Unto Death Crusade [New York: Harcourt Brace Jovanowich, 1973]); Gershon Shaked, *A New Wave in Hebrew Literature: Essays on Recent Hebrew Literature (Tel Aviv: Sifriyat Poalim, 1971), 136–40, 200–203. Nurith Gertz, *Amos Oz: A Monograph (Tel Aviv: Sifriyat Poalim, 1980), 147–58; Nurith Gertz, *Generation Shift in Literary History: Hebrew Narrative Fiction in the Sixties (Tel Aviv: Hakibbutz Hameuchad, 1983).

12. Gershon Shaked, *Wave after Wave in Hebrew Narrative (Fiction) (Jerusalem: Keter, 1985), 183. For the English translation of Late Love, see Amos Oz, Unto Death Crusade.

13. Yitzhak Shalev, *The Gabriel Tirosh Affair (Tel Aviv: Am Oved, 1964).

14. See A Survey of Palestine, prepared in December 1945 and January 1946 for the information of the Anglo-American Committee of Inquiry (Washington, D.C.: Institute of Palestine Studies, 1991), 1:141; Sabri Jiryis, The Arabs in Israel (New York: Monthly Review Press, 1976), 291, appendix table 4; Israel Statistical Abstract, 1990.

15. I found a very similar disposition toward the Christian Arab (Anton Shammas), portrayed as a "good Arab" who finds himself in a "minority group" among Muslim Arabs in Israel, and as such being shown sympathy—"as a Jew." See Sammy Mikhael, *"Arabesqaot ha Tsionutionut" (The arabesques of Zionism), comments on the debate between A. B. Yehoshua and Anton Shammas, *Moznaim* 60 (July-August 1986): 10–17.

16. M. Y. Berdichevsky, *"Revaluation of Values [after Nietzsche]," in *Writings: Essays* (Tel Aviv: Dvir, 1952; Maariv ed., 1960), 27–54.

17. For a critical comment regarding the "lachrymose Jew" as perceived by Zionists, see Salo W. Baron, *A Social and Religious History of the Jews* (New York: Columbia University Press, 1952), 1:297.

18. In response to the Kishinev pogroms, Bialik wrote the poem "On the Slaughter" (1903), and later he wrote "In the City of Slaughter" (1904). See H. N. Bialik, *Writings* (Tel Aviv: Dvir, 1962).

19. Rafi Pesakhson and Telma Eligon, eds., *Elef Zemer ve-Od Zemer: The Israeli Sing-Along* 4 vols. (Tel Aviv: Kineret, 1981).

20. Zeev (Vladimir) Zabotinsky, *"Dr. Herzl," in *First Zionist Writings* (Jerusalem: Ari Zabotinsky, c. 1948), 97–100.

21. Yehoshua Porat, *The Emergence of the Palestinian-Arab National Movement 1918–1929* (Tel Aviv: Am Oved, 1976), 169–95; Yehoshua Porat, *From Riots to Rebellion: The Palestinian-Arab National Movement 1929–1939* (Tel Aviv: Am Oved, 1976), 69–104; Muhammad Y. Muslih, *The Origins of Palestinian Nationalism* (New York: Columbia University Press, 1988), 158 and passim.

22. Ian Lustick, *Arabs in the Jewish State: Israel's Control of a National Minority* (Austin: University of Texas Press, 1980), 82–149; Sammy Smooha, *"Arabs and Jews in Israel: Minority-Majority Relations," *Megamot* 22 (September 1976): 397–423.

23. The early popular conviction among Zionists, of homosexual proclivities among Arabs, is indicated by Brenner's protagonist in his 1911 novella *Mikan u-Mikan (From here and there), in *Complete Works*, 2d ed., comp. Menachem Poznansky (Tel Aviv: Hakibbutz Hameuchad, 1955): "The natives are foxy and corrupt, slothful and contemptible, they are the majority in this place, they sell all kinds of food . . . they stole an animal and had sex with it" (p. ??). "But at night— where would you sleep? Ha? Would you sleep with Arabs? . . . With Arabs?—Hee! . . . Do you know what Arabs'll do to you?—Gentiles do obscenities" (p. 1:350).

In an interview Ehud Ben Ezer had with the magazine *Shdemot* in 1972, he spoke of his research on the image of the Arab in Brenner's fiction and, among other things, he said: "Brenner looked at otherness at its lower level, the erotic and violent level. He saw the threat of a twisted, pervert, and bestial eros. Homosexual relations, sex with animals, these were for him the diseases of the East. These, as he saw it, were the dangers of the encounter with Arabs. He thought these dangers were no less than those of the sword, and perhaps even more tempting. He feared the assimilation among them." "Between Romantics and Bitterness: The Arab Issue in Our Literature—A Discussion with Ehud Ben Ezer," *Shdemot* 46 (Spring 1972): 25.

Politicians had similar fears: "Zabotinsky, for example, contended that the assimilatory power of the majority could not, as a rule, be resisted, even if its cultural level was lower than that of the minority." Yosef Gorny, *Zionism and the Arabs, 1882–1948: A Study of Ideology* (Oxford: Clarendon, 1987), 171, quoted in Norman G. Finkelstein, "Zionist Orientations: A Study of Ideology," *New Politics* 2 (Summer 1988). Ben Gurion made much the same argument (Gorny, p. 217, cited in Finkelstein).

24. In the English edition the phrase that appears here is "to defeat his enemies."

25. "The Abyssinian eunuch, abu-al-Misk Kafur (musk camphor), was purchased from an oil merchant, by Muhammad ibn-Tuhj al-Ikhshid [who founded] a Turkish dynasty . . . in al-Fustat, Egypt. . . . Kafur became sole ruler from 966 to 968. He successfully defended Egypt and Syria

against the rising power of another petty dynasty in the north, the Hamdanid. . . . The case of this black slave, rising from the humblest of origins to a position of absolute power, was the first but not the last in Islamic history." Philip K. Hitti, *History of the Arabs*, 10th ed. (London: Macmillan, 1970), 456.

26. *Effendi* is an Arabic term meaning "master," "landowner," "sir." "The proletarian Zionists invariably saw behind Palestinian resistance the hands of feudalists and effendis, insisting that the Arab workers would at some point make common cause with the Zionist movement." Gorny, *Zionism and the Arabs*, 300, quoted in Finkelstein, "Zionist Orientations."

27. *Encyclopedia Judaica* (Jerusalem: Keter, 1972), 15:916.

28. Tel Hai is the Hebrew name of a Palestinian village, Talha, at the site in Upper Galilee where Joseph Trumpeldor (1880–1920) is buried. Since then, a kibbutz has been established near the Lebanese border. Trumpeldor died in battle with Palestinian villagers who resisted the French and Zionist settlers. The Zionist myth makes Trumpeldor a symbol of pioneering and the armed defense in Palestine. It is said that Trumpeldor's last words before dying were, "Never mind, it is good to die for our country." See Shulamit Laskov, **Yosef Tumpeldor: A Biography* (Haifa: Shikmona, 1972), 243.

The very idea that Betar should name itself after Trumpeldor turns the myths surrounding Tel Hai, Trumpeldor, and Zabotinsky even more grotesque if we consider that Zabotinsky not only had opposed Jewish settlement in this region of the country, but also opposed sending aid and support to Trumpeldor, holding that that was the job of the British troops, in line with his general ideology about the British government's obligation to conquer the land for the Jews (ibid., pp. 232–33). I am thankful to Professor Chomsky for drawing my attention to this irony.

29. This sentence is missing from the English edition.

30. Philip Mattar, *The Mufti of Jerusalem and the Palestinian Nationalist Movement* (New York: Columbia University Press, 1988), 87–88.

31. Charles D. Smith, *Palestine and the Arab-Israeli Conflict* (New York: St. Martin's, 1988), 100.

32. Mattar, *The Mufti of Jerusalem*, 124.

33. Luci Dawidowicz, *The War against the Jews 1933–1945*, 10th anniversary ed. (New York: Holt, Rinehart & Winston, 1985). On the *haavara* (transfer) agreements, concluded August 1933, see pp. 82–85. On the June 21, 1933, Zionist memorandum to the National Socialist government, proposing that the "new German state" recognize "the Zionist movement as the most suitable Jewish group in the new Germany with which to deal, that Jewish status in Germany thenceforth be regulated on the basis of group status rather than individual rights," see pp. 183–85. The Zionist movement "held out bait—in the event the Germans cooperated . . . to call off the anti-German boycott. The Zionists continued to pursue the idea of group rights for the Jews . . . from the start conceding individual rights and the achievements of the Emancipation" (see pp. 183–85). On the Eighteenth Zionist Congress resolution to exclude anti-Zionists as applicants for British certificates for immigration to Palestine, and the Zionist criteria for "suitable" applicants, see pp. 189–90. On the Kastner-Eichmann negotiations in Hungary (the rescue of 1,684 Jews in exchange for 450,000 who went to their deaths) and the 1953–54 Kastner trial in Israel, see Lenni Brenner, *Zionism in the Age of the Dictators* (Westport, Conn.: Croom Helm, 1983), 252–64. See also Hannah Arendt, *Eichmann in Jerusalem: A Report on the Banality of Evil* (New York: Penguin, 1976); Dina Porat, **An Entangled Leadership: The Yishuv and the Holocaust, 1942–1945* (Tel Aviv: Am Oved, 1986); Dina Porat, *The Blue and the Yellow Stars of David: The Zionist Leadership in Palestine and the Holocaust 1939–1945* (Cambridge: Harvard University Press, 1991); Tom Segev, *The Seventh Million: The Israelis and the Holocaust* (New York: Hill & Wang, 1993).

34. Lenni Brenner, *The Iron Wall* (London: Zed, 1984), 194–98. For a detailed bibliography, see p. 212.

35. *Encyclopedia Judaica*, 16:738.

5. The 1948 War: Irony and Self-Righteousness

1. The Arab Legion was the army of the state of Transjordan, and was then under British command. Until 14 May 1948, units of the Legion were stationed in Palestine as part of the deployment of British military forces. After that date the Legion stayed in Palestine under an agreement with the later-to-be Israeli government. This agreement was reached through long negotiations between the Zionist leadership in Palestine and King Abdullah of Transjordan, with the British government acting as mediator. In the process, Golda (Meyerson) Meir met with King Abdullah on 17 November 1948, in Naharyim (the Palestine hydraulic electrical station on the Jordan River). According to Avi Shlaim, "Abdullah secured Jewish agreement for annexing to Transjordan that part of Palestine that was to be allotted to the Arabs by the UN. Mrs. Meir . . . had returned home with what amounted to a non-aggression pact with one of the leading Arab states. The ruler of that state and master of the Arab Legion had promised that he would never attack the Jews or join with other Arabs in frustrating the establishment of a Jewish State." Avi Shlaim, *Collusion across the Jordan: King Abdullah, the Zionist Movement and the Partition of Palestine* (New York: Columbia University Press, 1988), 116; see also Appendices 1 and 2, pp. 625–27. This agreement was never violated by the Arab Legion, except where it contested Israeli aggression against an area controlled by the Legion in accordance with this agreement.

2. Philip Mattar, *The Mufti of Jerusalem and the Palestinian Nationalist Movement* (New York: Columbia University Press, 1988), 127.

3. Ibid., 112–13.

4. Walid Khalidi, "Plan Dalet: Master Plan for the Conquest of Palestine," *Journal of Palestine Studies* 18 (Autumn 1988): 4–37.

5. For purposes of analysis, I quote here from the English edition.

6. Tzadok Eshel, *The Carmeli Brigade in the War for Sovereignty* (Tel Aviv: Maarachot, Ministry of Defense Publishing, 1973), 174–84.

7. The Israeli six-inch mortar, the "Davidka," was known for its inaccuracy, and thus as an indiscriminate weapon that wrought havoc among civilians and had a tremendous terrorizing effect.

8. Quoted in Eshel, *The Carmeli Brigade*, 179.

9. The Israeli historian G. Z. Israeli makes the following curious comment about intentions: "It should be noticed that the leaders of the PCP generously dispensed *promises* among Arabs regarding travel and studies in Russia. Communist propaganda among Arabs was based not necessarily on class-conscious persuasion and personal ideals. The inducements for Arabs were different (spending time abroad for free, and the opportunity to meet with Jewish young women freely within the party, etc." (emphasis added). G. Z. Israeli, *MPS-PKP-MAKI: The History of the Communist Party in Israel* (Tel Aviv: Am Oved, 1953), 79.

10. In proposing the ideological principles for the movement's founding convention (1–3 April 1927), the program, *inter alia*, said: "Considering maximal magnitudes of Jewish immigration to the country which would result in the concentration of *the majority* of the people of Israel in the Land of Israel *and its environs*, and on the other hand—the existence of masses of Arab inhabitants in the country, future social developments following the era of national liberation would bring about a bi-national socialist society" (emphases added). Quoted in Yossi Amitai, *The United Workers Party (MAPAM) 1948–1954: Attitudes on Palestinian-Arab Issues* (Tel Aviv: Tcherikover, 1988), 22. I would like to point out that already in its inception, the territorial ambitions even of Hashomer Hatzair were wider than Palestine alone (to include its "environs"), and only after *the majority* of the "people of Israel would concentrate in the Land of Israel." In other words, after the existing Arab majority is turned into a minority, *only then*, and "following the era of national liberation," meaning the establishment of Jewish hegemony, "a binational socialist society" may come about. Hashomer Hatzair always spoke of "cooperation" and "friendship of

nations," but never offered equal membership for Palestinian Arabs in the movement. With the passing of time the qualifications for a binational society were made more restrictive. In June 1942, Hashomer Hatzair joined the League for Jewish-Arab Rapprochement and Cooperation, a group that counted intellectuals such as J. L. Magnes, M. Buber, A. A. Simon, and M. Reiner among its members. The Hashomer Hatzair directives for this union said: "The Zionist Organization political program should express willingness to establish a binational regime in the country, based on unhindered progress of the Zionist enterprise and *on a parity government, with no regard for the proportional demographic numbers of the two peoples*" (emphasis added). Quoted in Amitai, *The United Workers Party,* 23. It turns out, then, that the two most progressive organizations of the Zionist movement agreed on these points with Ben Gurion: unhindered Jewish immigration to Palestine and parity in government, which would deny the Palestinian majority proportional political representation. In spite of numerous suggestions by the Palestinian national leadership and the British government's qualified consent, the Zionist Organization never agreed to democratic, proportional elections for an Arab-Jewish legislative body in Palestine. On January 23, 1948, MAPAM (the United Workers Party) was established. Hashomer Hatzair was a major partner in it. For that union, Hashomer Hatzair gave up its ideological principle of a binational society—or state. Because of internal political tensions from right and left, which had very little to do with "the Arab problem," MAPAM broke up in 1954. During the years of its existence, Palestinian citizens of Israel could not join the party as equal members. A separate section was established for them: the MAPAM Arab Section. The Arab Section was headed by Jews; "Arabs," could not participate in electing the governing bodies of the party, nor, evidently, could they be elected. Following the breakup, MAPAM finally decided to allow membership for Arabs in the party, but it remained on paper only. Although the Arab Section was dismantled, the Department for Arab Activities remained. "For years to come," says Yossi Amitai, "this department functioned as the exclusive connecting link between Arab members and the party's institutions so that a direct contact was never possible. In addition, for all these years the heads of the Arab Department of MAPAM, with no exception, were Jews. The party made sure to have an Arab candidate for the Knesset elections in a safe spot, but the integration of Arab members in party institutions (the Department for Arab Activities included), or even as a 'pressure group,' remained problematic." Amitai, *The United Workers Party,* 165. See also Joel Beinin, "The Arabists of Hashomer Hatzair (MAPAM)," *Social Text* 28 (1991): 100–121. As for Weizmann and Ben Gurion, "in the mid-1930's, when prospects for the Zioinist enterprise brightened, [they] abandoned the parity principle in favor of a Jewish state *tout court.*" Gorny, *Zionism and the Arabs,* 227, 255, quoted in Finkelstein, "Zionist Orientations." Henceforth, the "sole significance" of the parity principle "was as a convenient political means of rejecting British proposals for the establishment of a legislative council." Gorny, 207, quoted in Finkelstein. Zabotinsky commented that "since Herzl first proposed the idea of the charter, the Zionist movement had acted on the premise that until Jews formed the preponderant element in Palestine the democratic principle of majority rule would have to be honored in the breach there." Cited by Gorny, 303, quoted by Finkelstein. And Chaim Arlozorov (the socialist) prepared a "tentative proposal to establish a *provisional* Zionist dictatorship in Palestine to expedite the territorial concentration of the Jews and the establishment of a Jewish majority." Gorny, 224, quoted in Finkelstein. Finkelstein provides a superb critical exposé of Gorny's text.

11. Hans Lebrecht, *Hapalestinaiim 'Avar veHoveh* (Israel: Mif'alim Universitaiim Publishers, 1987) (translation of *Die Palastinenser Geschichte und Gegenwart* [Frankfurt: Verlag Marxistische Blatter, 1982]).

12. Aharon Cohen, *Israel and the Arab World* (Boston: Beacon, 1976), 185, 353.

13. Israeli, *MPS-PKP-MAKI,* 201.

14. Marie-Helene Huet, *Monstrous Imagination* (Cambridge, Mass.: Harvard University Press, 1993).

15. The English edition uses the word "bedroom" (see Heb. 76; Eng. 107).

16. In 1948 Azouri's father must have been at least sixty-five years old, when we consider that his brother (Azouri's uncle), the famous abu-al-Misk Kafur Sherara, died in the same year at the age of sixty-seven, and that Azouri (who is not the eldest son) is himself forty-four years old in 1948.

6. "The Organizations"

1. The Mossad becomes, as it were, an analogous extremism to that of "the Organizations." This is one way the narrative establishes a symmetry between these two entities. But, in fact, they are not at all symmetrical, because the term "the Organizations" stands as a trope for all that "we know" is Palestinian as such, whereas the Mossad is a definite entity that the Israeli liberal Jewish Hebrew reader might well concede is of dubious character, an aberration.

2. Yosef thinks of Heine, "the German Jew who loved and hated his Jewishness and his Germanness, who lived in Paris and in revenge against himself wrote lines of love and accusation against himself" (Heb. 103; Eng. 147).

3. This issue cannot be raised in the English edition, notice: "with two young men whom the Israeli papers, would doubtless have described as 'minority group members.' "

4. Unlike the Hebrew version, the English translation does not name the airline.

5. Samikh el-Kassem and Mahmoud Darwish, two of the most distinguished Arab writers in Israel, appear in this novel with their real names. These writers are known for their radical Palestinian nationalist position. Much of their literary and poetic work is printed in Arabic, and their poetry and literature is highly regarded among Arabic readers. Some of their literary work is translated and published in Hebrew in literary magazines and in daily newspaper literary supplements. On different occasions in this narrative, Yosef repeats his criticisms of their work, which, in one way or another, are analogous to those of their Zionist critics. He faults them not so much on literary and aesthetic grounds but on their political militancy as such, or, "thus," their hatred of Israel. Mahmoud Darwish left Israel in 1973 following political harassment by Israeli authorities. He joined the PLO and assumed a leadership position in its Cultural Department.

6. This part of the paragraph is missing from the English edition.

7. The last three sentences in this paragraph are missing from the English edition.

8. This detail is missing from the English edition.

9. Typically, Yosef does not tell us that his uncle *is* a Maronite Christian, only that "he had lived as" one.

10. For another instance of compromised compassion for Palestinian refugees whose life in camps under Israeli occupation becomes meaningful only when compared with Jewish misery in Eastern Europe, and thus ending up being compassion only for oneself, see David Grossman, *Hazman Hatshov* (Tel Aviv: Am Oved, 1987) (trans. Haim Watzman, *The Yellow Wind* [New York: Farrar, Straus & Giroux, 1988]).

11. In Yehoshua's story "Facing the Forests," a silenced Arab is presented to the Jewish reader as an object of compassion, despite his hidden destructive intentions. He has had his tongue cut out, but the narrator, an Israeli Jewish ranger, apparently does not feel this character merits the attention necessary to inform the reader who has cut out this person's tongue, or why. See A. B. Yehoshua, *"Facing the Forests," in *Facing the Forests: Short Stories* (Tel Aviv: Hakibbutz Hameuchad, 1968) (trans. Miriam Arad in *Modern Hebrew Literature*, ed. Robert Alter [New York: Behrman House, 1975]).

12. That is, abu-al-Misk Kafur Sherara's.

13. For an argument to the contrary, consider the following by Yehoshua: "A Jew can best lead a normal, coherent and challenging life in Israel, and the Diaspora is essentially a neurotic solution to the identity conflict between the Jews as a people (like any other) and as the Chosen

People (like no other)." A. B. Yehoshua, *In Bezchut haNormaliut Hamesh Sikhot al Tzionut (Tel Aviv: Schocken, 1980) (trans. Arnold Schwartz, *Between Right and Right: Five Essays on Zionism* [Garden City, N.Y.: Doubleday, 1981]). Yehoshua began to develop this theme in his first novel, *The Lover* (Tel Aviv: Schocken, 1979). Gabriel, "the lover," in the course of the story, is "redeemed" twice: first, when he returns to Israel from France, where he had lived as a *yored* (emigrant from Israel); the second time, when he is "freed" from the ultra-Orthodox community Neturei Karta, in Jerusalem, where he had hid himself as a deserter from the military during the 1973 war. In his most recent novel, *Mr. Mani* (Tel Aviv: Hakibbutz Hameuchad, 1990), Yehoshua brings this theme to perfection. The novel slips backward in time from an Israeli kibbutz in 1982 to the mid-18th century in Turkey, tracing the Mani family through six generations. By a movement backward in time and geography, a teleological spin is effected whereby the reader's state of mind at "the end" (in the mid-18th century) has internalized a historical *condition* that had existed only at "the beginning," in 1982. Thus, in the process of reading, an as it were future existence of Israel through struggle and sacrifice is already "justified" in the reader's mind. This *coup de théâtre* is achieved through the writing of Jews into history while dewriting from it Arabs and Palestinians. For the concept pertaining to a critic of orientalist (geographic, demographic, and social) history of Palestine, see Beshara B. Doumani, "Discovering Ottoman Palestine: Writing Palestinians into History," *Journal of Palestine Studies* 21 (Winter 1992): 5–28. In this way, Yehoshua *de-Diasporizes* the Jews, and thus "normalizes" them at least one hundred years before Zionism. At the end, however, a critical reader ought to realize that this is a novel about taking possession of land, a novel that "affirms the primacy of geography and an ideology about control of territory." As Edward W. Said notes: "The geographical sense makes projections— imaginative, cartographic, military, economic, historical, or in general sense cultural. It also makes possible the construction of various kinds of knowledge, all of them in one way or another dependent upon the perceived character and destiny of a particular geography." Edward W. Said, *Culture and Imperialism* (New York: Alfred Knopf, 1993), 78.

14. See Yoram Kaniuk, *The Last Jew* (Tel Aviv: Hakibbutz Hameuchad & Sifriyat Poalim, 1981). In this novel the (Israeli Jewish) reader is confronted with a dilemma whether or not the *Israeli* is the "last Jew." Supposing that non-Zionist Jews are not able to maintain, or will be forced, sooner or later, to abandon their Jewish identity—Zionism, then, acts as a last station, the end of Jewish history—for how much "Jewish" is there if there is no Jewish identity left outside of Zionism? For a hilarious critique of this Zionist dilemma, see Philip Roth's novel *Operation Shylock: A Confession* (New York: Simon & Schuster, 1993). Ted Solotaroff regards this as "the first international contemporary Jewish novel," a comment that I find pertinent to this study. Ted Solotaroff, "The Diasporist, *Operation Shylock: A Confession* by Philip Roth," *The Nation*, 15 June 1993, 826–29.

15. *Kelippah* is the Hebrew word for "peelings." The term signifies a doctrine in Lurianic Kabbalism.

7. Oppositional and Insurgent Israeli Hebrew Literature

1. For such evaluations, see Avraham Shanan, ed., *Dictionary of Modern Hebrew and General Literature* (Tel Aviv: Yavneh, 1970), 90; Gershon Shaked, *Hebrew Narrative Fiction 1880–1980: In the Land of Israel and the Diaspora* (Tel Aviv: Hakibbutz Hameuchad & Keter, 1983), 68–98. For an excellent critique of these and similar evaluations, see Ammiel Alcalay, *After Arabs and Jews* (Minneapolis: University of Minnesota Press, 1993), chap. 3 and passim.

2. See Ella Shohat's powerful critique of Zionist ideology as it pertains to Sepharadim and Arab Jews in Israel, where, *inter alia*, she says: "An ideology which blames the Sepharadim (and their Third World countries of origin) has been elaborated by the Israeli elite, expressed by politicians, social scientists, educators, writers, and the mass-media. The ideology orchestrates an inter-

locking series of prejudicial discourses possessing clear colonialist overtones. It is not surprising, in this context, to find the Sepharadim compared, by the elite, to other 'lower' colonized people." Ella Shohat, "Sepharadim in Israel: Zionism from the Point of View of Its Jewish Victims," *Social Text* 19/20 (Fall 1988): 3.

3. For a broad discussion of this and related issues, see Alcalay, *After Arabs and Jews*, chap. 3 and passim.

4. Yacov Besser, *"Rehabilitation or Defamation: An Interview with Shmeon Ballas," *Massa*, 23 October 1992, 25. Besser is a poet, critic, and editor and publisher of the literary magazine *Iton 77*.

5. Gershon Shaked, *"In Combat against the Ashkenazi Establishment," *Massa*, 25 September 1992, 21; *"O, the Good Old Days," *Massa*, 2 October 1992, 25; *"Severance or Reconciliation," *Massa*, 9 October 1992, 25. These articles were excerpted from Shaked's forthcoming fourth volume of his *History of Hebrew Modern Fiction 1880–1980* (Tel Aviv: Keter, Hakibbutz Hameuchad, 1970-).

6. That is, World Zionist Organization Jewish Agency for Palestine, established in 1923. Although for many the Agency may seem unreal, still exists. Its functions are broadly defined as for "Zionist purposes."

7. For a critical discussion of these attributes of social life in Israel, and their representation in Israeli cinema, see Ella Shohat, *Israeli Cinema: East, West and the Politics of Representation* (Austin: University of Texas Press, 1987), chap. 3.

8. Sammy Mikhael, as I will discuss below, did attempt to address this need for glory and heroism, in Israel, within this community itself.

9. Ballas is a prolific writer of fiction, having to date published seven novels, three volumes of short stories, and numerous literary studies. Needless to say, the literary establishment in Israel did not lend its support to the translation of this novel into any other language.

10. This group includes Shimon Ballas, Sammy Mikhael, Amnon Shamosh, and Yitshak Gormezano-Goren.

11. Quoted in Besser, *"Rehabilitation or Defamation," 25.

12. Shimon Ballas, *The Last Winter* (Jerusalem: Keter, 1984); Shimon Ballas, *The Other One* (Tel Aviv: Zmora-Bitan, 1991). A more accurate translation of the second novel's title would be *And He Is Other*.

13. Describing a public meeting to honor the publication of *The Other One*, Iris O'ded said, "Continuous attacks were directed at the author, as if Ballas were actually Haroun-Ahmad himself, who arrived in Israel in disguise directly from the court of Saddam, King of the Scuds [this was June 1991]. The audience kept shouting at the author 'Be ashamed of yourself.' When eventually, the author was allowed to speak, he said: "You almost made me a non-Jew. . . . The issue is, though, the Jew among Gentiles. In this country the Gentile is the Arab, therefore, it is hard for you to accept someone who says that he is an Arab-Jew. Would you have objected to a French-Jew, or a British-Jew? Judaism has been wrestling for a long time with the otherness of the Jew. . . . It cannot be looked at as a one-sided issue, and you are aware of the existence, in this country, of more than one Exile." Quoted in Vicki Shiran, *review of *The Other One*, by Shimon Ballas, *Iton Aher*, 23–24 (March 1992): 24.

14. Sammy Mikhael, *Hasut* (Tel Aviv: Am Oved, 1977) (trans. Edward Grossman, *Refuge* [Philadelphia: Jewish Publication Society, 1988]. Page numbers cited in text refer to the English version.

15. Yoram Kaniuk (after Mikhael?) uses a similar figure, "the Party." See chapter 5.

16. The country from which Marduch came, not mentioned in the novel, is referred to as "there." In Kaniuk's *A Good Arab*, the Holocaust in Europe is also referred to as "there."

17. This too is an element used by Kaniuk.

18. The curse *Kus-emak* in Arabic is almost integral to the Hebrew vernacular in Israel. When necessary, my translation differs from the original.

19. Sammy Mikhael, *Shavim veShavim Yoter* (All men are equal, but some are more) (Tel Aviv: Boostan, 1974). A more accurate translation of the Hebrew title would be *All Are Equal—and Some Are More.* All translations from this novel are mine. In 1975, Mikhael published the prize-winning *Palm Trees in the Storm* (Tel Aviv: Am Oved), which, like his later book, *Shacks and Dreams* (Tel Aviv: Am Oved, 1979), was written for young people. *A Handful of Fog* (1979) depicts the dissolution of a Jewish family in Baghdad, in the mid-1940s. This family was divided by the opposing moral convictions of two sons. One was a member of the Communist party underground; the other was active in the Zionist underground. The novel articulates this difference as poles of a moral dilemma transformed by events into a family crisis. *Trumpet in the Wadi* (Tel Aviv: Am Oved) was published in 1987. It is, like most of his earlier work, concerned with relations between Arabs and Jews in the context of Israel's 1982 invasion of Lebanon.

20. As a matter of fact, most immigrants of that period came from North Africa, and thus from a geographic region that lay to the west of Israel. However, Arab Jews and Jews of the Balkan countries of Sephardi (Spanish) descent are termed Sepharadim (Spaniards) or Mizrahim (Orientals). Thus, the terms *East* and *West* are not defined geographically but politically. In explicitly derogatory instances in which they refer to various non-Ashkenazi groups and individuals, the term *blacks* (or, in Yiddish, *shvartzes*) is used. In this narrative the term *black* is used by speakers to address each other, and thus in a mood of self-irony, therefore, in a way implicitly critical of hegemonic Ashkenazi vernacular. For a rigorous analysis of this aspect of Israel's cultural dichotomy, see Ella Shohat, *Israeli Cinema* and "Sepharadim in Israel."

21. See Shimon Ballas's novel *Hama'abara* (The transition camp) (Tel Aviv: Am Oved, 1964).

22. Hanoch Bartov, *Each Had Six Wings* (Merhavia, Israel: Sifriyat Poalin, 1954).

23. It is interesting, however, that this character is the only one among Mikhael's male characters in this novel with an Arabic name, and it is a slightly derogatory nickname. For more on that, see chapter 8.

24. The Arabic name of the place is not questioned in the narrative, although Arabic-speaking Jews come to live there less then a year after the Palestinian village that had been there was demolished.

25. See Michel Foucault, *The Birth of the Clinic: An Archaeology of Medical Perception*, trans. A. M. Sheridan Smith (New York: Vintage, 1975), specifically chap. 8, "Open Up a Few Corpses," 124–46.

26. This is reemphasized later (through an Ashkenazi conspiracy of sorts). David's (now ex-) wife's mother, Tzipora, had first sabotaged David's application for a better and higher job than was already offered him in a large bank. Knowing personally the director of the Personnel Department who interviewed David, she then takes care to "arrange" a part-time job for her daughter, Margalit, at the same bank. After David and Margalit's divorce, Tzipora "arranges" her daughter's marriage with that same director, Mr. Zidowitz, who happens to be a widower. He is the age of Margalit's mother, and, once he marries Margalit, he becomes David's son's stepfather. There is another aspect of this complexity: David's last name is Asher (a biblical name). Although this is a popular last name among Arab Jews, it also fits well with the "Israelization" of names (see more on that in chapter 8). The name Zidowitz, on the other hand, is an Ashkenazi name, it has a Yiddish sound to it, and the first three letters of the name constitute the word *Zid*, which is an offensive anti-Semitic appellation. Whether or not this juxtaposition of names was a conscious act on the part of the author is, I think, irrelevant.

27. The child, as a product of failed union through "intermarriage," in some respects, may be compared to Yosef, the protagonist in Kaniuk's novel *A Good Arab,*.

28. Meaning "without prior Zionist indoctrination," as he later says to Reuben in one of their conversations.

29. This term is directed at Ashkenazi Jews in Israel. It takes its sound from a frequent Yiddish speaking tone of the word *vwoos* (what), used as a question.

30. Dan Horowitz and Moshe Lisak, **Trouble in Utopia: The Overburdened Polity in Israel* (Tel Aviv: Am Oved, 1990), see especially chap. 3, p. 119. See also Shlomo Swirski, *Israel: The Oriental Majority*, trans. Barbara Swisrski (London: Zed, 1989).

31. Horowitz and Lisak, *Trouble in Utopia*.

32. These are the concluding words of the novel.

33. In Arabic: Slaughter! Slaughter! Slaughter! See the opening page of the novel.

8. On the Morning of the *Aqedah*

1. *Hesder* is the Hebrew word for "arrangement"; the Hebrew term *Yeshivat-Hesder* denotes a political arrangement with Orthodox parties by Israeli coalition governments in which Orthodox students who are not conscientious objectors may complete their higher education in the *yeshiva* and join the service upon graduation.

2. Albert Swissa, **Aqud* (The bound one) (Tel Aviv: Hakibbutz Hameuchad, 1991). The title refers to the binding of Isaac by Abraham—in Hebrew, *aqedah*. All translations from this novel and all other related Hebrew materials are mine; page numbers are cited in text. I express my gratitude to Mr. J'il Amuyal for assisting me with the Archival Institute of the Israeli Hebrew Writers Guild in Jerusalem. At my request he sent me eight items of criticism and reviews of the novel *Aqud*. Mr. Amuyal teaches literature at the Science and Art High School in Jerusalem.

3. Given that the background for this novel is historic and autobiographical, and the name of this neighborhood is real, it might be considered an intended irony: in translation, the name would be something like Garden Town, Parkville, or Kew Gardens.

4. The three child protagonists of the novel are Yohai (a Hebrew name combining two words, and etymologically implying "God is alive," common among Sepharadi and Arab Jews), Beber (a Maghrab, Berber, nickname for Albert or Abraham), and Ayiush (an Arabic name also etymologically related to "life"—in Hebrew, Haiim).

5. See James Scott, *Weapons of the Weak: Everyday Forms of Peasant Resistance* (New Haven, Conn.: Yale University Press, 1986); Franz Fanon, *The Wretched of the Earth* (New York: Grove, 1968).

6. One of the most distinguished critical reviews of *Aqud* is Ariel Hirschfeld's essay **"A Word about Sales," *Haaretz*, 1 March 1991, 8(B). Hirschfeld is a writer, literary critic, editor, and professor of literature. He is one of the younger Israeli critics who have established themselves as new authorities. Another is Menachem Peri, who has a similar professional background, although he is of a somewhat older generation. For recent and relevant discussions of power in the Israeli literary "establishment," see Avi Katzman, **"He Is the Establishment," an interview with and about Gershon Shaked, *7 Days* (*Haaretz* weekly supplement), 27 December 1991, 21–23.

7. Hirschfeld, **"A Word about Sales."

8. Ibid.

9. As noted, the title of Hirschfeld's essay is "A Word about Sales"; approximately one-third of it concerns Menachem Peri.

10. Yehudit Orian, **"Albert Swissa, Go On—but Be Aware," review of *Aqud*, by Albert Swissa, *Yediot Aharonot*, 11 January 1991, Literary section, 22, 24; Batia Gur, **review of *Aqud*, by Albert Swissa, *Haaretz*, 25 January 1991, 8(B).

11. Within the first month of its publication (January 1991), *Aqud* had gone through two printings. In November 1991 it had a third printing. According to Hirschfeld, it sold a few tens of

thousands of copies—in Israel's marketing magnitudes, a substantial success. Hirschfeld, *"A Word about Sales."

12. I mentioned Amnon Navot's use of this term in chapter 2. The term *materia*, in this context, would mean "content."

13. It seems that the term *there* is applied by speakers of hegemonic culture as signifier of "pre-Israeli" space and time that should not be mentioned by name. When used, this term refers culturally to an earlier biography (time and place) one had lived or from which one came—to Israel. It is a "there/then" concept of fear associated with shame, which powerless Jewish "strangers" or "exiles" ought to have felt in their country of origin, in reference to the Holocaust (see the discussions of Kaniuk and Mikhael above), or in enemies' "untamed" territories, "where the jackals howl" (a literary title used by Amos Oz in 1982).

14. Hazaz is a writer from an older generation; I mentioned him briefly in the introduction to this book.

15. Orian, *"Albert Swissa, Go On," 22. Orian's own review, however, is ambivalent and even self-contradictory. She asks, for example: "If [the novel] is so bad how come it is so good?" But her answer is confusing. She also believes "that there is no protest in Swissa's writing," which may be why she finds it confusing.

16. *Jalabiyas* are long, hooded woolen robes.

17. Ariana Melamed, "Wild, Surprising and Overflowing," review of *Aqud*, by Albert Swissa, *Hadashot*, 4 January 1991, weekly supplement, Literary Criticism section, 45.

18. Yigal Sarna, "A Moroccan Novel," interview with Albert Swissa, *7 Days* (*Yediot Aharonot* weekly supplement), 4 January 1991, 16.

19. The phrase "walk together" is taken from the biblical story of the "binding." It is used in this narrative whenever a child and his father "walk together." The few lines I recite here are taken from a passionately poetic account of the father reproaching his son while at the same time actually being consoled by him, all in the language and conceptual framework of the "binding" myth (see pp. 92–95).

20. Hirschfeld, *"A Word about Sales."

21. It would be relevant to mention here Dorfman and Mattelart's discussion of Donald Duck's sterility and asexuality, "eliminating the biological link between the parent and the child's sexuality." See Ariel Dorfman and Armand Mattelart, *How to Read Donald Duck: Imperialist Ideology in the Disney Comic* (New York: I. G. Editions, 1984).

22. *Motacila Alba*, a singing migrating bird, nests during the winter in the eastern Mediterranean countries.

23. We should not forget that Yohai is about to be exiled.

24. *Ya bnini* means "my child" in North African Arabic.

25. Kinneret is the Hebrew name used for the Lake of Galilee. The poem about Kinneret, "Ve'uly" (Perhaps), by Rahel Bluwestien (1890–1931), has been put to music and is widely sung in Israel as a popular patriotic song. *Shulkhan Arukh*, "the prepared table," is the name of a code written by Joseph Caro. The book, first printed in Venice in 1565, is a synopsis of previous works on Jewish traditional law by the same author, and "was ultimately accepted as the code of Jewish law par excellence." *Encyclopedia Judaica* (Jerusalem: Keter, 1972), 14:1475.

26. Scott, *Weapons of the Weak*.

27. Gur, review of *Aqud*.

28. Quoted in Sarna, "A Moroccan Novel," 15–16.

29. In Hebrew, the word used is *herem*, which means boycott, excommunicate, destruction. The term is biblical.

30. *Rashi* is an abbreviation for the name of Rabbi Shlomo ben Isaac (1040–1105), leading commentator on the Bible. Rashi was born and lived in Troyes, France.

31. Bnei-Brak is a town in the vicinity of Tel Aviv that is known for its ultra-Orthodox major-

ity population and severely restricting rules of conduct. Certainly, living there would be a myste-rious and frightening experience for an eleven-year-old child from a slum neighborhood in Jerusalem.

32. *Tsadik* (pious) is both noun and adjective.

33. This is an abridgment of the following: "One should enhance, not lessen, the importance of holy matters" (Talmud, Brachot, 28).

34. The name is Hebreized from the Greek term *synegoros*: advocate, lawyer, champion of the right. The word entered the Hebrew language in the fourth century B.C., in the wake of Alexander the Great's conquest and the emergence of Helenism. In *Aqud* we have a French form of the Hebrew noun/name *sanegor*, which, etymologically, could mean "*my* advocate" and in the narra-tive could have an ironic intention.

35. *Aqedah* is the Hebrew term for "binding" (for sacrifice).

36. This is from Peri's comments on *Aqud*'s back cover.

37. *Aqud* opens with the words, "The boy rose early in the morning." The biblical story opens, "Abraham rose early in the morning" (see Genesis 22:3).

38. Hirschfeld, *"A Word about Sales."

39. Gersha is these children's only adult friend. He has created a garden fence of used junk, and his yard is the only place in which birds and animals and flowers are protected. He is the only adult these children do not fear, and some of them even take advantage of him; in their games they occasionally inflict pain on him, though Ayiush says that Gersha enjoys it. Gersha is their only protector and, in many respects, provider. He is a human being for these children, despite his appearance to critics as a "madman" or as "grotesque."

40. Orian, *"Albert Swissa, Go On," 24.

41. See Alexander Pen, *Along the Way: Selected Poems* (Tel Aviv: Mada Ve'chaim, 1956), 45–53.

42. See Shimon Ballas's novel *Hama'abara* (Tel Aviv: Am Oved, 1964). The novel presents the same theme, the struggle of the Iraqi Jewish immigrant community in the early 1950s. In it, all characters are introduced by their Arabic names.

43. In Ballas's novel *Hama'abara* the Arabic name of the place, Saqiya, is mentioned.

44. See Chapter 7.

45. This is Arabic for "happy holiday."

46. Alfred Schutz, *The Phenomenology of the Social World*, trans. George Walsh and Frederick Lehnert (Evanston, Ill.: Northwestern University Press, 1967).

47. The biblical episode relates as follows (Numbers 15:32–36). During the time that the Israelites were in the wilderness, a man was found on the Sabbath gathering sticks. The people brought him to Moses and Aaron and he was kept in custody, because it had not been decided what should be done with him. The Lord told Moses that the man must be put to death, stoned by all the community. This was done outside the camp, as the Lord commanded Moses.

48. Ayiush walks away with his nanny "from the *mlakh* to the *madina*" (from the Jewish ghet-to to the cosmopolitan city).

49. On the doctrine and its development, see Gershom Scholem, *Major Trends in Jewish Mysticism* (New York: Schocken, 1961), 287–324; see also his *Studies and Texts Concerning the History of Sabbatianism and Its Metamorphoses* (Jerusalem: Mossad Bialik, 1974), 9–76 and passim.

50. The Jewish Orthodox traditional blessing of a child by the father is profoundly significant. It derives directly from biblical sources. The biblical blessing is usually phrased in conditional terms, always implying a curse, in case the commands involved in the blessing are not fulfilled. Yet there are many instances where a curse is explicit in the phrasing of the blessing. In the context of this tradition, the blessing with the curse is very effective. It has the power of prophecy, and even of incantation. For further discussion, see, for example Yehezkel Kaufman, *The Religion of Israel from Its Beginnings to the Babylonian Exile* (Chicago: University of Chicago Press, 1960); Max

Weber, *Ancient Judaism*, trans. and ed. Hans H. Gerth and Don Martindale (New York: Free Press, 1952).

51. This term is taken from the name of Epikouros (B.C. 342–271), the Greek philosopher who taught liberation from the fear of gods and the fear of death. In Hebrew and in a Jewish traditional context, it indicates a heretic or an infidel.

52. Quoted in Sarna, "A Moroccan Novel," 15.

53. Ibid., 16.

Conclusion

1. Benedict Anderson, *Imagined Communities: Reflections on the Origin and Spread of Nationalism* (London: Verso, 1991).

2. R. Deutsche, "Boys Town," review of *The Condition of Post Modernity*, by David Harvey, *Environment Planning* 9 (1991): 5–30.

3. Michael E. Brown, "Introduction" in *New Studies in the Politics and Culture of U.S. Communism*, ed. Michael E. Brown, Randy Martin, Frank Rosengarten, and George Snedeker (New York: Monthly Review Press, 1993), 15–44.

4. See Edward W. Said, *Orientalism* (New York: Vintage, 1979).

Index

Compiled by Eileen Quam and Theresa Wolner

Yerach Gover is currently senior research fellow at the Center for Social Research at the City University of New York Graduate Center, adjunct professor of sociology at the College of Staten Island, and editor of *Social Text*. He has published several articles on Hebrew literature and ideology in various journals.